RIGHTS OF THE DISABLED

LIBRARY IN A BOOK

RIGHTS OF
THE DISABLED

David M. Haugen
with Susan Musser and Andrea DeMott

Facts On File
An imprint of Infobase Publishing

Rights of the Disabled

Facts On File, Inc.
An imprint of Infobase Publishing
132 West 31st Street
New York NY 10001

Library of Congress Cataloging-in-Publication Data

Haugen, David M., 1969–
  Rights of the disabled / David M. Haugen, with Susan Musser and Andrea DeMott.
      p. cm. — (Library in a book)
  Includes bibliographical references and index.
  ISBN 978-0-8160-7128-9 (alk. paper)
  1. People with disabilities—Legal status, laws, etc.—United States. I. Musser, Susan. II. DeMott, Andrea B. III. Title.
  KF480.H365 2008
  342.7308'7—dc22   2007034803

Facts On File books are available at special discounts when purchased in bulk quantities for businesses, associations, institutions, or sales promotions. Please call our Special Sales Department in New York at (212) 967-8800 or (800) 322-8755.

You can find Facts On File on the World Wide Web at http://www.factsonfile.com.

Text design by Ron Monteleone
Graphs by Dale Williams

Printed in the United States of America

Bang Hermitage 10 9 8 7 6 5 4 3 2 1

This book is printed on acid-free paper.

CONTENTS

PART III
APPENDICES

Acknowledgments

This book could not have been completed without the commitment and talents of my coauthors. Susan Musser, who drafted the chronology, glossary, and organizations and agencies sections, has a flair for packing a wealth of information into a small amount of space. And Andrea DeMott, who wrote the law and disability rights section, has a facility for making dense topics readable and approachable. I would also like to thank my wife, Hayley, a student of disability studies who contributed her time and expertise to this title. I appreciate the assistance you all have given me in making this a fine contribution to the growing body of disability literature.

PART I

OVERVIEW OF THE TOPIC

CHAPTER 1

INTRODUCTION TO DISABILITY RIGHTS IN AMERICA

Disability is often discussed as a medical condition or as a theoretical issue. Most of these discussions frame persons with disabilities as a separate caste in society, an "other" that requires attention, special services, and support. Rarely are the disabled conceived in inclusive terms, as one of many diverse populations of Americans that face family, health, social, and economic issues. However, as disability activists point out, the conception is unfortunate because millions of Americans will join the ranks of the disabled either as a result of injury or old age. Furthermore, although the disabled are a minority in America, they are the largest minority and the only one that anyone—regardless of race, color, creed, or gender—can join at any time in one's life.

People with disabilities are commonly portrayed as an "other" because they are often noticeably different than the able-bodied, independently mobile, and mentally competent individuals who compose the large segment of society that has, itself, defined the standards of physical and intellectual normality. However, granting that there exists such a readily apparent category of the "able," it has been difficult for policymakers, judges, and even disability groups to define who clearly should be classified as "disabled." Disability laws are often quite vague on defining disability, and this has sometimes meant that federal judges have had to decide who is covered by these laws on a case-by-case basis. While this could lead to restrictiveness, some disability advocates have found that the imprecision of legal definitions has meant that the "other" category is expansive and can include many sorts of disabilities as long as judicial bodies agree that the disabilities fit the terminology expressed in the letter or spirit of these laws.

The Americans with Disabilities Act (ADA), the foremost piece of legislation concerning disability rights, simply defines disability as a "physical or mental impairment that substantially limits one or more of the major life

3

activities." As suggested previously, determining what constitutes an impairment to a major life activity has been a matter for continual judicial appraisal; however, the U.S. Department of Justice (DOJ) has recognized that major life activities include seeing, hearing, speaking, walking, breathing, performing manual tasks, learning, caring for oneself, and working. Thus people with acquired immunodeficiency syndrome (AIDS), epilepsy, mental retardation, or visual or hearing impairments, for example, have met the criteria of disability as defined by the ADA and have been granted its protection. Others with non-chronic pains, broken bones, or temporary diseases have typically failed to meet the definition of disabled and consequently are commonly denied protection under the ADA.

Other organizations have maintained distinct definitions of disability. The Social Security Administration, for example, provides benefits for those who have an "inability to engage in any substantial gainful activity by reason of any medically determinable physical or mental impairment which can be expected to result in death or has lasted or can be expected to last for a continuous period of not less than 12 months." This somewhat less-restrictive definition of disability can include such medical conditions as peptic ulcers and heart disease as well as psychological disorders such as mental illness and mood disorders. The American Association on Mental Retardation (AAMR), on the other hand, has a more limiting definition of intellectual disability, stating that a person has an intellectual disability if he or she has an IQ below 70–75, has significant limitations in two or more adaptive skills (communication, self-care, home living, social skills, leisure, health and safety, self-direction, functional academics, community use, and work), and has lived with the disability at least since the age of 18.

The variety of such definitions makes it clear that disability has no singular set of criteria. In some respects, this has made those with disabilities feel less a part of a cohesive community, even as they feel excluded from participating in the larger society. Indeed, the disability rights movement—which advocated for and won civil protection in the form of the ADA in 1990—is a fractured conglomeration of interest groups representing various disability communities (the blind, the deaf, the mentally disabled, et al.). The unity that the disability rights movement achieved in the 1980s and 1990s did not come from any sense of collective vision but rather from a shared knowledge of what it meant to be excluded from participation in mainstream society.

The exclusion of the disabled in American society has deep roots in history. In colonial America, the physically disabled were considered unproductive burdens and the mentally impaired were often believed to be the victims of a divine scourge. For centuries, the handicapped were institutionalized, shut away from the mainstream to be cared for by doctors and good Samaritans. This separation has kept alive a sense of the disabled as helpless, imperfect people—a sense that continues to pervade current debate on disability issues. Only since the rise of modern industrialization have the disabled become a more recognizable feature of American life. Hundreds of thousands of machine workers, for example, suffered disabling injuries in the 1900s, leading to struggles over workman's compensation. In addition, the First World War added another 123,000 returning veterans to the ranks of the disabled. Such large numbers forced the government and welfare organizations to face issues of health care, rehabilitation, education, and employment. However, even the swelling ranks could be hidden away in hospitals, workhouses, and other institutions where their conditions could be attended—and in the case of disease-engendered impairments—perhaps cured. But two decades after World War I, the nation fell into an economic slump, and everyone—the able-bodied and the disabled—fought desperately to work as social welfare seemed ill-equipped to see the nation through the depression. At a time when unions struggled to find strength, some people with disabilities recognized the power of standing together to change the circumstances that had relegated them to wards of the floundering state.

EARLY AGITATION: THE LEAGUE OF THE PHYSICALLY HANDICAPPED

The first organization to champion the rights of the disabled was formed in 1935 during the midst of the Great Depression. The organization, known as the League of the Physically Handicapped, was a loose knit group originally built around a core of six members who argued that the Emergency Relief Bureau (ERB) of New York was unresponsive to the employment needs of people with disabilities. The six leaders requested a meeting with the New York City director of the ERB, Oswald W. Knauth, to discuss why the bureau was routinely denying disabled workers from seeking employment with the Works Progress Administration (WPA), a federal agency set up to provide opportunities for the nation's unemployed to find jobs in government service. At the time, government employers routinely stamped the applications of people with disabilities with a "PH" to denote physically handicapped—a mark that normally disqualified them without review of their talents or skills. When Knauth declined to hear any complaints until the following week, the six protestors staged a sit-in of the ERB office that lasted from May 29 through June 6, 1935.

The League of the Physically Handicapped was a unique advocacy organization in that the members were not seeking charity or assistance; they were insisting that their abilities were being unfairly overlooked because of the perception that their physical impairments would make them unemployable. The league knew it had no legislative recourse. The Social Security Act of 1935, for example, was being debated in Congress at the time, and even this monumental legislation, though providing vocational training and some assistance for disabled Americans, failed to consider that a vast number of disabled individuals were capable of performing jobs if given the chance. In addition, no government agency dealt with the discriminatory practices that kept most of the disabled out of the workplace. Thus, the league had to operate under a new paradigm. As disability rights historians Doris Zames Fleischer and Frieda Zames state, the members refused to see themselves as unfortunate victims but as "a minority unprotected by the law."[1]

The league was also quite distinct because its members possessed a variety of disabilities. Previous collectives championed the interests of specific subgroups such as the blind or the deaf. Members of the League of the Physically Handicapped were mainly mobility-impaired, but their conditions were brought on by a variety of illnesses including cerebral palsy, tuberculosis, heart ailments, and polio. Despite their impairments, the six league members who staged the sit-in were fully capable of handling jobs for which their disabilities would not interfere.

The League of the Physically Handicapped sit-in attracted some support and garnered attention from the press. With the media on hand, the six demonstrators began pressing a list of demands. Not only did they want to talk with Knauth, they now stipulated that 50 job openings would have to be made available to league members and 10 more positions added each week thereafter. They also demanded that the members placed in those jobs receive the same salary as their non-disabled peers and be integrated into existing working environments. Knauth rebuffed the demands. Over the next year and a half, protestors kept up the vigil, picketing New York employment offices and taking their message to the radio and newspapers. Eventually the city opened roughly 1,500 job positions in the WPA for disabled New Yorkers. This concession had much to do with unflattering press coverage and the pressure tactics of the league, but it did not signal a change in state or federal policy. New York City officials made it known that only Washington could do away with the "PH" stigma for government jobs.

TAKING THE FIGHT TO WASHINGTON

The League of the Physically Handicapped officially formalized itself quite soon after the events of early June 1935. The group acquired offices and elected officers to devise strategies to keep the fight going. In May 1936, league members made a pilgrimage to Washington, D.C., in hopes of bringing the issue of job discrimination—especially within government services like the WPA—to the attention of President Franklin Delano Roosevelt. The demonstrators occupied the offices of the WPA and refused to vacate until they had met with Roosevelt or some senior administrator who would take their complaints seriously and initiate some change in policy. On day two of their sit-in, the league members were granted a meeting with Harry L. Hopkins, the head of the WPA. Hopkins listened as the visitors demanded the institution of a government job program that would strictly serve people with disabilities. Hopkins rejected the plan, stating that the organization had no proof that job discrimination existed in the WPA. The league vowed to return with the proof.

Two months after the WPA siege, the League of the Physically Handicapped issued its "Thesis on Conditions of Physically Handicapped," a document that drew mainly on league members' own experiences in laying out the history of job discrimination against people with disabilities. The thesis charged that the government routinely considered all disabled people "unemployable" regardless of the degree of their disabilities. It criticized, for example, state and federal employment agencies for requiring needless physical evaluations of employees who were applying for positions that required no special physical skills. Although the league sent its thesis to Hopkins and President Roosevelt, it could not afford to immediately follow up on the issues. The jobs the league had won in New York were in danger; nationwide WPA cutbacks sent many employees—including several hundred New Yorkers with disabilities—back into unemployment. Hoping to redress this, the league went back to Washington in August 1937 to attempt another meeting with Roosevelt or Hopkins. The latter consented to meet with the league, but he maintained that the cutbacks were necessary and that new concessions to give WPA jobs to all disabled workers could not be granted.

Unable to effect lasting change in government policy, the league needed time to regroup and plan strategy. Instead, many of the leading members left the organization as they found work and began families. Internal dissension further fractured the membership, and accusations that the league—like other workers' rights groups—was a collection of communist agitators drove away new recruits. Without impetus and leadership, the League of the Physically Handicapped slowly dissolved and ceased to exist by 1940.

VICTIMIZATION AND THE PREVAILING MEDICAL MODEL

The League of the Physically Handicapped was a product of its times. Previous disability organizations focused on securing assistance for what were perceived as the "victims of fate." Schools for the deaf began in the United States as early as 1817, and workshops for the blind also arose in 19th-century America to help blind adults find gainful employment. Then, following

World War I, federally funded veterans' services developed to provide job training for the multitude of maimed soldiers who returned from overseas. Those Americans who had more severe physical or mental disabilities, however, were simply shut away in institutions where interaction with the larger public was minimal.

While the supposedly "hopeless" cases remained in secluded care, those who could more obviously benefit from living assistance and job training were given some opportunities. Progressive-era reformers proceeded under the belief that disabled people could be rehabilitated to take an active role in society. Thus, from roughly the 1890s through the 1920s, reformers worked to change the notion that disability equaled dependency. Some argued that society was to blame for this equation, but a vast number identified the victims as the source of the unhealthy relationship. The latter group believed the root problem of disability lay in the afflicted person; the body machine had broken down and needed to be repaired. They assumed that the disabled individual could achieve rehabilitation through surgery, physical therapy, and even moral education. These concepts became part of what is now referred to as the "medical model" of disability. Rehabilitation efforts reinforced tacit assumptions that disability was a personal affair, that the medical community had the primary authority and know-how to address the problem of disability, and that disability was defined as an imperfect or "abnormal" state that could be corrected or cured.

By the time the League of the Physically Handicapped formed, the medical model was a powerful force in shaping attitudes and policies concerning disability and the disabled. Furthermore, the medical model had its own figurehead in the form of the sitting president. Franklin Roosevelt had already built an impressive political career by the time he was struck with polio in 1921. He was assistant secretary of the Navy under President Woodrow Wilson, he served two years as New York state senator, and he ran as a vice-presidential candidate on the Democratic ticket in 1920. With such an active public and private life, Roosevelt would not let the paralysis he suffered in his legs slow him down. Though confined to a wheelchair, Roosevelt did not initially perceive himself as handicapped. He believed, as the medical model dictated, that rehabilitation and determination would restore his ability to walk. He moved to Warm Springs, Georgia, to undertake a regimen of mobility exercises. He would later establish a center in Warm Springs to help polio patients through counseling and physical therapy. Despite his positive outlook, Roosevelt's legs did not respond to his desires. He continued his political climb mostly from a seated position, though he could stand and walk with the aid of metal braces if the public eye was upon him.

Roosevelt kept his disability hidden as often as possible as he advanced his career, becoming governor of New York in the late 1920s and then president of the United States in 1933. Much of the secretiveness during his presidency had to do with Roosevelt's desire to be perceived at home and abroad as a symbol of strength and fortitude. His tenure, after all, carried Roosevelt through a bleak economic depression and a world war. Steering the nation through such crises required a person recognized for his ability, not his disability. According to historians, the public was also willing to ignore the president's paralysis. Even the press was complicit in perpetuating the deception by never photographing Roosevelt in his wheelchair. Hiding the president's impairment, however, reinforced the notion that his disability was a private concern. In addition, seeing the president stand and walk at ceremonies implied to onlookers that Roosevelt was winning his battle against polio. Such messages covered over opportunities to address disability as a social issue, and Roosevelt seemed completely content not to broach the subject. As Doris Zames Fleischer and Freida Zames suggest, Roosevelt simply manifested the axioms of the medical model, especially embodying—to himself and to the public—the belief that disability could be overcome. Fleischer and Zames claim that "the President fell victim to the same dissembling that he was perpetuating: disability equals weakness; therefore, he is in fact not 'really' disabled. The fiction the public was fed that he *could* walk without a great deal of human or mechanical aid became the internalized hoax that he would walk without assistance."[2]

Members of the League of the Physically Handicapped were as likely as the president to be influenced by the precepts of the medical model. The league certainly did not set out to force society to consider how disability was misperceived and often ignored in America. They did wish to draw attention to the social injustice that people with disabilities suffer, but the main focus of their protest was job discrimination. Choosing this target exemplified another way in which the league was responding to its time in history. During the mid 1930s, the nation was still in the grips of the Great Depression. A large portion of Americans were either out of work or underemployed. The league considered disabled Americans as suffering the worst of the economic crisis because they were not only unemployed, they were deemed unemployable. Though driven by economic necessity, the league's choice to target employment, however, was a significant—if nascent and probably unintentional—step in undermining the medical model. In America's capitalist society, work has social value, and thus the worker could not be worthless. By advocating for jobs and the right to compete in the workforce, the League of the Physically Handicapped insisted that many people with disabilities need not be dependent on the welfare of the state.

THE REHABILITATION MOVEMENT

Although the league and its influence ebbed by the time America entered the Second World War, the issue of disability rights did not disappear. In fact, by war's end, the host of returning disabled veterans was a visible reminder of this otherwise invisible segment of the population. America, however, was more inclined to integrate the veterans back into society than to address the injustices facing the larger disabilities community. The veterans had lost limbs or eyesight or been otherwise maimed in service of the nation, and the country felt obliged to repay them for their patriotic commitment. This commitment was evident at the end of the First World War when Congress enacted rehabilitation and vocational training benefits for returning veterans. These services were extended in 1943 during the Second World War. Then, in 1947, the President's Committee on Employment of the Handicapped held its first meeting to court public support for greater integration. The committee promoted a National Employ the Physically Handicapped Week (observed every October) that brought together business leaders with disability representatives and medical professionals to encourage the employment of disabled veterans and civilians. As author Fred Pelka writes, "The campaign was notable in that it did not use pity or urge businesses to hire disabled workers out of charity. Rather, the committee used research conducted by the Bureau of Labor Statistics to demonstrate that disabled employees rated high in efficiency, productivity, and safety and low in absenteeism, often outscoring their non-disabled coworkers."[3]

Disabled veterans also benefited from a relatively new trend in medical treatment that came to the fore in treating the war's wounded. Dr. Henry Kessler and Dr. Howard Rusk pioneered rehabilitative medicine after recognizing that military hospitals and recovery facilities were treating wounds but not the wounded. Though working independently, Kessler and Rusk each advocated a comprehensive approach to rehabilitation. As writer Joseph P. Shapiro explains, "They would go well beyond acute care to put together all the medical services—from physical therapy to occupational therapy—that a newly disabled person required to return to a normal life."[4] Rusk, who had joined the U.S. Air Force at the advent of World War II, established the first Air Force Rehabilitation Center in Pawling, New York, in 1944. The center offered physical therapy as well as occupational counseling, emotional counseling, and family support services. Part of Rusk's and Kessler's programs also included teaching disabled veterans how to become better informed about their own treatments and how to become more knowledgeable consumers when it came to the medical aids and services available to them. President Roosevelt was so approving of this new treatment approach that he ordered each branch of the armed forces to organize its own rehabilitation program. Rusk left military service at war's end and brought his methods to the general population. After opening the Institute of Rehabilitation Medicine at New York University Medical Center in 1951, Rusk and his colleagues worked at improving prosthetic limbs, wheelchairs, and communication devices for the many people who availed themselves of his innovative methods. The medical community was largely resistant to what some termed "Rusk's Folly," but over the next two decades rehabilitation medicine gained wide acceptance and did much to erode the prevailing power of the medical model of disability.

GRASSROOTS ORGANIZING

The link between disabled veterans and civilians with disabilities was reinforced in the postwar years as veterans began sympathizing with their often-overlooked counterparts in society. The disabled servicemen recognized that they were receiving more attention and medical aid than civilians who had similar debilities. Formed from various local organizations in 1947, the Paralyzed Veterans of America (PVA) was one of the first national advocacy groups that raised awareness of all Americans who live with paraplegia or quadriplegia due to spinal cord injuries. Only a year after its conception, the PVA sponsored the establishment of the National Paraplegia Foundation (NPF) as its civilian counterpart. Renamed the National Spinal Cord Injury Association in 1979, the NPF brought treatment breakthroughs in the military medical field to civilian practices. Spinal cord injury—a condition that was commonly terminal in the years prior to the war—quickly became survivable by large numbers of veterans and civilians, who entered the labor force, attended college, and forced attention to a host of accessibility issues that had previously been ignored.

While veterans' services contended with the needs of the physically disabled in the postwar years, other organizations turned to advocacy on behalf of the mentally handicapped. United Cerebral Palsy (UCP) began in 1946 when parents of children with cerebral palsy (CP) banded together in New York City to confront the lack of medical services available to disabled young people. Similar UCP organizations sprang up around the country, and by 1949, the individual entities merged into the United Cerebral Palsy Association (UCPA). The national organization—still very much a volunteer, grassroots association—brought attention to the disorder and how doctors routinely misdiagnosed cerebral palsy as a form of mental retardation, which unfortunately subjected many CP children to life in state institutions. The children who escaped this fate, Pelka states, experienced widespread discrimination. "Society encouraged parents to view their disabled children as a source of shame," he writes. "Doctors and dentists often refused to treat children with CP. Those children who were not institutionalized were often denied access to public schools."[5]

To correct the misperception, the UCPA began to lobby state legislatures for the establishment of special education programs for CP children and for funds for greater medical services. In 1950, the UCPA staged its first celebrity-backed telethon to raise money for research into the causes and treatment of cerebral palsy. Part of the proceeds from such fundraisers went toward the creation of the United Cerebral Palsy Research and Educational Foundation in 1955. The foundation and the UCPA continued to stress research in hopes of treating and preventing cerebral palsy, and the focus on "curing" the disorder had the beneficial side effect of convincing the public that those afflicted with cerebral palsy were not destined for institutionalization. The "cure" mentality, however, had the unintended consequence of reinforcing the notion that people with cerebral palsy were less-than-normal—medical model "patients" waiting to be corrected by a wonder treatment.

Various parent groups followed the lead of the UCP to bring together those who had children living with other specific disabilities. Ann Greenberg, the mother of a Down syndrome child, formed the New York Association for Help of Retarded Children (AHRC) in 1949. In the following year, family members and friends of children with developmental disorders founded the National Association of Retarded Children (NARC), which later became the Association of Retarded Citizens (and eventually "The Arc" in 1991) when it broadened its agenda to include the needs of developmentally delayed adults. Also in 1950, the Muscular Dystrophy Association (MDA) was established by concerned parents, adults with the disorder, and medical professionals. Each of these organizations offered tangible benefits to the children and adults living with physical and mental disabilities. "Medical and rehabilitation research, recreation training, and work programs provided avenues for socializing and expanding skills," notes Robert Funk, the former director of the Disability Rights Education and Defense Fund. However, these opportunities, as Funk mildly criticizes, were often enjoyed only "in segregated and sheltered settings."[6]

THE CURE MENTALITY

A more troubling criticism of these grassroots organizations—especially as they were originally conceived—was that they emphasized ridding humanity of a specific disorder instead of demonstrating how disability could be integrated into the patchwork of society. Inspired by the development of vaccines that virtually eradicated polio in the mid-1950s, groups such as the UCPA and the MDA raised funds largely under the premise that more research would hasten cures that waited just around the corner. One way these organizations sought to secure donations was by adorning fundraising advertisements with images of stricken children. A tactic that can be traced back to the March of Dimes campaigns to end polio in the 1930s, the exploitation of "poster children" gave each abstract-sounding disorder a very human face. More important, the vulnerability of children played upon the sympathies of the donors who wanted nothing more than to help the helpless. Of course, this reinforced the notion that the handicapped were, indeed, helpless, and furthermore imparted the "unstated, though erroneous, message . . . that disability was somehow limited to children," as Fleischer and Zames contend.[7]

Another controversial manner of selling a "search for the cure" mentality to the public also began in the 1950s, when television became a mainstay of many American homes. Lengthy televised fundraisers, or telethons, brought images of disabled children into the country's living rooms for the sake of disability charities. Like the persuasive power of poster children, the youngsters paraded across the telethon stage induced some viewers to donate out of sympathy. Others who tuned into these marathon productions conceded to the pleas of celebrities who lent their time and reputations to the various disability causes. Telethons were—and remain—an effective way of making disabilities visible while raising huge sums of money for research and improved services. However, the pandering and exploitation elements of telethons have aroused much criticism, a fact that has perhaps been best exemplified by the contentions surrounding the annual Muscular Dystrophy Association telethon.

The MDA Telethon

The MDA telethon was first broadcast in Cleveland, Ohio, in 1959. It did not reach national prominence (and, to some, notoriety) until 1966 when comedian Jerry Lewis became the celebrity spokesperson for muscular dystrophy and consequently took over the reins of the telethon. Lewis brought in major talent and built the event into a Las Vegas–style spectacle that raised millions every year from individual donors and corporate enterprises. Disability rights historian and journalist Joseph Shapiro acknowledges the benefits by stating, "Lewis's tireless fund-raising built MDA into an organization that would support important research." But the critics of telethon tactics viewed the MDA extravaganza with more horror than hope. For example, Shapiro recites the story of Evan Kemp, Jr., an individual with Kugelberg-Welander syndrome and a former adviser to President George H.W. Bush on disability rights. Kemp's parents were among the organizers of the first MDA telethon, at a time when Evan was 24 years old and earning a bachelor's degree from Washington and Lee University in Lexington, Virginia. According to Shapiro, Kemp "felt that . . . telethons fostered the stereotype that muscular dystrophy was a tragedy, its 'victims' childlike and perpetually sick, and that these misconceptions hurt disabled people more than the condition itself."[8]

In 1981, Kemp wrote an op-ed article for the *New York Times* that disparaged the MDA telethon, claiming that it conveyed the notion that handicapped people were ill and in need of a cure. Such beliefs, he argued, made the public fearful of muscular dystrophy and thus afraid of those who had it. It was not until the 1980s and 1990s that larger numbers of disability activists echoed Kemp's complaints. Some of these critics also charged that a fair portion of the money raised in the MDA telethon was used to pay for the extravagant affair, and not for research or disability services. Other critics noted that the money that found its way into research grants was often being used to enhance prenatal screening services that could identify fetuses exhibiting potential disabilities. In this way, the MDA telethon—which relies on heartfelt stories of disabled children meeting life's challenges—was raising money to ensure that other children like them will never be born. This insidious message infuriated many activists who had been fighting public perceptions that a life with disabilities was a fate worse than death. Few disability activists, then, believed that the money raised by telethons was worth the negative stereotypes these events were perpetuating in a society that already marginalized the handicapped. As Kemp wrote in his *New York Times* piece, "If it is truly to help, the telethon must show disabled people working, raising families and generally sharing in community life."[9] Not until the 1990s, however, would more representative reflections of disability be integrated into telethons—and even this did not placate some activists who insisted that the nature of all telethons is to divide society between the fortunate and unfortunate.

THE START OF THE DISABILITY RIGHTS MOVEMENT

Although early disability activists worked to counter nefarious images and push for expanded opportunities in the workforce, their efforts had not given birth to a collective disabilities movement by mid-century. Many struggles were localized, and the gains could be limited. Better rehabilitation techniques and service facilities, for example, certainly benefited handicapped individuals, but they did little to improve the outsider status of people with disabilities. The greatest strides had been made by veterans' organizations, but it was still easy for mainstream America to make distinctions between a wheelchair-bound war hero and a cerebral palsy victim. Such classifications kept the disability community fragmented, and in some cases the division was maintained from within as well as from without. In the 1960s, however, the entire concept of disability in America changed. Inspired by the tactics and goals of the civil rights movement, disabilities activists in many camps championed the notion that only a national or global disabilities movement could embolden the disabled to claim their rights in order to compel society to rethink its prejudices and fears.

Much of the new political activism taking shape in the early 1960s was fomented on college campuses as young Americans gained access to higher education in record numbers. The disability rights movement was no exception. Some U.S. colleges had experimented with handicapped accessibility in the late 1940s and 1950s. The Champaign-Urbana campus of the University of Illinois was one of the first academic institutions to experiment with a program for the disabled. Though providing no funds for the program, the school allowed activists—supported by grants from the American Legion and other veterans' groups—to build access ramps to school facilities to prove that the handicapped could easily attend classes and navigate the campus if given the opportunity. The project's instigator, Tim Nugent, also helped develop lift-access buses to accommodate wheelchairs, and he created a sports program for students with various disabilities. Quickly, the campus's facilities grew to keep pace with disabled enrollment. Historians Doris Zames Fleischer and Freida Zames note that "by the fall of 1962, students with severe disabilities shared responsibility for the operation of the newly established University of Illinois residence, the Guy M. Beckwith Living Center, renamed Beckwith Hall in 1992."[10] The authors state that the University of Illinois stood out throughout the 1960s as one of the few major universities to provide wheelchair access on campus and offer specially designed programs for the disabled.

BERKELEY AND THE ORIGINS OF INDEPENDENT LIVING

The year that the Beckwith Living Center opened proved to be a watershed year for civil rights, including disability rights. Just as a young African American named James Meredith integrated the University of Mississippi in 1962, Ed Roberts, a quadriplegic who had been disabled by polio, broke educational barriers by being admitted to the University of California at Berkeley. Unlike the University of Illinois's tolerance for its disability experiment, Berkeley was less welcoming to disabled students. One campus administrator reportedly informed Roberts, "We've tried cripples and it didn't work."[11] Roberts persisted, however, and after winning the support of a campus health official, he was finally enrolled. Joseph Shapiro views Roberts's admittance as a defining moment in the disability rights movement. He even claims, "The disability rights movement was born the day Roberts arrived on the Berkeley campus."[12]

Roberts's enrollment was not broadly significant in itself, but what he helped accomplish at the university lends some credence to Shapiro's enthusiastic claim. Entering a campus with limited disabled accessibility, Roberts relied on the help of his brother (also a UC student) to transport him to classes and otherwise assist him on a daily basis. He was also compelled to live in a wing of the campus's Cowell Hospital because the student dormitories did not have floors strong enough to hold the iron lung in which Roberts was confined at various times in the day. But meeting these challenges turned Roberts into something of a celebrity when a local newspaper carried his story. Within a few years, other severely disabled students followed Roberts's lead and joined him at Berkeley. In 1967, Roberts and 11 other wheelchair-bound and iron lung–confined students formed the Rolling Quads in Cowell's makeshift dorm. This tight-knit group absorbed the messages of the civil rights movement as well as the anti-Vietnam War movement and Berkeley's own Free Speech movement. They learned that students had the power to effect change on campus and influence national politics; they also believed that minorities can make their voices heard.

In 1968 Roberts was approached by his former college advisor, Jean Wirth, to help her create a national program to assist minority college students who were often forced by circumstance to drop out of higher education. Roberts accepted and began writing a federal grant application that would include the disabled in this definition of minority. In this way, federal money could be used to provide transportation, jobs, and other necessities to keep disabled students in academia. In 1970, the proposal translated into the inauguration of the Physically Disabled Students' Program (PDSP) at Berkeley. The agenda of the PDSP was to make Berkeley wheelchair accessible and to initiate services that would allow students with disabilities to live independently. The Rolling Quads were instrumental in determining what these services would entail and helming the departments that oversaw them. They concluded that the PDSP should hunt down and secure accessible housing, and it should hire a pool of personal assistants who could do everything from push wheelchairs to prepare meals (an element lacking, for example, from the University of Illinois's experiment). Shapiro adds, "The Rolling Quads also ran PDSP's advocacy department, walking students through the maze of red tape and bureaucracy that accompanied attendant-care funding and other benefits and services."[13]

The Berkeley program proved to be quite radical. Although some attempts at independent living programs had been tried as early as the 1940s, they often had limited scope, and lack of funds usually ensured their demise. In 1957 and again in 1961, bills advocating independent living even circulated through Congress, but neither was passed into law. Besides achieving federal recognition and support, Roberts and the PDSP redefined independent living to emphasize the role of the disabled in determining what types of assistance they needed to lead autonomous lives outside of institutional care. In addition, both Roberts and the organization wanted society to face the limitations it placed on the disabled and restructure itself to include people with disabilities as active members of communities. "Independence. Self-sufficiency. Mainstreaming. Disability as a social problem," Shapiro writes. "These were the principles that guided the PDSP and the disability rights movement of which the PDSP was the leading edge."[14]

In a short time, the PDSP moved Berkeley's students with disabilities out of Cowell Hospital and into the surrounding community. The program was so successful at demonstrating how independence, self-sufficiency, and mainstreaming could be achieved that many other disabled young people flocked to enroll at the university. People with disabilities in the Berkeley community also availed themselves of PDSP assistance. By spring 1971, the PDSP staff was overwhelmed with clients looking for housing, attendants, and other services. Roberts and the PDSP leadership decided to launch a new program to handle the needs of the non-students who wanted aid. They opened the Center for Independent Living (CIL) in 1972 and set it up to function along the same lines as the PDSP. The CIL had a rocky start, but by 1974 the center had enough federal grants to keep it in continuous operation. The success of the CIL brought attention to Berkeley and inspired other communities across the nation to attempt pilot programs of their own. According to Robert Funk, the CIL "became the model and symbol of what individual disabled people could achieve given the opportunity. It offered hope and dignity and had profound influence on disability professionals, Congress, and disabled people throughout the United States."[15] California governor Jerry Brown took particular interest in the program and appointed Ed Roberts the state's new director of the Department of Rehabilitation in 1977, the same agency that fifteen years previously had refused to fund Roberts's enrollment tuition at UC Berkeley.

THE REHABILITATION ACT OF 1973

The U.S. government began to take a serious interest in Americans with disabilities in the late 1960s and early 1970s. Not only were college campuses being integrated and physically altered, but disabled veterans were returning from Vietnam in large numbers and joining with the student groups and other political action organizations to make their voices heard. In addition, parents of the disabled were pushing politicians for expanded opportunities for their children. In response to this latter outcry, Congress created a federal bureau for the handicapped in 1966, which began funding special education programs that provided new teaching materials and trained teachers in disability instruction. Then, in 1968, Congress passed the Architectural Barriers Act, which required all buildings financed by federal funds to provide means of access to people with disabilities (though the act had no provisions to enforce compliance).

The most significant and far-reaching government measure came about with the passage of the Rehabilitation Act of 1973. Like many other significant pieces of congressional legislation, the Rehabilitation Act was pushed through Capitol Hill without much fanfare or debate. Since the beginning of the 20th century, seven other rehabilitation bills had passed Congress by the time the 1973 legislation came up for a vote. Most of these previous bills offered increased work opportunities for the disabled community, and the Rehabilitation Act was widely regarded as just another piece of expanded vocational rehabilitation legislation. However, the scope of the 1973 act was far more than vocational training and job placement.

The impetus for the bill grew out of complaints that the federal Rehabilitation Services Administration was not responsive enough to the needs of the disabled, especially the severely disabled who often received no rehabilitation services at all. Under the new act, federal and state authorities would coordinate programs in an effort to reach more people and expand services. To meet this goal, the first four titles of this five-title act spelled out how federal funds would be granted to state agencies, research facilities, and vocational rehabilitation services. As undoubtedly refreshing as these sections were, their significance paled in comparison, though, to that of the fifth title of the act. Bound up in Title V, a catchall section of the act given the prosaic name "miscellaneous," were a host of federal requirements that lawyer, activist, and historian Richard Bryant Treanor calls "novel, unprecedented, . . . and extremely broad in scope and results."[16]

TITLE V AND SECTION 504

Often referred to as the Bill of Rights for Americans with Disabilities, Title V of the Rehabilitation Act of 1973 contains four sections that define the government's commitment to the disabled. Section 501 states that the federal government would adhere to equal opportunity policies with regard to hiring, placement, and advancement of qualified disabled employees. Section 502 established the Architectural and Transportation Barriers Compliance Board (ATBCB) to enforce the Architectural Barriers Act of 1968. Section 503 extended the federal equal opportunity agenda by compelling government contractors to demonstrate affirmative action policies in the employment and advancement of people with disabilities. Finally, Section 504 is a deceptively simple sentence: "No otherwise qualified handicapped individual in the United States . . . shall solely by reason of his handicap, be excluded from participation in, be denied the benefits of, or be subjected to discrimination under any program or activities receiving Federal financial assistance." Of all four sections of Title V, this last proved the most groundbreaking. Although limited to programs receiving federal funds, Section 504 became the first federal measure to recognize and champion the civil rights of people with disabilities.

As soon as President Richard Nixon signed the bill into law in September 1973—after twice vetoing it on the grounds that its measures were too costly and ultimately veered the legislation away from its supposed vocational aims—activists sought to force the government to issue guidelines detailing how Section 504 was to be interpreted and regulated. James L. Cheery, a disabled student at Howard University, was the prime mover in petitioning the government for regulations. Cheery feared that without strict guidelines, the simple wording of Section 504 would be twisted or subverted as each new court case arose in response to civil rights violations. Securing legal counsel, Cheery brought suit against the Department of Health, Education, and Welfare (HEW) in 1976 to convince the government to act. Nationwide protests by disability activists arose in support of Cheery's lawsuit. HEW drew up guidelines after a judge ruled in Cheery's favor, but the department received a new director, Joseph A. Califano, Jr., in 1977 who withheld his signature from the document. As demonstrations swelled in response to the delay, newly elected president Jimmy Carter was hounded by disability activists who had supported his candidacy. Chief among these was the American Coalition of Citizens with Disabilities (ACCD), an advocacy group that had formed just two years prior. Headquartered in Washington, D.C., the ACCD had the ear of the president and established friendly contacts within various parts of the administration, including HEW.

The ACCD pushed for a resolution by early April 1977, but Joseph Califano, the reluctant signatory, made clear that his department needed more time to consider the regulations. Concerned that the delay tactic was veiling a plan to gut the guidelines, disability activists staged sit-ins at HEW offices around the nation on April 5. Most of the demonstrations subsided within a day, but the contingent that held the San Francisco offices remained unmoved for 25 days. The core of this group was made up mostly of employees or clients of the Berkeley Center for Independent Living. They were experienced organizers and activists, and they had already established a community in the Bay Area that garnered public and corporate support. As Joseph Shapiro writes,

> *Food donated by a local Safeway store, Goodwill Industries, McDonald's, unions, and civil rights groups was prepared by the Black Panthers, including an Easter dinner. . . . Several priests lived with the demonstrators to help out with everything from preparing food to doing pastoral counseling and celebrating Easter Mass. A rabbi came to lead a Passover seder. There was even clandestine help, including food smuggling, from some of the federal employees who kept working in the building through the twenty-five days of occupation.*[17]

Regardless of their preparedness and the public's good will, the San Francisco sit-in was a remarkable show of resistance and fortitude, given that several of the protestors had severe disabilities and yet decided to sit in vigil without their needed daily attendants or respirators, catheters, and other health devices. The demonstration of will was enough to persuade Califano to sign the regulations for Section 504. It was an important victory, one that revealed the growing unity of the disabled rights movement and the community's optimistic outlook that change would finally follow the implementation of such definitive civil rights legislation. Looking back on the event, Frank Bowe, the executive director of the ACCD, remarked, "For four years we had fought behind the scenes to try to get the law implemented and enforced. And at the beginning of 1977, for the first time, we had some reason to hope that the law was at last going to become effective."[18]

With the passage of the act and the signing of the Section 504 regulations, the Rehabilitation Act of 1973 became the cornerstone of the disability rights movement, and there was a general feeling that things were changing for the better. Less than two months after the guidelines were released, all federal buildings as well as public schools and universities receiving federal funds were under obligation to provide ramps, elevators, and curb cuts for handicapped access. Schools and colleges were also compelled to admit and provide education for disabled students. Borrowing from the language of the Civil Rights Act of 1964 and Title IX of the Education Amendments of 1972, Section 504 of the Rehabilitation Act outlawed discrimination against the disabled in the same way those other pieces of legislation banned discrimination against minorities and women. In 1978, amendments to the act sanctioned the use of federal funds for independent living centers (Title VII), a form of rehabilitation that was technically ignored in the wording of the act but many believed was implicit in the provisions for "Innovation and Expansion Grants" in Title I. Additional amendments in the 1980s and 1990s spelled out other employment issues as well as mandated that all rehabilitation agencies covered by the auspices of the act create advisory boards that retain a majority of disabled members.

LIMITATIONS OF SECTION 504

All of these worthwhile gains were not won overnight, however, and the disabled community was quick to realize that their optimism was countered by financial pragmatism and a non-disabled public that was sympathetic to the cause but less inclined to help foot the bill for needed changes in public facilities. In one example cited by Joseph Shapiro, citizens of Rudd, Iowa, become outraged when faced with having to spend $6,500 to build a ramp for the town's public library even though no one in the small community of 500 used a wheelchair. Critics throughout the nation complained that the price of compliance with the new laws was high. "This was quite different,"

Shapiro notes, "from the black civil rights movement, where the end of separate accommodations had meant financial savings."[19] Granting civil rights to people with disabilities was a reasonable, even dutiful, act in this period of sweeping social change, but recognizing that implementing these rights meant revamping sidewalks, modifying public restrooms, expanding administrative costs at all federally funded institutions, and paying for a host of other changes was another matter.

In addition to haggling over cost considerations—which disability spokespeople continually argued would be relatively inexpensive—the disabled community also worried whether the Rehabilitation Act would be the hoped-for vehicle of social change. As Fred Pelka notes, the all-important Section 504 "was limited . . . in that it did nothing about entities not receiving federal money." He also states, "Enforcement of 504 was spotty at best, and federal court decisions about its requirements were often confused and contradictory, tending to limit its effectiveness. As a result, entire aspects of American public life, for example, mass transit and housing, continued to be inaccessible to people with disabilities."[20]

There were also immediate challenges to the phrasings and definitions within the law. The first cases to reach the U.S. Supreme Court regarding Section 504 arrived in 1979. In *Southeastern Community College v. Davis*, 442 U.S. 397, the Court ruled that the Whiteville, North Carolina, school did not violate the law by denying the admittance of Frances B. Davis, a hearing-impaired woman, to its nursing program. Although Davis had filed the suit claiming that her Section 504 rights had been infringed, the justices unanimously concluded that Section 504 discrimination was clearly contingent. Because, as the college lawyers argued, Davis's hearing problems would make it difficult to attend to the needs of patients, she did not in the Court's view fit the definition of an "otherwise qualified handicapped individual" in this matter. As Pelka explains, the Court ruled that:

> *In order to be covered by the Rehabilitation Act, an individual must meet the program's basic requirements despite their disability and that a program or institution need not make fundamental alterations to facilitate the participation of people with disabilities if these would substantially alter the program's basic character or involve undue financial and administrative burdens.*[21]

Although the court noted that programs or institutions that failed to make reasonable modifications to accommodate people with disabilities could be cited for discrimination, it averred that the law did not imply that people with disabilities were to be the recipients of affirmative action. This rejection as well as the coining of the concept of "undue burdens" would haunt the progress of the disability movement and disability litigation for decades to come.

THE EDUCATION FOR ALL
HANDICAPPED CHILDREN ACT OF 1975

While the controversy surrounding the Rehabilitation Act was being settled, another great stride for the disabilities movement came in 1975 with
the passage of the Education for All Handicapped Children Act (EAHCA).
Building on Section 504 of the Rehabilitation Act, the EAHCA was drafted
after Congress determined that a million children with disabilities were
excluded from the public school system, and those who were permitted to
attend were not receiving educational benefits that would give them the
opportunity to be equal participants in society. Many of these children in
this latter group were remanded to special education classes that were typically set apart from the rest of the classrooms. There, they had little interaction with nondisabled peers and suffered through rudimentary teaching
exercises that did not test their abilities. By overwhelming majorities, both
houses of Congress chose to rectify the situation. The passage of the act,
which was signed into law by President Gerald Ford and went into effect in
1978, guaranteed that no child with disabilities could be denied access to
public education. The law also ensured that disabled students could no longer be segregated from the general school population unless the severity of
a disability made mainstreaming impractical. Additionally, the law made
educators responsible for learning the latest teaching methods and invited
parents to help plan for the overall education of their children.

The EAHCA (renamed the Individuals with Disabilities Education Act
in 1990) made clear that states are to determine which children require
special services—such as speech therapy, physical therapy, transportation,
and additional educational aids—and then provide these services through
tax money and government grants. Pelka adds, "The act recognizes that
school districts have limited resources. For this reason there is no requirement that they provide the *best possible* education, but rather one that provides opportunities for education roughly equivalent to those provided
nondisabled children."[22] Schools are expected to grant reasonable requests,
and parents do have recourse to challenge any decisions that they feel compromise their children's education.

Along with the Rehabilitation Act of 1973, the EAHCA proved another
important piece of legislation recognizing the civil rights of people with
disabilities. However, the EAHCA was not met with approbation from all
corners of the disabilities community. Some champions of Deaf culture assumed that bringing deaf children into mainstream schools would force
them to abandon sign language and compel them to take up lipreading and
speech. Such skills were not favored by some sections of the deaf community because they denied deaf people their own predilection for sign lan-

guage communication. The American Coalition of Citizens with Disabilities supported this claim despite the fact that the argument seemed to contradict the overriding mission to move people with disabilities into the mainstream. Backed by the ACCD, the deaf community earned the right to have American Sign Language interpreters be accepted as a special service required by deaf students under the EAHCA.

DEAF CULTURE AND BLIND ACTIVISM

The EAHCA was not the first issue to bring deaf advocates out to contend with disabilities concerns. Deaf activists, such as Frank Bowe, have been vital members of the disabilities community working to educate the public and bring about more responsive legislation. But deaf people have always had a unique position within the larger disabilities community. Deafness is not a disability that is readily apparent to observers; it has no physical tell-tale deformity or palsy, and deaf people do not require the aid of obtrusive mechanical devices to survive or get around on a day-to-day basis. Instead, that which sets deaf people apart from the nondisabled world relates to communication.

For centuries, deaf people were considered to be mentally deficient because they could not always understand or be understood in talking society. Given the obstacles to communication, many in the ancient world—including Aristotle—assumed deaf people simply could not be educated. Others, such as Saint Augustine in the fourth century A.D., preached that deafness in children was a sign of God's disfavor with the parents. Such widely held beliefs made deaf people outsiders in both society and the church. In the 1500s, however, Pedro Ponce de León, a Benedictine monk, began teaching speech to the deaf children of Spain's aristocracy. Now referred to as oralism, de Leon's method allowed Spanish heirs to learn how to approximate speech sounds, getting them to talk just enough to evade Spain's inheritance laws that viewed the deaf and mute incapable of owning property or discharging the legal duties of stewardship.

Oralism lingered through the centuries and eventually became the dominant teaching method in Europe and America in the late 19th and early 20th centuries. Institutions that utilized the method emphasized lip-reading and amplified sounds to ensure communication. But oralism could not be taught to the entire deaf community; only those who were not profoundly deaf or those who had experienced their deafness after being able to hear were likely candidates for the oral school. Their counterparts preferred sign language to communicate. Initially formulated in the early 19th century, American Sign Language was the primary means of instruction in many deaf schools until the rise of oralism. It remained the common avenue of communication for the profoundly deaf and even those students of oralism who simply found sign language convenient and easy.

Proponents of sign language cherish this means of communication because it is their own. They argue that being forced to participate in an oral culture devalues their own culture and language. But during the heyday of oralism, the defenders of sign language learned quickly that the ability to speak was prized not only by society at large but by many deaf advocates who saw it as a means of greater participation in a world dominated by speech. As Doris Zames Fleischer and Frieda Zames state, "Since the ability to speak was traditionally a source of political influence in the deaf community, those who used sign language were disadvantaged."[23] Sign language users were considered second-class citizens within their own deaf culture, in addition to being disparaged by outsiders. Alexander Graham Bell waged a campaign to abolish sign language, especially in education, because it supposedly inhibited deaf people's ability to lipread, speak, and integrate with hearing people. The noted inventor's influence coupled with that of other philanthropists persuaded several state legislatures to enact bans on sign language in federally funded schools. Sign language went underground, where it remained popular with deaf students who found it an easier means of communication among themselves when not at work in an oral classroom.

It was not until the 1960s that American Sign Language gained currency. By the middle of that decade, educators at Gallaudet College in Washington, D.C., published *A Dictionary of American Sign Language on Linguistic Principles*. Their work emphasized the distinctive syntactic structures of American Sign Language and revealed that it was a language in its own right, not just a pantomime of English. At roughly the same time, parents groups began showing concern that their deaf children were not receiving the promised benefits of oralism and were much better at communicating by signing. They pressed for reinstating a 100-year-old method of educating the deaf through a combination of sign language and oralism. Within a decade, pure oralism fell out of favor, and the majority of deaf people were educated at schools that taught the "Combined Method." However, oralism remained an active teaching doctrine and still is the preferred method at some schools today.

DEAFNESS AS IDENTITY, NOT DISABILITY

With oralism's decline in the 1960s and 1970s, deaf advocates took advantage of America's progressive political climate to reconceive deaf culture. In 1972, linguist James Woodward was the first to offer a distinction between deaf people and the Deaf. According to Woodward, the former phrase refers simply to those who are hearing impaired, while the latter term reflects a culture that shares traditions and values such as its preference for sign language. Therefore, the Deaf consider themselves a minority within the larger deaf community. Deaf culturists, however, are an active minority, and in the 1960s and 1970s, they invigorated the Deaf arts, including theater and American Sign Language poetry. Many insisted that deafness was not impairment and argued that the Deaf should be classed as an ethnic minority group in America, not as a segment of the disabilities community.

With this attitude, the Deaf reacted against the passage of the Education for All Handicapped Children Act of 1975 because they believed mainstreaming deaf children would negatively impact their heritage. This proffering of a unique cultural identity is also at the root of why the Deaf tend to alienate themselves from other people with disabilities. To embrace that larger community would be to admit that deafness is a disability and not a badge of cultural affiliation. To observers both inside and outside the deaf community, this self-imposed separatism smacks of elitism. As Frank Bowe has written, "Deaf culture advocates cannot have it both ways. . . . They cannot on the one hand benefit from [disabilities legislation with] provisions guaranteeing free public education, social services, and protection against discrimination—all of which costs money, and at the same time hold themselves apart from others who also benefit from such provisions."[24]

Deaf cultural activists, however, do not view themselves as elitist but as defenders of a traditionally oppressed minority. And this awareness spread throughout the deaf community even as great strides in disability legislation were being made. The most prominent eruption of deaf pride came in March 1988 when students at Gallaudet University, the only liberal arts college in the world that tailored its programs specifically to meet the needs of a largely deaf student body, demonstrated against a decision by the university's board of trustees to appoint a hearing president. For months, the students had been staging a "Deaf President Now" campaign and were shocked when the board chose the one hearing candidate, Elizabeth Ann Zinser, among three contenders to head the university. In response, the students rallied and staged a campus-wide takeover that closed the institution. They demanded that a new, deaf president be chosen and that the board of trustees take on a majority of deaf members. The trustees refused, but the contest was not ultimately decided by them. With the faculty and alumni—even the former university president—in favor of a deaf president, Zinser made clear that she did not have the support needed to be an effective leader. She resigned four days after being appointed. Within a week the trustees capitulated to the student demands, and Gallaudet earned its first deaf president. The victory was complete and its achievement had lasting impact. Indeed, the protests drew national and international attention not only because of the nature of the cause but because it was the first time a university had been immobilized by an organized and committed group of disabled individuals. The students revealed the power of a disabled minority and the misguided notions that the nondisabled world still harbored and propagated. Joseph Shapiro concludes that the Gallaudet demonstrations had perhaps the most impact on the disabilities movement itself. In his history of the movement, he writes, "The uprising . . . resonated for people of all disabilities, who empathized with the students' revolt against the paternalistic care of well-meaning but insensitive people who were not disabled."[25]

THE BLIND AND THE NEW YORK CITY SUBWAY GATES

Six years prior to the Gallaudet revolt, some of New York City's blind activists made their own bid for change—one that reflected a division within their own ranks. In that year, the American Council of the Blind (ACB) filed suit against the Metropolitan Transportation Authority (MTA) for putting into service subway cars that did not include gates between adjacent cars to keep people from falling onto the tracks. This danger is especially great for blind passengers who find the entrance doors on subway cars by tapping along the hull of each car until a gap is found. If the gap turns out to be the space between cars, the blind person may mistake it for the entrance and topple onto the tracks. Many such instances had occurred, leaving victims maimed or killed when unaware engineers set their trains in motion. The National Federation of the Blind (NFB) disapproved of the ACB's suit, arguing that blind people could easily be trained to distinguish the precipitous gap from the proper doorway.

The NFB was founded in 1940, and, unlike previous advocacy groups for the blind, it was the first to be chaired by blind leaders. Its first president, Jacobus tenBroek, organized the NFB to fight for economic and welfare justice for the blind. Similar to the League of the Physically Handicapped, tenBroek and his followers wanted access to the mainstream workforce, from which they were routinely denied. Most blind workers were shunted into special workhouses where they labored for substandard wages away from their mainstream peers. In 1948, the organization issued "A Bill of Rights for the Blind," which called for the blind to receive regular pay at ordinary jobs for which they were qualified. Like the Deaf movement, the NFB became more militant over time and soon waged its arguments from a position that blindness was not a matter of disability as much as it was an issue of social prejudice. This attitude was not shared by all members of the NFB, and eventually several broke away from the federation to organize the ACB and other blind advocacy groups in the early 1960s.

As the ACB pressed its lawsuit in 1983, NFB spokesperson Rami Rabby appeared on a television news program, insisting that the blind did not need safety gates. Rabby's argument was based on the belief that the gates would come to symbolize special accommodations for the blind, and the NFB took the position that if the blind eschewed special treatment, they would be more likely to achieve the social integration they desired. Although the two organizations' conflicting messages confused lawmakers, a U.S. district court eventually ruled in 1985 that the gates should go up in accordance with the protections offered by the Rehabilitation Act.

THE GROWTH OF THE INDEPENDENT LIVING MOVEMENT

The deaf students of the 1988 Gallaudet protests and the blind subway riders of New York were part of the first generation to benefit from the Rehabilitation Act of 1973 and the Education for All Handicapped Children Act of 1975. The decade in which the students came of age was one in which disability activists sought to capitalize on their legislative gains while continuing to advocate for greater civil rights recognition. The independent living movement was the prime mover of the period, as disability advocates recognized that living away from institutional care was the first step in achieving personhood in a society that either frowned on or paternalized dependency. As Joseph Shapiro claims, the spread of independent living centers "proclaimed a new ideal of independence. The centers argued that no one—not even doctors or therapists—knew more about the needs of disabled people than disabled people themselves."[26]

In the mid-1970s the nation could only count roughly 50 independent living centers built on the Berkeley model. Halfway into the next decade, the number would grow to almost 300, with at least one present in every state. In 1977, Lex Frieden, a car accident victim whose broken neck left him confined to a wheelchair, founded the Independent Living Research Utilization Project (ILRU) in Texas. The mission of the ILRU was to research independent living issues and to provide information, training assistance, and technical guidance to the government, schools, and all other interested parties. In the following year, thanks to amendments to the Rehabilitation Act, the government began funding independent living centers and ensuring that people with disabilities were involved in the management of these centers and the policymaking of related issues. Speculating on this significant decision, Richard Bryant Treanor suggests that "perhaps Congress was motivated by the well established fact that it costs far less to steer the disabled in the direction of independence than to simply spend money for maintenance and support."[27]

The nation's independent living centers are diverse in their organization, services, outreach capabilities, and funding. All commonly disseminate information on community housing issues, transportation plans, and state and federal benefit programs. Most work one-on-one with clients in providing peer counseling, skills training, and help in obtaining personal assistance services such as attendants or aids for the blind and deaf. Some centers even offer benefits such as legal aid and technical assistance and repair for wheelchairs and other assistive devices. In addition to providing services and programs, the independent living centers are often rallying points for political action. They bring people together to discuss disability issues and unite them to take action against injustices. In more recent years, however, disability activists have urged the centers to become even more militant, arguing that these institutions—now more than 30 years old—have grown complacent and are less willing to do anything that might upset their federal, state, and independent benefactors.

Independent living centers have always been an extension of rehabilitation services. Their goal is to bring people with disabilities out of state facilities to become active members of their communities. The transition has never been easy. As independent living took center stage in 1978, the Rehabilitation Institute of Chicago created a committee to address the needs of recently disabled patients who were ready to move out of the institute and into the community. The committee understood that beyond temporary housing, the rehabilitated had no place that was affordable and accessible to set down more permanent roots. In 1980, the committee set in motion a program called Access Living. The new program established a unique independent living center that not only catered to the patients at the Rehabilitation Institute but also responded to the needs of the disabled throughout the city. Access Living retained a legal team that fought against housing discrimination, among other disability issues, to get its clients into Chicago's neighborhoods. It has since taken part in lawsuits against new building developers who have not adequately adhered to the codes of "adaptable design," a requirement under the 1988 Fair Housing Amendments Act that mandates all new dwellings designated to house four or more families be equipped with permanent access features and be adaptable to the future needs of any disabled resident who may live there.

Thanks to the work of Access Living and all other independent living centers, people with disabilities have found housing outside of nursing homes and other care facilities. Because of this, the independent living movement has had a significant impact on shaping the future of disability rights in America. As Fleischer and Zames state, if it was not for the push toward independent living, "many of the individuals who would become prime movers in the ongoing civil rights struggle for equal rights for people with disabilities might have remained hidden away in institutions or confined in their homes."[28] Many of these activists made it their mission to educate the public about misconceptions concerning people with disabilities and to further educate the disabilities community about the benefits of empowerment. Judith Heumann, a pioneer in the independent living movement and the deputy director of the Berkeley Center for Independent Living, clarified the value of the program when she said, "We have a vested interest in its survival; without it our services disappear." She argues how independent living has given people with disabilities the freedom to be active in pursuit of their rights. "What it amounts to is that disabled people are getting services, feeling secure about the fact that services are not going to be taken away, feeling free to speak out on issues, but then also being able to get into other issues apart from those dealing with sheer personal day-to-day survival [such as] curbcuts [in sidewalks], integrated housing, SSI [social security insurance], accessible transportation, education, jobs." Independent living saves people with disabilities time, time that they can use to advocate for political change. "That is where I feel my energy needs to be invested," Heumann concludes. "That is where I feel the energy of all disabled people needs to be invested."[29]

THE FIGHT FOR ACCESSIBLE PUBLIC TRANSPORTATION

In the 1980s, the disability rights movement, flush with the Section 504 victory and emboldened by the freedoms brought on by independent living programs, began investing more time in turning political gains into practical change. The first target was transportation accessibility. Given the freedom to live anywhere, people with disabilities recognized how vital it was to be able to get to everywhere. In order to achieve that freedom of mobility, public transportation would have to become accessible. However, transportation authorities were not so amenable to changes; installing wider doors and wheelchair lifts as well as broadening the interior aisles on buses would cost money and time. To compel compliance, disability activists filed lawsuits in several different cities to see that Section 504 antidiscrimination policies were enforced among public transportation services receiving federal money.

THE TRANSBUS SETBACK

The first lawsuit to tackle public transportation was attempted in Philadelphia in June 1976. This class action suit was filed in federal court on behalf of 13 united disability groups led by the state's branch of Disabled in Action. In the case, *Disabled in Action of Pennsylvania, Inc. v. Coleman*, the plaintiffs contended that Section 504 of the Rehabilitation Act of 1973 mandated that the disabled not be "denied the benefits of" public transportation services.

Therefore, in their view, the secretary of transportation under the Gerald Ford administration, William T. Coleman, should compel public transportation authorities to see that all mass transit vehicles be made accessible. To achieve this, the plaintiffs stipulated that the transit authorities adopt a new model bus, the Transbus, built by General Motors (GM). The prototypes of this bus featured a retractable boarding lift, a wider body, and other benefits to facilitate disabled riders.

In 1977, six months after the case began, the Jimmy Carter administration took the reins of government, and Coleman was replaced by Brock Adams. The new secretary agreed with the plaintiffs that the law required bus lines to adopt an accessible vehicle model and ordered transit authorities to comply. With the lawsuit now irrelevant, the federal court dismissed the case. Disabilities activists counted their first victory in the fight to make public transportation accessible. However, the euphoria of the moment was short-lived. General Motors soon declared that it would not go ahead with Transbus production because the prototype buses had design flaws. GM argued that the low undercarriage—designed to accommodate a lowered floor for easier accessibility—might make them prone to breakdown in snowy climates. The company also claimed that the expense of retooling their plants to manufacture the Transbus would be prohibitive, especially given that not all of the design problems had been solved. The American Public Transit Association (APTA)—which counted GM among its membership—convinced Congress to reconsider the Transbus mandate in light of these unresolved issues.

Facing such delays, Frank Bowe, the director of the American Coalition of Citizens with Disabilities—one of the groups represented in the Transbus lawsuit—shopped the Transbus concept around to other auto manufacturers. Though most offered the same resistance that GM had, the newly created DeLorean Motor Company, which began operation in 1975, accepted the contract. DeLorean created its own prototype, which it demonstrated for Congress. Yet just as the plans seemed to be moving forward, the entire DeLorean company began to fold. Experiencing cost overruns and manufacturing problems that had nothing to do with the Transbus project, DeLorean was forced to file for bankruptcy in 1982 before any buses were built. The united transit authorities capitalized on the demise of DeLorean by arguing that they could not comply with any enforcement of accessibility if no company was willing to provide these novel buses. The APTA had even filed suit against the Department of Transportation (*APTA v. Lewis*) two years earlier, claiming that the secretary had no power to force public authorities to comply with accessibility. The APTA argued that the costs of accommodating a very few (as the APTA suggested) disabled riders would make public transportation a more expensive and therefore less desirable service for all. As Richard Treanor states, the APTA "estimated the cost of capital improvements, retrofitting stations and vehicles and the like, at 3 to 5 billion dollars."[30] Buoyed by the outcome of the 1979 *Southeastern Community College v. Davis* case, the APTA claimed that the Department of Transportation was exceeding the law in demanding that buses be lift-equipped under Section 504. In 1981, the District of Columbia Circuit Court of Appeals agreed. Mirroring the *Davis* terminology, the court concluded that the regulations placed undue financial burdens on transit systems. The Department of Transportation was directed to revise its regulations. It did so not only in the spirit of court mandate, but also in tune with the directives of the country's newly elected president, Ronald Reagan.

Only three months before the conclusion of the APTA case, Reagan had signed Executive Order 12291, which compelled all federal agencies to make a cost-benefit analysis of any proposed regulations and opt for the least expensive means of achieving the desired result. With this in mind, the Department of Transportation issued new guidelines that suggested transit authorities make "special efforts" to accommodate people with disabilities. The watered-down phrase was a fallback to the wording of the Urban Mass Transit Act of 1970, which promoted the idea of accessibility but provided no specific enforcement strategy to bring about compliance. The new 1981 guidelines also gave individual transit agencies the option ("local option," as the privilege was defined) to adopt whatever type of accessible transportation system it saw fit—whether it be the implementation of lift-equipped buses in its standard fleet or the creation of a segregated paratransit system that would keep disabled riders from sharing buses with the rest of the public.

A BREAKTHROUGH IN NEW YORK

Despite the Transbus setback, disability rights activists did not give up the struggle to win accessibility in public transportation. Some cities such as Seattle and San Francisco had voluntarily embraced accessibility and ran fleets of lift-equipped buses, and activists touted these as models of how all mass transit systems should be operated. But to make the necessary impact, the disabilities community had to breach the nation's largest urban commuter service—the public transportation system of New York City. In 1979, James Weisman, an attorney representing the Eastern Paralyzed Veterans Association (EPVA), took on New York's Metropolitan Transportation Authority (MTA) in *Eastern Paralyzed Veterans Association v. Metropolitan Transportation Authority*. Weisman chose not to argue that the MTA had violated federal law by ignoring wheelchair accessibility on public buses and in the city's subway system; instead he asserted that the transit authority had discriminated against people with disabilities in violation of New York State's human rights law. That law asserts that the state bears the responsibility "to act to assure that every individual within this state is afforded an equal opportunity to enjoy a full and productive life" and that the state must "eliminate and prevent discrimination" in public services among other public sectors. The state court, however, disagreed with Weisman's claim, concluding that buses with boarding lifts and wheelchair-accessible subway stations were a form of "affirmative action" not required by law.

In 1980, as the EPVA case was being settled, the New York City contingent of Disabled in Action (DIA) pursued the accessibility issue through federal channels. Bringing suit against the federal, state, and city transportation services under Section 504, the DIA argued that accessibility of public transit was a right for New York's disabled residents. In the resulting case, *Dopico v. Goldschmidt*, the district court was not convinced of the plaintiff's claim. An appellate court, however, did find upon reexamination that the transit services are required under Section 504 to take at least "modest, affirmative steps" to facilitate disabled riders on public transportation. The decision forced the transit authorities to agree to equip new buses with boarding lifts as older buses were retired from service. But the MTA still proved resistant to implement any rapid change. After working with disability representatives to devise a broad-based plan for accessibility, the MTA stalled for time to consider what it believed were staggering costs that would disrupt service for all transit riders. Unwilling to condone such delays, a troop of disability activists led by the DIA staged a sit-in at the MTA building in Manhattan in November 1980. The protestors had a list of demands for the MTA, but they further hoped that the event would garner media attention and bring the issue before the public at large. Building authorities had the protestors removed, but the MTA was acutely aware of how much bad press would follow the police-led eviction of disabled people in front of television cameras. Indeed, media coverage was critical of the MTA in the days that followed, and news stories made clear the Section 504 issues at stake. As a result, the city's disabilities community believed that the demonstration was successful for three reasons, as Fleischer and Zames enumerate:

> *First, disability activists believed that they had gotten the "real" facts on Section 504 requirements for accessible mass transit to the public. Second, many people with disabilities who had never before participated in social action were motivated to continue their involvement in disability rights issues. And finally, lift-equipped buses that MTA had recently purchased to comply with Section 504 began to appear on the streets of New York City.[31]*

Even after the transit authority appeared to accede to public outcry, problems still dogged the implementation of the new lift-equipped buses. Disabled patrons complained that not enough transit options were put in service throughout the day, leaving many people stranded for hours in their daily travels. Others noted how frequently the lifts did not operate either because they were broken or because the bus drivers failed to have the right key to work the mechanism. After further lawsuits and a war of words carried out in the *New York Times* and other city newspapers, the issue was finally resolved in a compromise that engendered the New York State Handicapped Transportation Act of 1984. This piece of legislation required that 65 percent of all buses in the city be equipped with functioning lifts. It also created a new paratransit system to cater specifically to disabled individuals. Finally, the act compelled the city to make major subway terminals accessible to the disabled.

SETTING STANDARDS FOR REASONABLE ACCOMMODATIONS

The breaching of New York's transit system was a decided victory for disability rights activists and the disabilities community. However, other cities were not so easily persuaded to follow New York's lead. Accessibility advocates continued to argue that Section 504 mandated equal access to public transportation systems that received federal funding, but many transit authority diplomats countered that they were required only to make "special efforts" as the Department of Transportation stipulated. To keep up the pressure, demonstrators from American Disabled for Accessible Public Transit (ADAPT) staged protests outside the various convention centers where the APTA held national conferences. The ADAPT protestors, many riding in wheelchairs, linked arms and blocked entranceways to the convention sites. Several were arrested, bringing their plight before news cameras and resurrecting images of black civil rights disobedience. One Atlanta activist, Mark Johnson, stated, "Black people fought for the right to ride in the front of the bus. We're fighting for the right to get on the bus."[32]

As the contest waged, the transit options for people with disabilities floundered. Local authorities employed some accessible buses but did not run them at all hours of the day. Some determined that only specific routes—those supposedly most frequented by disabled riders—merited such buses. Disability lobbyists took the fight to Washington where they found sympathetic listeners in Alan Cranston and Donald Riegle, two democratic senators discontented with the Reagan administration's Department of Transportation guidelines. Senator Cranston was particularly outspoken, stating that the vague interim guidelines led people with disabilities into "third class citizenship." In 1982, Cranston and Riegle cosponsored a bill that Congress passed as the Surface Transportation Assistance Act. The legislation set standards for service provided by accessible buses and paratransit vehicles, but the standards were leisurely hashed out over the next three years. Then in 1985, the accessible transportation issue received a favorable push when the U.S. Supreme Court ruled in *Alexander v. Choate.*

The *Choate* verdict was the result of a suit by disabled Medicaid recipients who contended that the government of Tennessee violated Section 504 of the Rehabilitation Act when it decreased the number of in-hospital days the Medicaid program would cover. The Supreme Court disagreed with the plaintiffs by stating that Section 504 was not at issue. Though the Court rejected their complaint, the assessment handed down by the majority of justices made clear that the Court believed Section 504 had been misinterpreted in *Southeastern Community College v. Davis*. The majority opinion, led by Thurgood Marshall, contended that accommodations for people with disabilities must be made by federally funded organizations as long as these accommodations are reasonable. Thus, although the case had nothing to do with transportation, transit authorities recognized that the "reasonable" argument would soon plague future suits brought against them.

In May 1986, after much prompting from the courts and federal legislators, the Department of Transportation published revised guidelines concerning the implementation of Section 504. The new regulations were still lacking in enforcement remedies, but they adopted a list of minimum service criteria in accordance with the Surface Transportation Assistance Act of 1982. Yet even these minimum requirements could be ignored by transit systems that spent at least 3 percent of their budgets on transportation services for the disabled. In addition, the "local option" proviso was maintained, granting transit providers the final say on how to distribute services over their routes. In 1986, ADAPT and other organizations sued Secretary of Transportation Elizabeth Dole because the "local option" left accessibility rights at the mercy of transit authorities who might deem it most effective to implement a paratransit-only service in certain cities. This outcome, disabilities spokespeople argued, was not the intent of the law, for it did not strive for inclusion of the disabled but segregation similar to the "separate but equal" policies once dividing the nation along racial lines. The Pennsylvania District Court that heard the case, however, maintained that the "local option" stipulation was valid. A follow-up case argued in 1989 before the Third Circuit Court of Philadelphia (*ADAPT v. Skinner*) supported that decision, reaching, as Richard Treanor claims, "the shocking conclusion that 'separate but equal' transportation facilities are permissible."[33] Both the district and circuit courts, however, found in the same judgments that the 3 percent budgetary limit was capricious and could not hope to serve the needs of disabled riders in small cities where budgets would be likewise small. Therefore, the Department of Transportation was forced again to amend its Section 504 regulations, leaving the decision a mixed blessing for the disability rights community.

Section 504 of the Rehabilitation Act of 1973 was the first piece of legislation to conceive of people with disabilities as full participants in society. And as Fleischer and Zames note, the struggle for inclusion into the mainstream "was played out primarily in the transportation arena."[34] Resistance to accessibility policies proved that not everyone agreed that mainstreaming the disabled community was the government's objective, yet congressional testimony and judicial interpretation suggest the federal government was leaning toward mainstreaming. Even in the *Skinner* case, Judge Carol L. Mansmann wrote that the Section 504 regulations in question required "if not immediate and complete mainstreaming of the handicapped then affirmative steps in that direction."[35] When the Department of Transportation, then, went back to revise its guidelines in 1990, it tried to be forward thinking. When it issued its revisions in March, it factored in pending federal legislation that had the support of Congress and the newly sworn-in president George H. W. Bush. That legislation, the Americans with Disabilities Act (ADA), promised to build upon the civil right protections afforded people with disabilities. Expecting that the ADA would deliver on its promise, the Department of Transportation purposefully left much of the Section 504 legislation open to further debate and refinement. In October 1990, roughly three months after the passage of the ADA, the Department of Transportation finalized many of its regulations in accordance with the rights of people with disabilities as recognized and expounded under the new act. By that time, however, these long-fought-for changes would be overshadowed by the sheer breadth and scope of the Americans with Disabilities Act.

THE AMERICANS WITH DISABILITIES ACT (ADA)

Although years of fighting over accessible transit, employment issues, independent living concerns, and other controversies blazed a trail for the eventual passage of the Americans with Disabilities Act, more than one historian traces the genesis of the act to the changing of the guard at the National Council on the Handicapped (NCH), an office of the Department of Education. That seemingly inconsequential event occurred in 1982 when President Ronald Reagan vacated the department of all the Carter administration appointees—including Judith Heumann who was still also serving as the deputy director of the Berkeley Center for Independent Living. The new Reagan-era replacements were Republicans led by Joseph Dusenbury, the South Carolina Commissioner of Rehabilitation. Serving as his vice chair was Justin Dart, Jr., a disabilities activist and a member of the Texas Governor's Committee for Persons with Disabilities and other state disabilities organizations. Dusenbury—with the president's approval—charged Dart with assessing the current state of federal disability policy and drafting recommendations for needed changes. Well connected with activist organizations, Dart staged public forums with disability representatives from every state to get their input. As Joseph Shapiro writes, "At every meeting the consensus was the same: people of various disabilities all said they suffered from discrimination." Shapiro adds, "Sometimes Dart would bring along members of the council, who would be surprised to find people defining protection of rights—not, say, government welfare or health benefits—as their most pressing issue."[36]

Convincing the National Council of the need for stronger civil rights protections was the first step to encouraging new legislation. The council had been packed with conservatives whom President Reagan anticipated would follow his agenda. That agenda, author Richard K. Scotch states, "articulated a commitment to decreasing substantially the role of government in the lives of Americans, and particularly the role of regulations such as those promulgated for Section 504, which he perceived as unduly intrusive."[37] Adhering to this policy, Reagan had even pushed the Department of Justice and the Office of Management and Budget within the Executive Office of the President to review and rewrite Section 504 regulations in 1981 with the aim of cutting costs. This process was halted, though, after disability organizations lobbied and won support from executives within the administration. Ironically, the administration's attempts to erode the gains already made under Section 504 helped persuade the conservatives on the NCH to back improved disability rights legislation. As Fleischer and Zames suggest, the president's plans to build a cooperative NCH were miscalculated because he "may not have realized that disability issues often transcend liberal-conservative ideology."[38]

DETERMINING THE NEED FOR NEW LEGISLATION

In 1983, Dart's canvassing work was eagerly published by the NCH as a policy report calling for Congress to "act forthwith to include persons with disabilities in the Civil Rights Act of 1964 and other civil and voting rights legislation and regulations." The matter was never acted upon, however, as the council reconsidered its proposal and subsequently resolved that an entirely new piece of legislation would be needed to cover the unique discrimination encountered by people with disabilities. In 1984, the NCH was made an independent federal agency through amendments to the Rehabilitation Act. Sandra Parrino, the mother of a disabled son and the director of the New York Office for the Disabled, took over the chair of the council, and Lex Friedan, an organizer and officer of many disability organizations, was appointed its executive director. The pair ordered the drafting of some recommendations that might lead toward a new legislative act. Over the next three years, Friedan—with the assistance of Parrino, Dart, and legal counsel Bob Burgdorf—compiled past legislation, assistance program data, and personal testimonies of people with disabilities into one grand report entitled *Toward Independence: An Assessment of Federal Laws and Programs Affecting Persons with Disabilities—With Legislative Recommendations.* This new report was sent to Congress and the president in 1986, while Burgdorf began drafting a bill to fit the recommendations.

Support for *Toward Independence* and its companion bill was tentative among lawmakers and activists alike. Even those who wanted to see more comprehensive disability rights legislation enacted feared that a backlash was bound to arise, especially after the recent battles to keep Section 504 afloat. Two congressmen, however, did bring Burgdorf's Americans with Disabilities Act before their peers in 1988. One cosponsor was Tony Coelho, a California Democrat who served as the majority whip in the House of Representatives. Coelho was an epileptic who had faced discrimination throughout his life. In his congressional bid, his opponent even asked voters if they wanted a representative who might suffer a seizure during the debate over vital legislation. Apparently voters did, as Coelho won the election. The other cosponsor was Senator Lowell Weicker from Connecticut. Weicker was a moderate Republican who often refused to adhere to the conservative ideology of his party colleagues. His maverick politics, however, helped garner support for the Burgdorf bill from senators of all stripes, including Republican Bob Dole and Democrat Edward Kennedy. Despite the backing, the bill died at the end of the congressional session. Some, including Justin Dart, attribute its failure to its strong wording and infeasible demands. One such requirement was to compel all public buildings, stores, and restaurants to be accessible within two years of the bill's passage. Another clause gave people with disabilities the right to sue businesses for punitive damages if convicted of discrimination practices. These protections and requirements were too much to haggle over in an election year, when most members of Congress were busy stumping for votes at home. As Shapiro writes, even "Ronald Reagan, in the dwindling days of [his] presidency . . . , apparently did not even know of the bill's existence."[39]

CONGRESS CONSIDERS THE ACT

In 1989, a revised version of the bill was brought back to the Senate by Edward Kennedy (D-MA), Tom Harkin (D-IA), and John McCain (R-AR). After minor quibbling, the new ADA passed through the Senate in September by a vote of 76 to 8. Few were sure, however, how the bill would fare in the House because of the various special-interest committees—including the Surface Transportation Subcommittee—that had to weigh the merits of the law and the precision of its language. In late September, investigation committees began holding hearings on some of the provisions, and more revisions were made. The right to sue for punitive damages was removed, while the definition of what buildings had to be made accessible was expanded to include nearly all structures open to the public. There was also some debate about the inclusion of people with AIDS under the aegis of the ADA. Some legislators attempted to exempt people with AIDS from protection, but their opponents successfully barred the exclusionary language, leaving it unstated whether AIDS specifically qualified as a disability. In the surrounding debates, transportation representatives fought against the bill, stating that complete accessibility was too expensive. Some members of Congress who had strong ties to business interests suggested that small proprietors might also face inordinate costs to make their shops accessible. In addition, some public testimony was harsh if honest. Richard Treanor records one business owner as stating, "A lot of other people . . . like myself . . . do not want to go and be around a lot of other people in wheelchairs or other handicapped."[40] Still, the bill was pushed along in the House by Steny Hoyer (D-MD) and Hamilton Fish, Jr. (R-NY), as Tony Coelho left office facing a financial scandal.

In March 1990, when the House hearings on the bill ended, some disability activists believed that the lackluster results of these debates signaled that the act would be mired in Congress again. A group of demonstrators organized by ADAPT gathered in Washington, D.C., to pressure Congress to keep up progress on the bill. The protestors had come from all over the country and descended on the national capital in fleets of accessible vans. The self-titled Wheels of Justice crusaders represented various disability interests, and more than 700 of them marched or rolled from the White House to Capitol Hill on March 12 to listen to speeches from Justin Dart and other disability leaders. At one pivotal moment, Mike Auberger, a co-founder of ADAPT, uttered the following words before the crowd assembled at the base of the steps up to the Capitol building:

> *The steps we sit before represent a long history of discrimination and indignities heaped upon disabled Americans. We have faced what these steps have represented. . . . We will not permit these steps to continue to be a barrier to our rights and equality. . . . The preamble to the Constitution does not say, "We, the able bodied people." It says, "We, the people." We are the people.*[41]

At the conclusion of his address, the crowd began climbing the 78 steps of the Capitol with many wheelchair-bound attendees leaving their chairs and crawling up the stone flight. Over the next two days, activists continued to flood the Capitol, sitting in at the offices of some members of Congress and suffering arrest.

Despite such grand displays, the fight for passage of the ADA was mostly a grassroots effort. As a collective undertaking it lacked the defining elements of most successful movements in history. In the words of Joseph Shapiro, "It had no Martin Luther King, Jr., to bring it together, no Betty Friedan to write its manifesto. It had no unifying touchstone moment of courage or anger like the Montgomery Bus Boycott, the Freedom rides, or the Stonewall riots. . . . The fight for disability civil rights was a largely invisible, almost underground, movement."[42] Yet for being "invisible," the movement that pressed for the ADA was manifold. Richard Scotch contends that "a broad coalition endorsed the legislation, including virtually every major disability rights group and many other organizations with constituencies beyond disabled people, including the Leadership Conference on Civil Rights and the American Civil Liberties Union."[43] Having such outsider groups represented helped lend credence to the notion that civil rights were at stake. In addition, because many leaders in Washington had firsthand experience confronting disabilities among friends and relations, they worked tirelessly to drum up political support for the ADA. Yet of all the champions of the ADA, Shapiro asserts, "the most surprising, and perhaps the most important, too, turned out to be President George Bush."[44]

A Sympathetic President

George H. W. Bush, who had recently assumed command of the State, had been Ronald Reagan's vice president. He was familiar with some of the politics of disability because it was Bush whom Reagan chose to lead the Task Force for Regulatory Relief, the budget-conscious watchdog agency that was charged with trimming costs from Section 504 and other seemingly expensive legislation. Bush was also personally connected to disability issues. His daughter Robin died of leukemia at age three. His son Neil had a severe learning disorder, and his youngest son, Marvin, had a section of his colon removed and subsequently became a spokesperson for the Crohn's and Colitis Foundation. In addition, Bush's uncle, John Walker, became a quadriplegic after being stricken with polio while at the height of a promising career as a surgeon. According to Shapiro, "Bush spoke with admiration of his uncle's total absence of bitterness."[45]

In the role of vice president, Bush met with disability leaders when contemplating cost-cutting Section 504. He was swayed by their arguments that disabled Americans wanted the opportunities provided by Section 504 so that they could become more independent and cease being reliant on government handouts. The vice president was also overwhelmed by the sheer volume of protest mail he received when Section 504 came under budgetary examination. Bush recognized how vast and committed this overlooked segment of the population was, and he rightly guessed that the political power of the disabled was bound to grow during the years that he would perhaps make a bid for the Republican party's presidential nomination. Indeed, when Bush sealed his victory in the 1988 election, analysts determined that disabled Americans made up a significant percentage of the popular vote that gave Bush the edge over his opponent Michael Dukakis. This swing in votes may have had much to do with Bush's speech at the Republican National Convention in which he stated, "I'm going to do whatever it takes to make sure the disabled are included in the mainstream." Emphasizing the importance of this pledge, Shapiro asserts, "Those simple seventeen words . . . marked the first time that an American presidential nominee had acknowledged disabled people as a political force."[46]

With the president broadly in favor of disability legislation, it was only up to the House of Representatives to ratify the Americans with Disabilities Act. In May 1990, the House took up the bill in earnest. From May 17 to May 22, representatives haggled over eight amendments to the proposed ADA. After hashing out these matters, the bill was put up for a vote. In a few hours the result of years of effort passed through the House by an overwhelming majority vote of 403 to 20. The House bill and the Senate bill were then reconciled and the final version was sent to President Bush. On July 26, Bush held a ceremony on the south lawn of the White House. During a brief speech before an audience that included some 2,000 disability rights advocates, the president stated, "Let the shameful wall of exclusion finally come tumbling down." With that, he signed the Americans with Disabilities Act into law. Representatives of 180 different disability groups then endorsed the act. As Shapiro describes, "There were groups representing all the major disabilities, including spinal cord injuries, deafness and visual handicaps, mental retardation and mental illness, as well as those for newer or less-well-known conditions, such as AIDS, Tourette's syndrome, and chronic fatigue syndrome."[47] Many in attendance had been with the movement for years, and as Treanor concludes, "They had much to be proud of and much to be thankful for."[48]

THE ADA AND ITS MANDATES

As Richard Treanor asserts, "The Americans with Disabilities Act was the most significant federal legislation relating to civil rights for the disabled since the Rehabilitation Act of 1973. It complemented that act, and provided in the private sector what the 1973 act provided in the federal sector."[49] Its language and philosophy borrowed from the Civil Rights Act of 1964 and Section 504 of the Rehabilitation Act of 1973. Unlike Section 504, however, the ADA is quite extensive in order to preempt the types of challenges brought against the hazy wording of the Rehabilitation Act. The ADA has been codified as Public Law 101-336, and its precepts are laid out under five title headings.

Title I

Title I prohibits businesses with more than 15 employees from discriminating against people with disabilities who are qualified to perform the tasks of a given employment position. In part the law reads, "No covered entity shall discriminate against a qualified individual with a disability because of the disability of such individual in regard to job application procedures, the hiring, advancement or discharge of employees, employee compensation, job training, and other terms, conditions, and privileges of employment." Employers are also expected to make "reasonable accommodation" for disabled workers, but the employers may deny such accommodation if it would bring "undue hardship" upon the business. Since the expense of these accommodations—which might include jobsite accessibility or the modification of needed tools and machinery—was the burden of the employer (that is, federal funds were not provided), the employer could seek federal intervention to bar excessively costly changes.

Title II

Title II of the ADA declares that people with disabilities cannot be excluded from "participation in or denied the benefits of the services, programs or activities of a public entity." The services covered under this title include all federal, state, and local communication services, transportation services (including Amtrak, the national railroad), and public programs and facilities. The focus of this part of the act is on accessibility and transportation. It mandates structural changes in public places, including the requirement that all public sidewalks must have curb cuts for wheelchairs and other mobility devices. It states that all public programs and events must be accessible to the disabled or the venue must be changed to an accessible location. It builds on Section 504 to compel that all buses, trains, and train stations be made accessible (although some hardship complaints are tolerated and implementation times are not uniform). The act also prompts transportation authorities to create paratransit services to individuals who cannot access fixed-route commuter lines. Furthermore, through various lawsuits and complaints, the term "accessibility" under Title II has been broadened to include equal access to public services such as police, fire, and emergency response systems. For example, 911 distress switchboards had to be made accessible to users of teletypewriters.

Title III

Title III prohibits discrimination against people with disabilities in places of public accommodation or by services operated by private entities. Therefore, just as the Civil Rights Act of 1964 banned segregation or any form of discrimination against African Americans in public and private establishments,

41

the ADA extends that protection to the disabled. Restaurants, hotels, gas stations, stores, malls, theaters, hospitals, libraries, museums, and private schools, for example, must be made accessible to people with disabilities as far as needed changes are "readily achievable." As Treanor explains, "'Readily achievable' means easily accomplished and able to be carried out without much difficulty or expense." He also states:

> *In determining whether an action is readily achievable, factors to be considered include the nature and cost of the action, the overall financial resources of the facility, the number of persons employed in such a facility, the effect on expenses and resources, the size of the business and the number, type, and location of its facilities, the type of operation including the composition, structure, and functions of the work force, and the geographic separateness, administrative or fiscal relationship of the facility.*[50]

Buildings erected after 1993 had to be wheelchair accessible. All multilevel shopping malls had to have elevators. Retrofitting of existing buildings had to be done in accordance with the "readily achievable" maxim. In addition, Title III dictates accessibility rules for some forms of transportation. Whereas Title II applies to public transportation, Title III regulates private transportation services such as privately owned bus lines, taxi services, hotels with operating shuttles, and limousine companies. Finally, Title III specifies that litigants who bring noncompliant entities into court over matters of accessibility cannot sue for damages; they can only—if found in the right—compel the entities to make the needed changes to meet accessibility requirements.

Title IV

Title IV contends with telecommunications issues for the deaf and speech disabled. Most of these individuals use teletypewriters to send messages over the phone. A message can be read if the recipient also uses a teletype machine, but if the recipient is not hearing or speech impaired and uses a standard voice phone, the message would not get through. Title IV, therefore, requires that telecommunications services provide relay centers where users of teletypewriters can have their written phone messages translated into speech so that they may reach recipients who are not speech or hearing impaired. Fleischer and Zames note that the operators who provide the translation services "cannot change the content of conversations, limit the length of calls, maintain records, or disclose to others the contents of relayed conversations."[51] In addition to aiding phone services, Title IV mandates that federally funded television broadcasters provide closed captioning for the hearing impaired.

Title V

Finally, Title V of the Americans with Disabilities Act is a catch-all of provisions and clarifications not made explicit under the other titles. It defines those who cannot claim protection under the ADA for professed disorders. For example, the title states that pedophiles, voyeurs, transvestites, and transsexuals are not covered by the ADA for their sexual or identity disorders. Similarly, persons with criminal disorders are also excluded from protection. The title also protects those who have filed claims under the ADA and allows for some recompense of litigation expenses for those who win suits that pertain to ADA violations. Most significantly, though, Title V states that nothing in the ADA is meant to limit existing protections under the Rehabilitation Act of 1973 or any other disability rights laws. Such laws include state and local regulations that may provide greater protections than the ADA itself.

RESISTING THE SOCIAL MODEL OF DISABILITY

Many in the disabilities community were overjoyed with the passage of the Americans with Disabilities Act. Not only did it secure the rights and protections of people with disabilities under the law, it also brought the issue of disability rights to public attention. Indeed, the disability rights movement had already gained much sympathy from the nondisabled public, and the appearance of more independent disabled individuals in society brought greater acceptance of the mainstreaming of this previously invisible segment of the population. But, as Fred Pelka and others have noted, passage of the law "brought with it some disillusionment." Pelka observes, "People who expected to see an overnight change in the way society treated those with disabilities were disappointed."[52]

Perhaps part of the disillusionment was due to a shift in theoretical approach to disability that the ADA demanded. Mary Johnson, the founder of the *Disability Rag* magazine, argues succinctly, "To understand its tenets, one must use a new model." The ADA does not configure disability within those who are disabled. Instead, it eschews the medical model of disability in favor of a social construction. As Johnson explains, the socio-political model of disability "sees the problem as the society which fails to accommodate to individuals and groups who are deemed different, abnormal, 'they.' The socio-political model says that separating people out into a group, labeling them and denying them access and accommodation on the basis of that label, has nothing to do with medicine. It says that it is simply a political act."[53] The social model challenges society to recognize that disability is not a biological matter; it is an environmental, social, and political concern. People with disabilities, then, are only "disabled" in the sense that society and its way of doing things has made them less able to participate in business, recreation, public events, and other aspects of day-to-day life. Or as Professor of Political Science Iris Marion Young illustrates, "Moving on wheels is a 'disadvantage' only in a world full of stairs."[54] Society has yet to embrace this worldview primarily because it shifts the blame for impairment upon society as a whole. In the aftermath of its passage, therefore, some elements were resistant to the philosophy of the ADA and others argued that the act was an unnecessary piece of legislation.

Retail and service businesses largely approved the passage of the ADA. Making minor alterations to building design and facilitating the disabled, they realized, brought more customers to their shops, restaurants, and other outlets. Hotels and movie theaters, however, have been among the most resistant commercial facilities to make accessibility changes. Since the Title III provisions went into effect in 1992, many hotels have been sued for failing to provide ramps or other accessibility considerations to the disabled. In 1996, the Justice Department filed suit against the Days Inn chain of hotels after receiving dozens of complaints from disabled travelers. Days Inn franchise owners argued that they had built their hotels in compliance with the corporation's design standards; however, these standards were drafted well before the ADA took effect. Days Inn of America—the parent company—maintained that it bore no responsibility for the noncompliance of the individual franchises. The Justice Department believed otherwise, stating that Days Inn was required to provide building standards that adhered to the ADA mandate. Lawyers for the department even pointed out that the costs of making such changes during the building of hotels was negligible, and therefore plans should include necessary alterations before franchise owners end up bearing the considerable expense of retrofitting. In 1999, Days Inn of America settled the lawsuit by agreeing to provide interest-free loans to franchise owners who had to make postconstruction accessibility alterations. The settlement was significant because Days Inn is the largest hotel chain in America, and other corporate hotel enterprises will likely follow its lead or face similar litigation.

Despite such examples of forced compliance, Richard Scotch asserts that some providers of public accommodations as well as some business owners have been slow to accede to the trend. "This delayed response," he writes, "has been due, in part, to the perceived ambiguity of several statutory provisions and the desire for judicial clarification of how and to whom the law specifically applies." He concludes, "Many affected entities have taken a wait-and-see approach or have responded to individual situations on an ad hoc basis, while others have resisted change unless forced to comply by government agencies or the courts."[55]

ADA BACKLASH

Backlash against the ADA did not occur merely in response to the passage of the law; resistance to this type of legislation remained constant for decades before the bill's proposal and well after its implementation. In the words of CNN correspondent Raju Chebium, "Critics say they are not against equal rights for the disabled. But the ADA, they say, may not be the best vehicle to ensure and expand those rights."[56] Some of the main contentions are that compliance with the ADA is too expensive and the required turnaround times for compliance are too short. Writing in a 2005 issue of *Fortune: Small Business*, Justin Martin relates the story of Dave Mock, a saddle maker in California, who was sued under the ADA for several alleged violations including the fact that his counter was too high for customers in wheelchairs. According to Martin, Mock settled out of court when his lawyers' fees reached $27,000. Instead of making the needed alterations to his store—which would have cost at least another $20,000, Mock chose to close his business. The decision was a "great irony," Martin asserts, because the store was founded by Mock's uncle, a paraplegic, back in 1914.

Martin also claims that small business owners are often the most adversely affected by the ADA. Because the Justice Department and the Equal Employment Opportunity Commission (the two federal agencies that administer the ADA) do not routinely send inspectors on rounds to warn of potential violations, small businesses are forced to navigate the history of court interpretations of ADA statutes on their own if they wish to know if they are conforming to the law.[57] Those who cannot keep abreast are in peril, critics say. In 1997, film actor and director Clint Eastwood was hit with a lawsuit by a patron who stated that the parking lot and at least one of the bathrooms in his Mission Ranch Hotel in Carmel, California, were not accessible to people with disabilities. Facing more than $570,000 in legal fees, Eastwood took his plight to Congress in 2000 to see if the ADA could be amended to end such costly proceedings and to give business owners 90 days to make lawful changes that adhere to accessibility codes. Some members of Congress took up Eastwood's challenge and proposed the ADA Notification Act, which would amend Title III to include the 90-day compliance timeframe. The bill has yet to pass. In the meantime, Eastwood won the lawsuit brought against him. After determining that the plaintiff, Diane zum Brunnen, had never tried to use the Ranch Hotel facilities, the jury concluded that her accessibility claims were unsupported. The actor told interviewers that he was in favor of disability rights, but he believed Brunnen had been persuaded by money-hungry lawyers to file the suit.

This contention that some lawyers and disabled individuals are out to get rich off noncompliance issues is another motivation for the backlash against the ADA. Some critics maintain that a host of frivolous lawsuits have reached the courts in regard to noncompliance and other ADA matters, and a healthy proportion of these, the critics charge, have been enacted by people who may not have lasting disabilities. Because pursuing these court battles can be expensive, especially for small businesses, many owners choose to settle immediately. Martin writes, "Of particular concern for small businesses are so-called frequent fliers—disabled customers who go from establishment to establishment, uncovering alleged ADA violations and filing suits." Martin tells of one California restaurant entrepreneur's experience with a frequent flier named Jarek Molski. Molski, a wheelchair user, visited the restaurateur's three establishments within a three-week period (two of the restaurants on the same day, and one two weeks later) and then slapped the owner with an ADA lawsuit in which Molski claimed that all three establishments had inaccessible bathrooms and that he had injured himself "not once, but in each of the three bathrooms." According to Martin, a federal judge marked Molski as a "vexatious litigant" who used his suits as a means of extortion. He has since been banned from making any more claims in California without the approval of a judge. However, Molski still has access to state courts, where he already won $18,000 in a lawsuit against one of the three restaurants.[58]

In addition to fearing lawsuits from disabled customers, business owners are also reportedly shy of hiring people with disabilities as employees. This disinclination supposedly stems from similar apprehensions that disabled employees may sue businesses for not catering to whatever "reasonable accommodations" a disabled worker may require. Chebium states that "some employers might reject disabled applicants under some pretext other than the disability in order to avoid the potential for ADA lawsuits."[59] In support of this argument, critics of the ADA point to the fact that the employment of people with disabilities actually dropped in the years after the enactment of the law. However, as defenders of the ADA note, businesses win an overwhelming 98 percent of lawsuits brought against them by disabled employees. Llewellyn H. Rockwell, Jr., the President of the Ludwig von Mises Institute, argues that this fact merely proves that the law invites excess litigation. He concludes most businesspeople reject the provisions of the ADA because "the ADA is utterly incompatible with a free society, which has ironclad rules against interfering with the right of free contract between employers and employees."[60]

CURRENT AND ONGOING DISABILITY RIGHTS CONCERNS

In March 1998, the U.S. Supreme Court heard the first case pertaining to the ADA. In *Bragdon v. Abbott*, dentist Randon Bragdon refused to treat

Sidney Abbott in his dental office because the patient had acknowledged that she was HIV positive. Abbott sued Bragdon under the ADA for discrimination. She claimed protection under the act because her HIV status was a disability that, she argued, limited a major life activity—reproduction. Abbott won the case in federal court and then again in appellate court. Bragdon petitioned the Supreme Court to review the case. The Court agreed to address three fundamental questions in the case: whether HIV is a disability according to the ADA; whether reproduction is a major life activity as defined by the ADA; and whether the courts should defer to the opinions of health care providers who refuse treatment based on perceived threat to their own health. On June 25, 1998, in a five to four ruling, the Court determined that Abbott's decision not to have children because of HIV infection made her eligible for ADA protection. The Court did not, however, make a blanket statement that HIV was always a protected disability. It also concluded that the courts are not compelled to defer to the judgment of medical professionals who refuse treatment of patients based on suspected health threats. The *Bragdon* case seemed to exemplify the benefits of ADA protections, while setting a precedent for allowing those infected by HIV to be covered by the act. In subsequent cases, however, the Court ruled that impairments—such as hypertension and poor vision—were not eligible for ADA protection because they could be corrected so as to not limit a major life activity.

INCLUSION AND ELIGIBILITY

Defining who is and who is not disabled according to the Americans with Disabilities Act (and society in general) is one of the issues that remain current in the post-ADA world. Society most often equates the term "disability" with physical impairments; specialized accommodations for the disabled, for example, are marked with blue signs displaying a white wheelchair outline. The presence of ramps and widened bathroom stalls also reinforces the notion that the modern world has had to adapt physically to the needs of this minority. In addition, most people can easily extend the concept of "people with disabilities" to include the mentally disabled—especially those who possess disabilities that have physical signatures. However, the disability community encompasses a larger segment of the population than suggested by constrictive, popular conceptions of the wheelchair-bound and the mentally challenged. Many within the broader disabilities community have invisible disabilities, impairments and conditions that have no obvious physical hallmarks. Besides deafness and blindness, the definition of disability has been applied to conditions such as epilepsy, diabetes, sleep apnea, learning disorders, and a host of other ailments. The Equal Employment Opportunity Commission (EEOC) has also established guidelines that protect those with psychiatric impairments that include bipolar disorders, schizophrenia, and major depression.

Regardless of the conditions put forth, a person who claims disability protection under the ADA must demonstrate that the impairment restricts some major life activity. Courts have in some instances, though, denied plaintiffs protection under the ADA if their impairments could be mitigated by medicines or corrective devices. The EEOC, however, has often disagreed with the courts over this matter, insisting that many psychiatric conditions, for example, often go undiagnosed and therefore unchecked by medicine or therapy, leaving sufferers effectively disabled. Still, the Department of Justice and other federal agencies involved in the administration of the ADA do not maintain a list of disabilities that are covered by the law. Critics find this a shortcoming because it ostensibly allows an inordinate amount of people to claim a disability of some sort and therefore receive special benefits and protections. In a 1998 *U.S. News & World Report* article, John Leo remarked,

> *Hypersensitivity to tobacco smoke is a "handicap" under the Rehabilitation Act of 1973, infertility has qualified as a disability, and multiple chemical sensitivity [MCS—in which sufferers claim to be allergic to chemicals used to make rugs, furniture, and other common items in their home or work environment], about which everything is known except whether it really exists, is sometimes recognized as a disability by the Social Security Administration. As one doctor said about MCS cases: "Too many people are walking around thinking they have a medical problem when they just have life."[61]*

Champions of a broad definition, however, argue that the ADA was designed to include more than the visibly disabled. Wendy E. Parmet, a professor of law, states:

> *Indeed, the evidence that the ADA's drafters and supporters understood the definition's potential breadth is overwhelming. Perhaps most apparent is the statute's own preamble, with its estimate that there are forty-three million Americans with disabilities. . . . That the definition was to be expansive, moreover, was evident from a series of committee reports discussing the construction of the term. True, the application of the definition to certain specific conditions was not fully delineated. However, that uncertainty was inevitable, given an understanding of disability as a socially constructed phenomenon.[62]*

Without a set list of disabilities, the courts have often had to decide what constitutes a disability in terms of the ADA. Occasionally, this has led to some confusion. For example, in *Toyota Motor Mfg. v. Williams*, a former assembly line worker claimed that the repetitive tasks of a newly assigned position reawakened carpal tunnel syndrome that she acquired while working on the plant's assembly line. Unable to perform her duties, Williams was dismissed. A district court heard Williams's case for ADA discrimination protection but ultimately denied her plea. The court attested that carpal tunnel had not limited a major life activity and that Williams had no record of a substantially limiting impairment. A circuit court, however, reversed that decision, citing that Williams's manual impairment did limit her ability to perform requested job tasks, and therefore Toyota should have made accommodation for her disability. Finally, the U.S. Supreme Court heard the case and decided in 2002 that the circuit court had reached an erroneous conclusion. The Supreme Court justices rendered an opinion making clear that the impairment must be long-term or permanent.

One unique feature of the ADA is that eligibility of coverage is not limited to those who have a verified disability. The language of Title I stipulates that the ADA also protects those who are perceived as having a disability—even if they do not actually possess one or claim to possess one. This provision was included to ensure that no person could be discriminated against based on the perceived limitations of disability.

CRIMES AGAINST THE DISABLED

Maintaining a broader definition of disabilities—and affording protection to those whom are perceived to be disabled—has helped in discrimination cases involving employment and housing issues. It has done nothing to protect people with disabilities from violent or hateful crimes. Disability advocates argue that people with disabilities are often the victims of vicious crimes that are directed at them because they are disabled. Like other minorities, the disabled suffer their share of hate crimes, which include firebombing of group homes, vandalizing of accessibility devices, and personal assault. The Bureau of Justice Statistics records that 53 of a total of 7,163 incidents of hate crimes in the United States were directed against the disabled in 2005. Professor Jacqueline Vaughn Switzer contends that such numbers do not accurately represent the true scope of crimes motivated by disability. She states, "Some observers refer to persons with disabilities who are the victims of physical abuse, violence, or intimidation as the 'invisible victims.' Their exact numbers are unknown because many crimes against disabled people are not separately categorized or, more commonly, are unreported or never prosecuted." Switzer cites reports that suggest the rate of crimes against people with disabilities may be "four to ten or more times higher than the rate against the general population."[63] The *Boston Globe* did its own investigation in 2001 of crimes against the disabled in Massachusetts. The paper found that of 342 cases launched between 1997 and 1999, only 18 (about 5 percent) ended in conviction. "By contrast," the *Globe* notes, "about 70% of crimes involving able-bodied victims resulted in convictions during that period." The paper stated that the low conviction rate had much to do with the fact that police and prosecutors refused to push cases forward because of "concerns about how disabled or retarded victims would hold up in court."[64]

Until the mid-1990s, the federal and state governments did not categorize disability as a characteristic of a crime victim. In 1994, New York became the first state to gather statistics on hate crimes against the disabled, and in 1998 the federal government passed the Crime Victims with Disabilities Awareness Act, which mandated the collection of crime statistics involving people with disabilities. In 2000, President Bill Clinton reauthorized the Violence Against Women Act (originally passed in 1994). The newer version contains specific rewording to emphasize protections for women with disabilities. Women are a highly vulnerable segment of the disabled community. Of particular note among the criminal offenses suffered by disabled women are domestic violence and sexual assault. To emphasize this problem, Switzer relates the highly publicized rape of a mentally disabled woman in Glen Ridge, New Jersey, in March 1989. In this case in point, a group of high school athletes lured a 17-year-old woman with an IQ of 49 into a basement recreation room where they raped her with a broomstick and a baseball bat. During some stages of the violent act, the room was crowded with more than a dozen onlookers who reportedly did nothing to stop the assault. Although the defense attorney argued that the woman went willingly into the basement and flirted with the boys shamelessly, the court eventually convicted three of the attackers of sexual assault and one on conspiracy charges.

WOMEN AND MINORITY REPRESENTATION

Disabled women are a distinct subgroup of the larger disabilities community. Their unique plight has often been overlooked in disability literature and policy. Adrienne Asch and Michelle Fine write in the introduction to their book on the subject, "Women with disabilities traditionally have been ignored not only by those concerned about disability but also by those examining women's experiences."[65] The authors state that the feminists have abandoned them because they are doubly stigmatized as weaker and more helpless than their peers. And many activists have also purposefully avoided promoting disabled women's issues because being both disabled and female has traditionally run counter to the notion of independence that disabilities advocates are endorsing. For these reasons, disabled women have been hovering at the bottom of the economic and social ladder—earning the lowest incomes, obtaining the fewest jobs, and not always knowing about or availing themselves of the services offered to people with disabilities. Writing for the Center of Human Policy at Syracuse University, Rannveig Traustadottir asserts that women with disabilities are also "likely to have received less education than both non-disabled women and men with disabilities."[66] These disadvantages, Asch, Fine, and Traustadottir claim, are not statistically well-reported, and the literature on disabled women's issues remains scant—further demonstrating, these authors maintain, how often this segment of the disabled population is disregarded.

Other minority subgroups under the disabilities umbrella also have been overlooked or ignored in disabilities literature. Typically, these groups exist at the intersections of multiple minority labels. For example, ethnic/racial minorities who are disabled often face identity issues and social discriminations not shared by the entire disabilities community. Likewise, homosexual people with disabilities must come to terms with being doubly stigmatized in society and perhaps even ignored within the larger disabilities population. Several authors who have explored minority subgroups among the disabled have noted that black women with disabilities are the most disadvantaged within society and have had the least written about their position both in society and in the disabilities community. Asch and Fine can do little more than note, for example, that this subgroup occupies the lowest rung on the economic ladder in America. All of these groups, however, have specific rights issues (pertaining to reproductive rights, sexual discrimination, racial segregation, etc.) that tend to be subordinated to the rights issues supposedly shared by the larger disabilities population. As Traustadottir points out, "Almost all research on people with disabilities has assumed the irrelevance of gender as well as other social dimensions such as race, class, ethnicity, and sexual orientation."[67] This is certainly true of most histories of disabled rights in print and even of many of the sociological studies that address the intersection of disability, culture, and public policy.

REPRODUCTIVE ISSUES

Some of the major gender issues to gain prominence in recent years have to do with reproductive technology and reproductive rights and their relationship to people with disabilities. For example, with advancements in prenatal testing, there is a greater chance of detecting birth defects, Down syndrome, and other physical and mental disabilities affecting fetuses. Disability activists have argued that such testing is a disservice to people with disabilities because a diagnosed disability can become reason enough for many parents to abort a fetus. To those concerned, this reinforces the dangerous notion that a disabled life is a defective life and therefore one not worth living. Switzer adds that "the problem is exacerbated, some observers believe, by the fact that few people have contact with individuals with disabilities and consequently may overestimate their cost to society and underestimate their contribution to society."[68] She argues that doctors may be among the "few people" because they may have little sense of how disabled people function and succeed in their lives outside the medical office. Doctors may therefore unintentionally "complicate" parental decisions about the feasibility of raising a child with disabilities.

Switzer also notes that doctors have become fearful of lawsuits involving women who claim that they were not properly informed about the risks of fetal defects or the genetic testing that could detect such defects. As a result, medical professionals have become very cautious in providing as much information as possible to patients on potential risks. Some disability groups argue, though, that the preponderance of information emphasizes to parents that disability is something to be identified and weeded out. Fred Pelka quotes Adrienne Asch as stating, "When information about life with disability is described at all, it usually is a description filled with gloom and tragedy and limited opportunities completely at odds with the views of the disability rights movement."[69]

Today, however, supplying information is all that doctors can do to help parents make pre- and postnatal decisions about the fate of infants with disabilities. This is a direct result of the passage of 1984 amendments to the Child Abuse Prevention and Treatment Act of 1974. As recently as the 1980s, doctors often advised parents of children born with disabilities to withhold life sustaining treatment if the parents could not financially support the special needs of the child and if the impairment was expected to be so grave as to severely limit the child's quality of life. In 1982, a child referred to as Baby Doe made national headlines when her parents—taking advice from a physician—opted to deny her lifesaving treatment after discovering that the infant was born with Down syndrome and a blocked esophagus. Disability activists reacted to the news in horror. They prompted the court to intervene on the newborn's behalf, but before any legal action could be taken the child died. The furor was enough to cause the presidential administration of Ronald Reagan to decry this type of infanticide. The president directed the Department of Health and Human Services (HHS) to draw up regulations that would allow for the monitoring of disabled infants and the mandated posting of warnings in federally funded medical facilities that disabled children were protected under Section 504 of the Rehabilitation Act. The American Hospital Association and other major medical organizations challenged the HHS in court and eventually won a Supreme Court decision (*Bowen v. American Hospital Association, et al.*) that struck down the guidelines in 1986. By then, however, President Reagan had signed the Child Abuse Prevention and Treatment Act, which broadened the definition of child abuse to include medical infanticide—making the HHS regulations superfluous.

Euthanasia and Assisted Suicide

Besides showing concern over infanticide, the disability rights community has also taken issue with the practice of euthanasia and assisted suicide. Euthanasia (Greek for "good death") implies a merciful end to a life that is no longer worth living. Who decides whether the life under scrutiny is worth living is the subject of much controversy, as are the moral implications of choosing to end a life prematurely. These concerns vary slightly between the two common forms of euthanasia. "Passive" euthanasia typically refers to the removal of life-sustaining devices (feeding tubes, respirators, etc.) from a terminally ill patient, while "active" euthanasia involves the direct intervention of a third party in aiding a terminally ill person to end his or her own life. The latter term is often interchangeable with the phrase "assisted suicide," especially if a doctor is present at the deathbed (physician-assisted suicide) to administer drugs to hasten death. Such an end requires the participation of the patient who decides that an illness has made his or her life unendurable and is willing to ingest drugs or have drugs injected to bring about death. Passive euthanasia puts that decision-making power in the hands of relatives or guardians because the patient is comatose or otherwise unable to make such a choice. All of these factors make euthanasia and assisted suicide a complex subject for all people facing end-of-life decisions, yet as Switzer writes, "For people with disabilities, the issue has become literally life-threatening."[70]

Several right-to-die organizations have championed the notion of a "good death" in America since the 1930s. The issue became permanently wedded to the disabilities community in the 1960s and 1970s as the concept of disability rights emerged out of the national civil rights climate. Some disabled individuals maintained that they had the right to decide their own fate, and parents of vegetative patients argued that they had similar powers if they deemed their loved one's quality of life would never improve. In 1989, this right seemed to have been validated in *State of Georgia v. McAfee*. In that case, the state argued that it had a duty to safeguard individuals' lives, even though Larry James McAfee, the victim of a motorcycle accident, insisted that he wished to die rather than endure despondency as an institutionalized quadriplegic. The Georgia court upheld McAfee's plea to be able to turn off his own respirator and be given a sedative to end his life. The justices made clear that the state's powers did not trump individual liberty and the personal control over one's own fate. After winning his case, McAfee later changed his mind when he talked with disabilities advocates who persuaded him that there were opportunities for a life with greater freedom.

In 1990, the U.S. Supreme Court affirmed a Missouri Supreme Court decision that the parents of Nancy Beth Cruzan did not have the right to have a feeding tube removed from the vegetative body of their daughter.

Rights of the Disabled

The U.S. Supreme Court stated that Cruzan's parents did not have "clear and convincing evidence" that Nancy would have wanted life-support discontinued. That same year, three friends of Cruzan testified to the Missouri lower courts that Nancy would not have preferred to live in a now-seven-years-long vegetative state. Missouri then granted that testimony as compelling evidence and authorized the removal of the tube, allowing her to die in December.

The disabilities community was torn by these decisions. Many terminally ill and disabled patients applauded the right to have control over the time of their deaths should they feel their pain or disability had become too much to bear. A large segment, though, claimed that government-sanctioned euthanasia simply perpetuated the belief that death was preferable to living with a disability and that a disabled life was no life at all. This latter group asserts that many disabled people who desire to end their lives come to that conclusion for reasons other than pain. Like McAfee, some people with disabilities face isolation and depression; others—especially those who may have not availed themselves of services to increase their independence—may see themselves as a burden to loved ones or society.

In 1996 several activists—including attorney and former ADAPT leader Diane Coleman and author and psychologist Carol Gill—formed an anti-euthanasia organization called Not Dead Yet to reach those disabled people considering the "good death" option. Their main effort was to protest society's apparent tolerance for this unhelpful "solution." One of their targets was Jack Kevorkian, a former doctor and proponent of assisted suicide, who reportedly had helped some 130 terminally ill people end their lives, typically via a device that would administer lethal drugs at a time of the patient's choosing. Kevorkian was dubbed "Doctor Death" by an ambivalent media, but he was hailed by some as a folk hero who helped the terminally ill retain the dignity of choosing their own end instead of lingering in pain under family or state care. In 1996, Coleman and Gill, representing the newly formed Not Dead Yet, went before Congress in hopes of preventing the federal government from passing laws in support of assisted suicide. In their testimony, the pair argued, "Assisted suicide will *not* remain confined to the imminently dying. Individuals and groups who have spearheaded this push for assisted suicide have clearly intended people with disabilities to be targeted once laws are relaxed for terminally ill people." Then, Coleman and Gill foisted much of the blame for this "push for assisted suicide" upon Doctor Death:

> *Kevorkian has openly admitted that he designed his suicide device as an answer for quadriplegics. He has said that he perceives physical disability as a cause of extreme human suffering that can be addressed by "medicide." He also argued, as did the Nazis, that society will benefit from the deaths of in-*

curably disabled people. Chillingly, he wrote: "... the voluntary self-elimination of individual and mortally diseased or crippled lives taken collectively can only enhance the preservation of public health and welfare." The courts have not prevented this man from following through on his intention to "enhance" society by eliminating people with disabilities who despair in the face of society's crushing oppression.[71]

In 1999, Kevorkian was sentenced to prison for the poisoning of one of his patients. Even with Kevorkian behind bars, disability activists were vigilant.

In 1994, Oregon voters had passed an initiative that legalized assisted suicide in the state. The law was challenged, but Oregonians overwhelmingly favored the policy. Disability advocates feared that other states would follow Oregon's lead and breed a culture of death in the United States. Between 1997 and 1998, assisted suicide initiatives were put forward in 26 states. All were defeated, however, with the aid of disability groups. In 1997, the U.S. Supreme Court weighed in on the matter. In two cases, *Washington v. Glucksberg* and *Vacco v. Quill*, the Court rendered opinions that there was no constitutional "right to die," yet it maintained the states ultimately had dominion over the legalization of assisted suicide. In 2006, the Court heard a case that tried to bring down Oregon's law, but the majority of justices upheld the state's right to fashion its own policies in the matter of assisted suicide. Not Dead Yet and other activist groups remain active in fighting right-to-die measures, and no other state has yet successfully adopted an assisted suicide law.

THE HARMFUL IMAGE OF THE SUPERCRIP

"Although Jack Kevorkian undoubtedly is one of the most despised and cursed individuals by many disability rights activists," Jacqueline Vaughn Switzer contends, "he shares that distinction with Christopher Reeve, the actor best known for his portrayal of Superman." Reeve earned that notoriety, Switzer wrote three years before the actor died in 2006, because he had championed a cure for spinal cord injuries and because of "his belief that living with a disability is a fate worse than death."[72] The robust and active Reeve was paralyzed after spinal injuries he suffered when he was thrown from a horse in 1995. After facing depression and contemplating suicide, Reeve—with the support of family and friends—worked through rehabilitation and gained a respect for those around him who also struggled to overcome their spinal injuries. Deciding to use his celebrity status to bring attention to spinal cord research, Reeve helped raise funds for treatment and the search for a cure. In his first public appearance after his accident, Reeve told interviewer Barbara Walters of television's *20/20* that upon learning of his disability, he briefly felt that he was no longer a human being. That image lingered through the interview, but Reeve quickly turned his condition into something that he would eventually overcome. As Mary Johnson writes in her book that deals in part with the problematic image of Reeve, the *20/20* interview gave Reeve "a stage to launch the message that he would walk again."[73]

Reeve's professed self-loathing and subsequent push for a cure angered many people with disabilities because these views seemed to hearken back to the Franklin Roosevelt administration and the dominance of the medical model of disability. As Switzer reiterates, disability activists were dismayed because "Reeve's approach simplifies a complex issue, making it seem as if all one has to do is wait for medical science to make everything in their lives perfect—that disabilities can be 'fixed' just as someone would fix a broken toaster."[74] A consequence of this, she notes, is that disability issues such as accessibility and discrimination get overlooked as the search for the cure takes center stage. Reeve did set up the Christopher Reeve Foundation to secure donations for spinal cord research, and the organization has received more than $65 million for that purpose. He also returned to acting and directing in the late 1990s. In 2002, Reeve even became tied to the federally funded Christopher and Dana Reeve Paralysis Resource Center, a facility that teaches independence to paralyzed clients. His visibility, his tireless efforts to raise money, and his perseverance in his profession established him as a near-mythic figure who would not let his disability stop him.

Some disability advocates, however, painted Reeve as a celebrity pawn of spinal researchers—the well-known token who could be paraded in front of likely donors. They defamed him as perpetuating the myth of the "Supercrip," a disabled person who could overcome impairment and stand as a testament to the spirit of those who had been cruelly wronged by fate. Beth Haller, a journalism professor, warns in a 2000 issue of the *Ragged Edge* (a disabilities periodical), "The power of the Supercrip is a false power. People with disabilities are put on pedestals because of their inspirational quality in doing ordinary things, which is actually a patronizing way to laud people, imbued with charity. Presenting someone as inspirational is just another way of pitying them or the 'tragedy of their fate.'"[75]

ACCESSIBILITY IS STILL AN ISSUE

To most disability activists, the need to find cures for various disabling ailments is secondary to the pressing need to address discrimination and other barriers that still hamper the inclusion of people with disabilities into the full workings of society. The U.S. government has spearheaded changes in accordance with Title II of the ADA to ensure that federal agencies, public services, and other civic programs meet the needs of people with disabilities.

Introduction to Disability Rights in America

Under Project Civic Access, the Department of Justice is working to make sure that courthouses and public meeting venues are accessible to disabled citizens, that civic sidewalks have curb cuts for wheelchair access, and that communication systems are in place to assist the blind and the hearing impaired in contacting emergency services, understanding what is transacted at public functions, and even utilizing government Web services. One of the major issues Project Civic Access is designed to address is the accessibility of polling places. This matter became a major concern in the contentious 2000 presidential election when disability advocates in several states—including the then pivotal state of Florida—noted that voting machines were not designed for people with disabilities. The notorious punch-tab voting cards of Florida were particularly cited as less-than-conducive to the blind and the physically impaired. In addition, people with disabilities in several cities argued that not all polling places were wheelchair accessible; churches used for polling venues, for example, are not required to adhere to the accessibility guidelines of the ADA.

Access to health care is another concern among people with disabilities. Part of this concern is lingering discrimination among health care facilities against disabled patients. In 2001, for example, the Department of Justice responded to complaints that New York's Staten Island University Hospital had unresolved accessibility and discriminatory issues relating to its dental clinic. As the complaints alleged, the dental clinic lacked accessible parking, shunted disabled patients through a separate entrance, and maintained a separate waiting room for patients with developmental disabilities. In 2003, the Justice Department eventually negotiated a settlement in which the hospital remedied these matters and agreed to pay $8,000 in penalties. Another medical problem faced by people with disabilities is the lack of accessible equipment in doctors' offices and hospitals. In 2005, the Department of Justice settled a complaint that a female patient in a wheelchair brought against the Valley Radiologists Medical Group of California. The patient stated that she could not get a needed bone density X-ray because the facility did not have a mechanical lift to help transfer her to the examination table. As a result of Department of Justice involvement, Valley Radiologists agreed to purchase lifts and to train the medical staff in the use of these devices. Many such changes are taking place across the country as cases are filed and settled.

People with disabilities are also continuing to bring attention to transportation services that have yet to measure up to the standards set by the ADA. While many public transit authorities bowed to pressure in the 1980s and 1990s to provide fleets of buses equipped with mechanical lifts, not all have maintained the smooth functioning of these assistive devices. One group of litigants in Detroit felt compelled to file suit against the city because many of the lifts on its transit fleet were inoperable or in poor repair.

In 2005, Detroit authorities agreed to keep its lift-equipped buses in good repair and to maintain logs of services and maintenance to improve its commitment to the principles of the ADA.

Perhaps the most notable case in the last decade involved Greyhound Bus Lines, which in 1999 finally agreed to make its buses accessible and to remove barriers in its boarding facilities. It also had to pay the 14 complainants individual damages that ranged from $500 to $4,000.

Other transportation services such as taxi companies and airport shuttle operators have also come under fire in recent years for either lacking assistive devices for people with disabilities or denying them transit entirely. Some of these cases have been handled by the Department of Justice, which has resolved complaints in numerous locations throughout several states. As Switzer contends, "Complaints to the U.S. Department of Justice (DOJ) and litigation seem to have become the most effective strategies used by disability rights groups to gain access to transportation."[76] In addition, the high-profile victories—such as the acquiescence of Greyhound Bus Lines—tend to push other transportation providers to measure up to the ADA guidelines for fear of bad publicity and costly penalties.

SOCIAL INTEGRATION

The struggle for accessibility is part of the disability community's larger fight for greater integration into society as a whole. In this fight, people with disabilities do not seek exceptional status; they want only the same access to the privileges and promises afforded to their nondisabled peers. As Joseph Shapiro writes, "People with disabilities want neither pity-ridden paternalism nor overblown admiration. They insist simply on common respect and the opportunity to build bonds to their communities as fully accepted participants in everyday life."[77] In 2001, President George W. Bush pledged his administration to promoting this attitude in America. He launched the New Freedom Initiative to reinforce the guarantees his father made in signing the ADA. Speaking before an audience that included many members of the disabilities community, Bush explained the aims of the New Freedom Initiative. Noting that discrimination and disadvantages had not disappeared with the protection of disabled rights, the president said:

> *Wherever a door is closed to anyone because of a disability, we must work to open it. Wherever any job or home, or means of transportation is unfairly denied because of a disability, we must work to change it. Wherever any barrier stands between you and the full rights and dignity of citizenship, we must work to remove it, in the name of simple decency and simple justice.*[78]

The administration promised to provide federal assistance in getting assistive technologies on the market and into the hands of the disabled. It also pledged to work with business leaders to create opportunities—including telecommuting options—for employing more people with disabilities.

Few disability advocates, however, believe that Washington has made good on these promises. Switzer, for one, concludes that Congress and the president have "moved on to other causes, other issues."[79] And such critics suggest that in the absence of strong executive and legislative commitment, the Supreme Court has continued to narrow the applicability of the ADA in successive court cases. The American Association of People with Disabilities (AAPD) believes that the Court's rulings have been so restrictive—especially in cases involving employment—as to endanger the ADA. Noting that the court system has sided with businesses in the overwhelming majority of discrimination cases, the AAPD has issued a call for people to come forward and record their personal experiences with job discrimination in order to bring this catalog of testimony before Congress so that legislative changes in the ADA can help remedy this imbalance.

To many activists, the high rate of failure in bringing a successful suit against employers under the ADA indicates that little has changed in the nearly two decades since the passage of that definitive legislation. Although many hoped that people with disabilities would now have the legislative support to assume a more participatory role in society, many trends have not changed significantly since the pre-ADA days. People with disabilities are still largely unemployed, underpaid, ill-housed, and undereducated. Paul T. Jaeger and Cynthia Ann Bowman point out in their 2005 work *Understanding Disability* that one of the more "glaring examples" of society's lack of inclusion is its treatment of children with mental disabilities. Referring to statistics gathered by a CNN news report, the authors assert, "Tens of thousands of youths with mental illness around the United States are housed in jails or juvenile detention centers every year as they await community mental health services because the number of available treatment options is insufficient."[80] Such inattention suggests that society is still comfortable with the idea that when the disabled cannot be treated and repatriated into the mainstream, they can simply be shut away out of the public view.

While many people with disabilities are physically shut away or feel that they have physical barriers to social inclusion, the digital age—with its expanding information and communication technologies (ICTs)—would seem to hold the promise of freedom and some degree of interaction. Jaeger, Bowman, and others, however, have noted that the Internet and its barrier-free virtual space have not lived up to its potential as a remedy for social exclusion. "Many computer technologies, many Internet service providers, most government web sites, and virtually all commercial web sites are inaccessible in some way to persons with a range of disabilities," Jaeger and Bowman contend. "As ICTs continue to play greater roles in everyday life, and as they become increasingly vital to education and employment, lack of access will have the potential to create electronic barriers that parallel the physical barriers that predate disability rights laws. These electronic barriers threaten to greatly reduce the social presence and inclusion of persons with disabilities."[81]

In a 2002 suit waged by a blind man who found it difficult to purchase airline tickets from the Southwest Airlines web site, a judge further ruled that the ADA did not cover virtual space. This significant ruling established a precedent that nongovernmental web site operators were not required by law to make their Internet pages accessible to people with disabilities. In a C/Net news piece, Andrew Langer, manager for regulatory policy at the National Federation of Independent Business, applauded the judge's decision and stated, "The ADA is supposed to help people who are disabled in truly egregious circumstances, to help them live a normal life. One should not have a cause of action to change everything about someone's business practices to make it simple to do things."[82] To disability activists, however, this case is not only another case in which the courts have sided with businesses in matters involving the ADA, it also exemplifies how people with disabilities may be excluded from the fastest growing and most important communication venue in the information age.

AN ONGOING STRUGGLE

Although society may be slow to change and accept its own culpability in perpetuating exclusionary practices and paternalism in regard to people with disabilities, the future may bring more rapid transformations. Most recent polls indicate that there are roughly 54 million people with disabilities in the United States, and as the introduction to this essay suggests, that number will continue to climb as medicine prolongs human life without doing away with the disabilities that commonly attend old age. More than one disability advocate has noted that most people, at some point in their lives, will experience a disability. In terms of understanding disability rights, the sheer numbers are perhaps likely to improve upon society's largely out-of-sight, out-of-mind attitude.

Another important factor that may help speed changes is the political power that the disability rights movement has built up over its long history. Disability groups have never failed to come together to fight for issues that they deem important, and national organizations with headquarters in Washington, D.C., have access to Congress and even the White House to keep abreast of new legislation. While power and interests remain fragmented across the various disability rights organizations—each promoting its own agenda and fighting for federal grants and assistance—the core notion of disability rights remains imperative to their survival.

Even if some activists argue that the ADA has not lived up to its potential, few would wish to turn back the clock. Noting that disability rights is still a process in America and other countries, Jaeger and Bowman attest, "The social world that a person with a disability experiences today in the United States, Europe, Australia, and a number of other places is radically different than the social world even thirty years ago." Disability rights is now the subject of a law in the United States, and social awareness—and even acceptance—of disability has never been greater. Society has yet to dismantle its negative preconceptions about disability, but shifting definitions, debating legislation, and general consciousness-raising has done much to improve the lives of many people with disabilities. And as Jaeger and Bowman maintain, "Each individual who experiences these social and legal changes reinforces the value and importance of these changes," emphasizing that the perpetuation of rights has a positive effect not only on the disabled who now have expanded opportunities in a less restrictive world but also upon society as a whole that reaffirms its commitment to protecting the rights of all.[83]

In the conclusion to his book, *We Overcame: The Story of Civil Rights for Disabled People*, Richard Bryant Treanor looks forward to the day when disability will no longer be exceptional. He writes, "If a blind student graduates from a high school for the blind and is accepted into a regular college along with non-disabled students, this accomplishment should, in the future, be regarded as not particularly newsworthy." The goal of access, independence, and civil protections, he insists, is not "newspaper publicity but rather an absence of publicity."[84] America (and the rest of the world) is far from "normalizing" disability, but it has made strides in ensuring people with disabilities have the right to participate in society instead of being merely isolated and abandoned. This assessment may be more accurate in theory rather than practice; however, few would deny that the nearly eight decades of this civil rights struggle have yielded tangible results. Disability rights activists recognize and celebrate these accomplishments, while acknowledging that more work needs to be done before Treanor's vision of the future comes to pass.

---

[1] Doris Zames Fleischer and Frieda Zames. *The Disability Rights Movement: From Charity to Confrontation*. Philadelphia: Temple University Press, 2001, p. 5.

[2] Fleischer and Zames, *The Disability Rights Movement*, p. 4.

[3] Fred Pelka. *The ABC-CLIO Companion to the Disability Rights Movement*. Santa Barbara, Calif.: ABC-CLIO, 1997, p. 248.

[4] Joseph P. Shapiro. *No Pity: People with Disabilities Forging a New Civil Rights Movement*. New York: Times Books, 1993, p. 63.

[5] Pelka, *The ABC-CLIO Companion to the Disability Rights Movement*, p. 310.

[6] Robert Funk. "Disability Rights: From Caste to Class in the Context of Civil Rights." In Alan Gartner and Tom Joe, eds. *Images of the Disabled: Disabling Images*. New York: Praeger, 1987, p.10.

[7] Fleischer and Zames. *The Disability Rights Movement*, p. 10.

[8] Joseph P. Shapiro, *No Pity*, p. 21.

[9] Evan Kemp. "Aiding the Disabled: No Pity, Please." *New York Times*, September 3, 1981. Available online. URL: http://query.nytimes.com/gst/fullpage.html?sec= health&res=9902E5D8133BF930A3575AC0A967948260. Downloaded January 1, 2007.

[10] Fleischer and Zames, *The Disability Rights Movement*, p. 37.

[11] Pelka, *The ABC-CLIO Companion to the Disability Rights Movement*, p. 266.

[12] Shapiro, *No Pity*, p. 41.

[13] Shapiro, *No Pity*, p. 51.

[14] Shapiro, *No Pity*, p. 52.

[15] Funk, "Disability Rights: From Caste to Class in the Context of Civil Rights." In Alan Gartner and Tom Joe, eds. *Images of the Disabled: Disabling Images*, p. 15.

[16] Richard Bryant Treanor. *We Overcame: The Story of Civil Rights for Disabled People*. Falls Church, Va.: Regal Direct, 1993, p. 49.

[17] Shapiro, *No Pity*, p. 67.

[18] Frank Bowe. "Handicapping America: Barriers to Disabled People." In John P. Hourihan, ed. *Disability: Our Challenge*. New York: Columbia University, 1979, p. 89.

[19] Shapiro, *No Pity*, p. 70.

[20] Pelka, *The ABC-CLIO Companion to the Disability Rights Movement*, p. 279.

[21] Pelka, *The ABC-CLIO Companion to the Disability Rights Movement*, p. 287.

[22] Pelka, *The ABC-CLIO Companion to the Disability Rights Movement*, p. 112.

[23] Fleischer and Zames, *The Disability Rights Movement*, p. 15.

[24] Frank Bowe, quoted in Fleischer and Zames, *The Disability Rights Movement*, p. 27.

[25] Shapiro, *No Pity*, p. 75.

[26] Shapiro, *No Pity*, p. 73.

[27] Treanor, *We Overcame*, p. 229.

[28] Fleischer and Zames, *The Disability Rights Movement*, p. 47.

[29] Judith Heumann. "Handicap and Disability." In John P. Hourihan, ed. *Disability: Our Challenge*. New York: Columbia University, 1979, pp. 14–16.

[30] Treanor, *We Overcame*, p. 293.

[31] Fleischer and Zames, *The Disability Rights Movement*, p. 59.

[32] Mark Johnson, quoted in Shapiro, *No Pity*, p. 128.

[33] Treanor, *We Overcame*, p. 304.

[34] Fleischer and Zames, *The Disability Rights Movement*, p. 69.

[35] Treanor, *We Overcame*, p. 304.

[36] Shapiro, *No Pity*, p. 108.

[37] Richard K. Scotch. *From Good Will to Civil Rights: Transforming Federal Disability Policy*. Philadelphia: Temple University Press, 2001, p. 170.

[38] Fleischer and Zames, *The Disability Rights Movement*, p. 89.

[39] Shapiro, *No Pity*, p. 114.

[40] Treanor, *We Overcame*, p. 116.

[41] Mike Auberger, quoted in Pelka, *The ABC-CLIO Companion to the Disability Rights Movement*, p. 33.

[42] Shapiro, *No Pity*, p.117.

[43] Scotch, *From Good Will to Civil Rights*, p. 175.

[44] Shapiro, *No Pity*, p. 119.

[45] Shapiro, *No Pity*, p. 119.

[46] Shapiro, *No Pity*, p. 122.

[47] Shapiro, *No Pity*, p. 127.

[48] Treanor, *We Overcame*, p. 133.

[49] Treanor, *We Overcame*, p. 133.

[50] Treanor, *We Overcame*, p. 144.

[51] Fleischer and Zames, *The Disability Rights Movement*, p. 101.

[52] Pelka, *The ABC-CLIO Companion to the Disability Rights Movement*, p. 22.

[53] Mary Johnson. *Make Them Go Away: Clint Eastwood, Christopher Reeve & the Case against Disability Rights*. Louisville, Ky.: Avocado, 2003, p. 174.

[54] Iris Marion Young. "Foreword." In Mairian Corker and Tom Shakespeare, eds. *Disability/Postmodernity: Embodying Disability Theory*. New York: Continuum, 2002, p. xii.

[55] Scotch, *From Good Will to Civil Rights*, p. 177.

[56] Raju Chebium. "Is the Disabilities Act Working?" CNN.com. Available online. URL: http://edition.cnn.com/2000/LAW/07/25/ada.anniversary/index.html. Posted July 25, 2000.

[57] Justin Martin. "Why the Disabilities Act Exasperates Entrepreneurs." *Fortune: Small Business*. Available online. URL: http://money.cnn.com/magazines/fsb/fsb_archive/2005/05/01/8259751/index.htm. Posted May 1, 2005.

[58] Martin, "Why the Disabilities Act Exasperates Entrepreneurs."

[59] Chebium, "Is the Disabilities Act Working?"

[60] Llewellyn H. Rockwell, Jr. "The ADA." Ludwig von Mises Institute web site. Available online. URL: www.mises.org/story/172. Posted March 12, 1999.

[61] John Leo. "Let's Lower the Bar." *U.S. News & World Report*, October 5, 1998, p. 19.

[62] Linda Krieger Hamilton. *Backlash against the ADA: Reinterpreting Disability Rights*. Ann Arbor: University of Michigan Press, 2003, p. 128.

[63] Jacqueline Vaughn Switzer. *Disabled Rights: American Disability Policy and the Fight for Equality*. Washington, D.C.: Georgetown University Press, 2003, p. 167.

[64] Raja Mishra. "In Attacks on Disabled, Few Verdicts." *Boston Globe*. Available online. URL: http://www.vachss.com/help_text/archive/in_attacks.html. Posted June 10, 2001.

[65] Adrienne Asch and Michelle Fine, eds. *Women with Disabilities: Essays in Psychology, Culture, and Politics*. Philadelphia: Temple University Press, 1988, p. 3.

[66] Rannveig Traustadottir. "Women with Disabilities: The Double Discrimination, Part 2." Center of Human Policy at Syracuse University web site. Available online. URL: http://thechp.syr.edu/womdis2.htm. Posted in 1990.

[67] Rannveig Traustadottir. "Women with Disabilities: The Double Discrimination, Part 1." Center of Human Policy at Syracuse University web site. Available online. URL: http://thechp.syr.edu/womdis1.htm. Posted in 1990.

[68] Switzer, *Disabled Rights*, p. 147.

[69] Pelka, *The ABC-CLIO Companion to the Disability Rights Movement*, p. 4.

[70] Switzer, *Disabled Rights*, p. 148.

[71] Diane Coleman and Carol Gill. "Testimony before the Constitution Subcommittee of the Judiciary Committee of the U.S. House of Representatives, April 29, 1996." Not Dead Yet web site. Available online. URL: http://www.notdeadyet.org/docs/house1.html. Downloaded January 15, 2007.

[72] Switzer, *Disabled Rights*, pp. 154–155.

[73] Mary Johnson, *Make Them Go Away*, p. 10.

[74] Switzer, *Disabled Rights*, p. 155.

[75] Beth Haller, "False Positive," *Ragged Edge Online*. Available online. URL: http://pages.towson.edu/bhalle/rag-article.html. Posted January–February 2000.

[76] Switzer, *Disabled Rights*, p. 198.

[77] Shapiro, *No Pity*, p. 332.

[78] George W. Bush, "Remarks by the President in Announcement of New Freedom Initiative," White House press release. Available online. URL: http://www.whitehouse.gov/news/releases/20010201-3.html. Posted February 1, 2001.

[79] Switzer, *Disabled Rights*, p. 229.

[80] Paul T. Jaeger and Cynthia Ann Bowman. *Understanding Disability: Inclusion, Access, Diversity, and Civil Rights*. Westport, Conn.: Praeger, 2005, p. 122.

[81] Jaeger and Bowman, *Understanding Disability*, p. 124.

[82] Declan McCullagh, "Judge: Disabilities Act Doesn't Cover Web," C/Net. Available online. URL: http://news.com.com/2100-1023-962761.html. Posted October 21, 2002.

[83] Jaeger and Bowman, *Understanding Disability*, p. 136.

[84] Treanor, *We Overcame*, p. 323.

CHAPTER 2

THE LAW AND DISABILITY RIGHTS

The following chapter discusses legislation and court cases that have significantly impacted disability rights in America. These rights have in general been the product of congressional mandate; the Rehabilitation Act and the Americans with Disabilities Act, for example, have sought to clarify the civil protections of people with disabilities. Many of these rights, however, and the extent to which they apply to people claiming protection have been scrutinized and sometimes narrowed in the court system. Thus, the federal courts have become the arena in the last two decades in which disability rights have been truly defined. Enforcement of disability rights as legislated by Congress is carried out by select agencies including the Equal Employment Opportunity Commission (EEOC) and the Department of Justice.

This chapter will begin by examining the federal laws that relate to disability rights, then move on to discuss relevant state laws, and finally identify important federal court cases that have defined disability rights in the United States.

FEDERAL LEGISLATION

Federal disability laws are codified in a few sections (called "titles") of the U.S. Legal Code. The Americans with Disabilities Act, for example, is codified as Chapter 126 of Title 42, the U.S. code title that deals with the public health and welfare. Wartime disability compensation is covered in Title 38. The laws and statutes outlined hereafter have all become part of this large and ever-changing body of federal regulations.

ARCHITECTURAL BARRIERS ACT OF 1968 (ABA)

Background

In 1959, the President's Committee on Employment of the Physically Handicapped and the National Easter Seals Society for Crippled Children and Adults cosponsored the development of the first national standards for architectural accessibility, the American National Standards Institute (ANSI) A117.1, entitled "Making Buildings Accessible to and Usable by the Physically Handicapped." These standards were intended to create a barrier-free building design. They provided technical specifications for building elements such as doorways, ramps, and elevators to make all parts of any facility accessible to wheelchair-bound persons and others with physical disabilities.

Congress encouraged public facilities to comply with ANSI A117.1 and established a commission to determine the extent to which architectural barriers prevented access to public facilities and to report on what was being done to eliminate them. This commission concluded that the public was largely ignorant of disability access problems and that little was being done to provide access. Recognizing that voluntary compliance was ineffective, Congress then passed the Architectural Barriers Act (ABA) in 1968.

Key Aspects of Legislation

The ABA requires that buildings and facilities designed, constructed, or altered with federal funds or leased by federal agencies be made accessible to handicapped persons. A wide range of facilities are covered by the ABA, including post offices, social security offices, prisons, and national parks. The law also applies to nongovernment facilities that have received federal funding, such as certain schools, public housing, and mass transit systems.

Compliance with the ABA was uneven at first, until Congress established the U.S. Architectural and Transportation Barriers Compliance Board in 1973 to enforce its guidelines. Later, the Americans with Disabilities Act of 1990 added accessibility standards applicable to places of public accommodation, commercial facilities, and state and local government facilities. Extensive, consolidated accessibility guidelines from both acts were published in 2004.

Impact

The ABA was the first measure by Congress to ensure access to the built environment, and it became the basis for all other successive architectural accessibility laws. More importantly, though, the ABA was the first national law to recognize that structural barriers prevent disabled persons from participating in federal programs, making it one of the first pieces of U.S. legislation supporting the civil rights of the disabled. It began the legislative shift toward removal of attitudinal and physical barriers that discourage participation by persons with disabilities in society, although its impact was limited to newer buildings in the public sector.

The Law and Disability Rights

REHABILITATION ACT OF 1973

Background

The complicated history of the Rehabilitation Act began in the early 20th century, when large numbers of disabled veterans were returning from World War I, and government and welfare organizations were confronting increased health care, rehabilitation, education, and employment demands. In 1918, the Smith-Sears Act established a federal vocational rehabilitation program for disabled soldiers; in 1920, the Fess-Smith Act followed up by creating a similar vocational rehabilitation program for disabled civilians. Subsequent amendments to what later became the federal Vocational Rehabilitation Act continued to expand the available services and the definition of who can receive them. National awareness of discrimination against Americans with disabilities grew as the numbers of veterans of the major wars of the 20th century increased. Congress responded to this growing awareness by passing amendments to what became the Vocational Rehabilitation Act after World War II, the Korean War, and the Vietnam War, continuing to expand the available services.

By the early 1970s, Congress was faced with a growing national recognition that the millions of Americans who have one or more physical or mental disabilities constitute one of the most disadvantaged groups in society. In response to this awareness, in 1973 Congress again amended the Vocational Rehabilitation Act, but with such sweeping changes that the legislation was renamed the Rehabilitation Act of 1973 to reflect its significance.

Key Aspects of Legislation

The purpose of the Rehabilitation Act of 1973, as stated in the statute itself, is to maximize economic self-sufficiency, independence, and community integration for individuals with disabilities, and to ensure that the federal government plays a leadership role in promoting the employment of individuals with disabilities, especially when those disabilities are severe.

As with the amendments from the preceding 50 years, the 1973 amendments to the law are primarily designed to promote job opportunities and training for disabled adults. The Rehabilitation Act contains five titles. The first four titles provide for funding and administration of federal and state vocational rehabilitation programs (Title I); research and training to promote inclusion and integration of individuals with disabilities into society (Title II); competitive grants and contracts for professional development and special projects (Title III); and the establishment of a federal agency, the National Council on Disability, to address, analyze, and make recommendations on issues of public policy that affect people with disabilities (Title IV).

Groundbreaking Title V, however, signaled a profound shift in federal policy by establishing a crucial link between disabilities and antidiscrimination protections. This title creates affirmative action programs for people with disabilities and assures equal opportunity in federal employment. The last sentence of Title V, now referred to as Section 504, has become the most important clause, establishing for the first time that discrimination against people with disabilities is illegal: "No otherwise qualified individual with a disability in the United States . . . shall, solely by reason of her or his handicap, be excluded from participation in, denied the benefits of, or be subjected to discrimination under any program or activity receiving Federal financial assistance or under any program or activity conducted by any Executive agency or by the United States Postal Service."

Since 1973, Congress has continued to amend the Rehabilitation Act about every five years, most often to provide clearer definitions of or updates to issues in previous amendments. For example, in 1998 the act was amended to require that the electronic and information technology developed or used by the federal government is accessible to people with disabilities, including both federal employees and members of the public.

Impact

The Rehabilitation Act, together with the Individuals with Disabilities Education Act and the Americans with Disabilities Act (ADA), has become one of the most important protections of the civil rights of Americans with disabilities. Section 504 in particular is widely recognized as the first civil rights statute in the world for individuals with disabilities. After its passage, advocates for the disabled began working immediately for its implementation.

The Rehabilitation Act was also influential in paving the way for the ADA in 1990; much of the language and many of the concepts in the Rehabilitation Act eventually found their way into the ADA. For example, the standards for determining employment discrimination under the Rehabilitation Act are the same as those used in Title I of the ADA.

FAIR HOUSING AMENDMENTS ACT OF 1988 (FHAA)

Background

Elimination of racial discrimination in the sale and rental of housing was one of the primary goals of the civil rights movement of the 1960s. Congress enacted Title VIII of the Civil Rights Act, commonly known as the Fair Housing Act, only six days after the assassination of civil rights leader Martin Luther King, Jr., in 1968. This landmark legislation outlawed for the first time public as well as private discrimination in housing practices based on race, color, religion, or national origin. In 1974, the struggle for equal rights for women spurred Congress to add sex as a protected class under the Fair Housing Act.

Twenty years after passage of the original act, the disability rights movement began to create a national awareness that persons with disabilities face not only physical barriers in housing but also negative stereotypes and prejudice that limit them from housing options. In response, the Fair Housing Amendments Act (FHAA) was passed in 1988 to extend the civil rights protections of the original act to families with children and persons with disabilities.

Key Aspects of Legislation

The Fair Housing Act made it illegal for direct providers of housing, such as landlords and real estate companies, and other entities such as banks and lending institutions to discriminate in any aspect of selling or renting housing or to deny a dwelling to a buyer or renter based on race, color, religion, national origin, or sex. These provisions helped to reduce certain forms of housing discrimination that had been common in the decades preceding the act's passage, including:

- refusing to sell or rent a dwelling or refusing to negotiate for the sale or rental of a dwelling to a member of a minority group
- setting higher prices for sale or rental of a dwelling to minorities than to non-minorities
- giving false information about availability of housing, for example by saying to minorities that no housing is available when in fact something is
- steering home buyers to certain neighborhoods or areas of a housing complex based on race

The FHAA prohibits housing discrimination against individuals with disabilities, using the same definition of disability as Section 504 of the Rehabilitation Act of 1973. The FHAA expanded the aforementioned list of prohibited activities to include actions that relate directly to discrimination based on disability. For example, housing providers must permit reasonable access-related modifications of existing premises if such modifications are necessary for a disabled person to be able to live in and use the premises.

Housing providers must make reasonable modifications in rules, policies, or services necessary to give persons with disabilities equal opportunities to use and enjoy the dwelling. For example, a landlord with a "no pets" policy may be required to grant an exception to allow a blind individual to keep a seeing-eye guide dog in the residence.

Beginning in March 1991, all new multifamily housing with four or more units must be designed and built to allow access for persons with disabilities. The requirements include accessible entrances and common use areas, doors that are wide enough for wheelchairs, kitchens and bathrooms that allow a person using a wheelchair to maneuver, and other adaptable features.

Furthermore, municipalities and other local government entities are prohibited under the FHAA from making zoning or land use decisions that exclude or otherwise discriminate against individuals with disabilities. An example would be denying a building permit for a home because it was intended to provide housing for persons with mental retardation.

Impact

When the FHAA was signed into law, people with disabilities were included for the first time under the provisions of a law banning discrimination against other minority groups. The Fair Housing Act of 1968 began to eradicate a wide range of discriminatory practices that had resulted in the segregation of minorities in ghettoes in America's major cities, and the goals of the FHAA were similar: to end segregation of the housing available to people who have disabilities, to give people with disabilities greater opportunity to choose where they want to live, and to assure that reasonable accommodation and modifications are made to the individual needs of people with disabilities in securing and using housing.

INDIVIDUALS WITH DISABILITIES EDUCATION ACT OF 1990 (IDEA)

Background

Before the disability rights movement began to change attitudes in the late 1960s, children with disabilities were often completely denied an education or were given one with severely limited expectations. This educational shortcoming led to several important lawsuits, including *Pennsylvania Association for Retarded Citizens (PARC) v. Pennsylvania* (343 F. Supp. 279, 1972) and *Mills v. Board of Education of the District of Columbia* (348 F. Supp. 866, 1972), in which the courts found the states to be violating the equal protection clause of the Constitution when providing education for children without disabilities but not for children with disabilities. These landmark cases spurred Congress to enact the Education for All Handicapped Children Act (EAHCA) in 1975, which was expanded and renamed the Individuals with Disabilities Education Act (IDEA) in 1990.

Key Aspects of Legislation

EAHCA mandated that all children with disabilities are entitled to a free, appropriate public education. The IDEA extended EAHCA and provides federal financial assistance to state and local governments to guarantee the education of children with disabilities. To ensure compliance, the IDEA sets out detailed requirements for the provision of special education and related services. These requirements include that states and school districts:

- make a free, appropriate public education available to all children with disabilities between the ages of 3 and 21
- identify, locate, and evaluate all children whose disabilities make them eligible for special services, regardless of the extent of those disabilities
- plan an individualized education program (called an IEP) for each child receiving special services under the act, with parents' help
- educate children with disabilities in the "least restrictive setting," that is, to the maximum extent possible, along with children who are not disabled

Conditions that are specified in the act as disabilities are mental retardation, hearing impairments, speech or language impairments, visual impairments, serious emotional disturbance, orthopedic impairments, autism, traumatic brain injury, and specific learning disabilities.

Impact

The EAHCA and IDEA codified the revolutionary notion that all children can be educated, regardless of disability, and the combined acts remain the most significant special education law to the present day. By extending the principle of equal educational opportunity to disabled students, these acts of Congress established education as one of the civil rights of people with disabilities. Difficulties in implementation of these two acts have often stemmed from lack of funds or lack of services available to schools, especially in cases of children with multiple disabilities. Thus the legislation continues to evolve. For example, Congress enacted significant revisions to IDEA in 1997 (P.L 105-17) and reauthorized the act in 2004, with new implementation regulations being published in 2006.

AMERICANS WITH DISABILITIES ACT OF 1990 (ADA)

Background

In 1990, the U.S. Senate and House of Representatives both approved the Americans with Disabilities Act (ADA) with over 90 percent majorities. President George H. W. Bush signed the bill into law before an audience of more than 3,000 disability activists, Congressional supporters, people with disabilities, and their families and friends on the South Lawn of the White House on July 26, 1990, in what the National Council on Disability has referred to as the largest signing ceremony in history. Passage of this historic legislation was achieved through decades of effort on the part of so many diverse organizations and individuals that an exact origin is impossible to pinpoint, although some see the White House Conference on Handicapped Individuals in May 1977, a gathering of disabled individuals for input into the federal policies that affected their lives, as an original catalyst. The shift in Americans' perception of people with disabilities as a group deserving of legislative protection is best summed up in the text of the ADA itself, in which Congress stated that:

> *Some 43,000,000 Americans have one or more physical or mental disabilities, and this number is increasing as the population as a whole is growing older; historically, society has tended to isolate and segregate individuals with disabilities, and, despite some improvements, such forms of discrimination against individuals with disabilities continue to be a serious and pervasive social problem. . . . Unlike individuals who have experienced discrimination on the basis of race, color, sex, national origin, religion, or age, individuals who have experienced discrimination on the basis of disability have often had no legal recourse to redress such discrimination; . . . Individuals with disabilities are a discrete and insular minority who have been faced with restrictions and limitations, subjected to a history of purposeful unequal treatment, and relegated to a position of political powerlessness in our society, based on characteristics that are beyond the control of such individuals and resulting from stereotypic assumptions not truly indicative of the individual ability of such individuals to participate in, and contribute to, society.*

Key Aspects of Legislation

The purpose of the ADA was to provide a national mandate for the elimination of discrimination against individuals with disabilities, to provide standards addressing that discrimination, and to employ the power of the federal government in addressing the major areas of discrimination faced every day by people with disabilities. The structure of the ADA was modeled after the Civil Rights Act of 1964 and the Rehabilitation Act of 1973.

The ADA broadly defines disability as any impairment, either mental or physical, that limits one or more major life activities, such as the ability to care for oneself, learn, work, walk, see, hear, speak, breathe, or maintain social relationships. People who currently have a disability, people who have a history of disability, and people who are perceived as disabled by others (whether or not they actually have a disability) are covered by the law's protections. Like the 1965 Civil Rights Act, the ADA consists of titles, each of which governs a separate area of discrimination.

Title I prohibits both public and private sector employers with more than 15 employees from discriminating against qualified individuals with disabilities. Employers are required to make reasonable accommodations to the known physical or mental limitations of applicants or employees who are otherwise qualified, unless such accommodation would impose undue hardship on the operations of the business.

Title II prohibits discrimination in public services offered by state and local government agencies, whether or not they receive federal assistance. This title also covers public mass transportation systems, such as city buses and subways, which are required to be made accessible to all people with disabilities.

Title III covers public accommodations offered by businesses and non-profit service providers, such as restaurants, retail stores, hotels, movie theaters, private schools, convention centers, doctors' offices, homeless shelters, transportation depots, zoos, funeral homes, day care centers, and recreation facilities including sports stadiums and fitness clubs. Transportation services provided by private operators are also included. These public accommodations must comply with basic nondiscrimination requirements that prohibit exclusion, segregation, and unequal treatment.

Title IV requires common carriers to establish telephone and television access for people with hearing and speech disabilities. Telephone companies are required to maintain telecommunications relay services (TRS) 24 hours a day; these allow callers with hearing and speech disabilities who use telecommunications devices for the deaf (TDDs, also known as TTYs) and callers who use voice telephones to communicate with each other through a communications assistant. Closed captioning of federally funded public service announcements is also mandated by Title IV.

Title V addresses miscellaneous provisions: the relationship of the ADA to other laws, development of technical assistance materials, coverage of congressional agencies, and prohibition of state immunity from remedies. This title also specifies certain disorders that are not covered by the ADA, such as transvestitism or other sexual behavior disorders, compulsive gambling, kleptomania or pyromania, and current illegal use of drugs.

Impact

The ADA is the most comprehensive and influential piece of legislation ever adopted to prohibit discrimination against people with disabilities. For the first time in history, the lawmakers offered disabled Americans broad civil rights protection at the federal level. The ADA did not solve every problem facing people with disabilities, but it represented giant steps forward, shattering barriers in the workplace, in schools, in places of public accommodation, in government, and in the courts that had kept people with disabilities from enjoying the same social and economic opportunities as other people and from participating fully in society. Litigation under the ADA and regulations to ensure ADA compliance continue to help achieve its sweeping mandate.

HELP AMERICA VOTE ACT OF 2002 (HAVA)

Background

Individuals with disabilities have faced many obstacles in exercising their fundamental right to vote. For instance, they can be prevented from entering a polling place that is not wheelchair accessible, or they may be unable to follow the spoken directions of a polling-place official due to a hearing impairment, or they might be unable to read the print on a ballot due to a visual impairment. The struggle to end discrimination against racial minorities in voting laws and practices in the mid-1960s also began to draw attention to the disenfranchisement of this other large group of voters.

The Voting Accessibility for the Elderly and Handicapped Act of 1984 (VAEHA) was the first piece of legislation adopted by Congress specifically to assure voting access for the disabled. The VAEHA requires that polling places across the United States must be physically accessible to people with disabilities for federal elections, or, in precincts where this is not possible, an alternate means of casting an Election Day ballot must be provided. States must also make registration and voting aids available to disabled and elderly voters. Although the VAEHA established the right to vote as a civil right of people with disabilities, it relied on voluntary compliance by voting precincts and provided neither standards for accessibility nor enforcement mechanisms, causing this act to be viewed by many observers as largely ineffective.

The sweeping Americans with Disabilities Act of 1990 prohibits public entities from denying people with disabilities the benefits of their programs, services, or activities in Title II. Being public entities, the state and local governments that administer elections are also required to comply with this statute. Therefore, polling agencies are required to provide reasonable modifications to voting practices to allow individuals with disabilities to benefit equally from them. They are also prohibited from making polling site selections that exclude people with disabilities and from imposing voting eligibility criteria that would tend to screen out people with disabilities. The ADA empowered disabled voters for the first time to lobby for change, often through lawsuits, when their voting rights were not being met.

In the presidential election of 2000, the closest and one of the most controversial elections in U.S. history, speculators maintained that millions of Americans were denied the right to vote or had their votes not counted, leading to unprecedented scrutiny of the voting process. Studies at the time showed that even 10 years after passage of the ADA, people with disabilities were still much less likely than other groups to exercise their right to vote, and this voting bloc, as many as 10 million people, could have had a profound effect on the outcome of the 2000 election had this disparity been addressed. Thus the Help America Vote Act (HAVA), which was passed by Congress to prevent the problems of the 2000 election from recurring, contains important voting-access reforms specifically targeted at disabled voters.

Key Aspects of Legislation

The broad purpose of the HAVA is to make changes in the voting process to make ballot-casting and the electoral system as inclusive as possible. This act provides for improvements in voting equipment, voter registration, casting of provisional ballots, and training for polling place workers. HAVA also mandates that by January 1, 2006, every precinct in the United States must provide at least one voting device that is accessible for individuals with disabilities, and it allocates millions of dollars to the states for implementation of this regulation.

Impact

Voting rights for people with disabilities have been evolving for more than four decades in the United States. The cumulative impact of the several acts of Congress had been to gradually eliminate the impediments the disabled have in voting. Because the administration of elections is primarily a state and local responsibility, HAVA has been most significant in providing federal funds to the states to implement the accessibility requirements established in previous federal legislation.

STATE LEGISLATION

The need for sweeping national change has ensured that the primary struggle for disability rights has taken place in the federal arena. Since most public institutions—such as schools, courthouses, museums, and transit authorities—receive federal funds, the easiest way to bring about compliance with proposed rights such as accessibility and equal treatment has involved the enactment of federal laws. In addition, the comprehensive auspices of the ADA extended federal mandates to nearly all private companies, services, retail outlets, and institutes, leaving little need for individual state legislation to contend with such facilities within their individual borders. However, several states have passed their own disability legislation that mirrors, reinforces, or extends federal laws; in fact, state statutes must be consistent with the ADA in order to pass. Few of these laws are worth detailing, since they do not fundamentally alter policies promoted by the federal government.

In addition to these laws, though, many states have adopted some laws that go beyond federal jurisdiction. Uniform or model acts, for example, are promulgated by the National Conference of Commissioners on Uniform Laws, a nonpartisan body that strives to provide laws that will have uniform applicability across state borders. Two important uniform laws that pertain to people with disabilities follow.

UNIFORM DUTIES TO DISABLED PERSONS ACT OF 1972

This uniform code requires that when law enforcement officers, medical practitioners and others find a person who is unconscious or otherwise unable to communicate, they try to make a reasonable effort to determine whether that person suffers from diabetes, epilepsy, or other types of illness that may cause blackouts or unconsciousness and to get the person medical care if so.

UNIFORM VETERANS' GUARDIANSHIP ACT

This law, originally proposed by the U.S. Veterans Bureau in 1928 and revised in 1942, provides national standards for the appointment and accountability requirements of persons who act as guardians for veterans. Such acts outline the process of appointing guardians, as well as the duties, responsibilities, limits, taxing of costs, and fees of guardianship. The act has been adopted entirely or in part by a majority of states.

Many states also have adopted non-uniform, state-specific laws that relate to issues not covered by the federal government. Two significant laws of this kind that relate to people with disabilities follow.

ASSISTIVE DEVICE LEMON LAWS

These state statutes govern defective assistive devices that the purchaser or user has attempted to have repaired multiple times, but the defect persists. If a device is a "lemon" under the state's definition, the purchaser or user may be entitled to a replacement, refund of the purchase price minus a deduction for usage, and/or refund of other costs such as the cost of renting a "loaner" device while the defect is being repaired. Assistive devices as defined by these laws are those that help a disabled individual with a major life activity such as communicating, seeing, hearing, or maneuvering. Examples include wheelchairs, telephone TTY devices, and optical scanners. Most states also prohibit manufacturers from reselling "lemon" devices without full disclosure to the consumer.

TEMPORARY DISABILITY BENEFITS LAW

This law requires payments to be made to eligible workers who suffer a loss of wages when they are temporarily unable to work due to a nonwork-related illness or injury.

The following list of states and the District of Columbia illustrate which of the aforementioned state laws, if any, are operative within each jurisdiction.

Alabama

[no relevant state laws]

Alaska

Assistive Device Lemon Law: covers most assistive devices when they are repaired four or more times or are out of service 30 days or more for the same defect during a one-year warranty period.

Arizona

Assistive Device Lemon Law: covers most assistive devices when they are repaired two or more times or are out of service for 30 days or more for the same defect during a one-year warranty period.

Arkansas

Uniform Veterans' Guardianship Act: adopted
Assistive Device Lemon Law: covers only wheelchairs, motorized scooters, or van lifts costing more than $750 when out of service for 30 days or more for the same defect during a one-year warranty period.

California

Temporary Disability Benefits Law: state benefits are funded through employee payroll deductions.
Assistive Device Lemon Law: covers most assistive devices when they are repaired four or more times or are out of service for 30 days or more for the same defect during the warranty period, which varies by type of device.

Colorado

Uniform Duties to Disabled Persons Act: adopted
Uniform Veterans' Guardianship Act: adopted

Assistive Device Lemon Law: covers only wheelchairs and motorized scooters when they are repaired three or more times or are out of service for 10 consecutive business days or a total of 30 days for the same defect during a one-year warranty period.

Connecticut

Assistive Device Lemon Law: covers most assistive devices when they are repaired three or more times or are out of service for 30 days or more for the same defect during a two-year warranty period.

Delaware

[no relevant state laws]

District of Columbia

[no relevant district laws]

Florida

Assistive Device Lemon Law: covers most assistive devices when a reasonable number of attempts at repair have been made for the same defect during a one-year warranty period.

Georgia

Assistive Device Lemon Law: covers all assistive devices costing over $1,000 and all motorized wheelchairs when they are repaired four or more times or are out of service for 30 days or more for the same defect during a one-year warranty period.

Hawaii

Assistive Device Lemon Law: covers most assistive devices when they are repaired two or more times or are out of service for 30 days or more for the same defect during a one-year warranty period.
Temporary Disability Benefits Law: employers are required to provide partial wage-replacement insurance.

Idaho

Assistive Device Lemon Law: covers most assistive devices when they are repaired two or more times or are out of service for 30 days or more for the same defect during a one-year warranty period.

Illinois

Assistive Device Lemon Law: a proposed law is being considered that covers most assistive devices when they are repaired three or more times or are out of service for 30 days or more for the same defect.

Indiana

Uniform Veterans' Guardianship Act: adopted

Iowa

Assistive Device Lemon Law: covers most assistive devices when they are repaired two or more times or are out of service for 30 days or more for the same defect during a one-year warranty period.

Kansas

Assistive Device Lemon Law: covers most assistive devices when they are repaired four or more times or are out of service for 30 days or more for the same defect during a one-year warranty period.

Kentucky

Uniform Veterans' Guardianship Act: adopted
Assistive Device Lemon Law: covers most assistive devices when they are repaired two or more times or are out of service for 30 days or more for the same defect during a one-year warranty period.

Louisiana

Uniform Duties to Disabled Persons Act: adopted
Uniform Veterans' Guardianship Act: adopted
Assistive Device Lemon Law: covers most assistive devices when they are repaired two or more times or are out of service for 30 days or more for the same defect during a one-year warranty period.

Maine

Assistive Device Lemon Law: covers most assistive devices when they are repaired three or more times or are out of service for 30 days or more for the same defect during a one-year warranty period.

Maryland

Assistive Device Lemon Law: covers only wheelchairs when a reasonable number of attempts at repair have been made for the same defect.

Massachusetts

Assistive Device Lemon Law: covers only wheelchairs when they are repaired four or more times or are out of service for 30 days or more for the same defect during warranty period.

Michigan

Assistive Device Lemon Law: covers only wheelchairs when a reasonable number of attempts at repair have been made for the same defect during a one-year warranty period for new wheelchairs (or 60 days for used wheelchairs).

Minnesota

Uniform Duties to Disabled Persons Act: adopted
Assistive Device Lemon Law: covers most assistive devices when a reasonable number of attempts at repair have been made for the same defect during warranty period of at least one year.

Mississippi

[no relevant state laws]

Missouri

Uniform Veterans' Guardianship Act: adopted
Assistive Device Lemon Law: covers most assistive devices when they are repaired four or more times or are out of service for 30 days or more for the same defect during a one-year warranty period.

Montana

Assistive Device Lemon Law: covers only wheelchairs when they are repaired three or more times or are out of service for 30 days or more for the same defect during warranty period.

Nebraska

Assistive Device Lemon Law: covers most assistive devices when they are repaired two or more times or are out of service for 30 days or more for the same defect during warranty period of at least one year.

Nevada

Assistive Device Lemon Law: covers most assistive devices when they are repaired three or more times or are out of service for 30 days or more for the same defect during the warranty period.

New Hampshire

[no relevant state laws]

New Jersey

Assistive Device Lemon Law: covers only wheelchairs when repaired three or more times or are out of service for 20 days or more for the same defect during a one-year warranty period.

Temporary Disability Benefits Law: employers are required to provide partial wage-replacement insurance.

New Mexico

Uniform Duties to Disabled Persons Act: adopted

Assistive Device Lemon Law: covers most assistive devices when they are repaired four or more times or are out of service for 30 days or more for the same defect during a one-year warranty period.

New York

Assistive Device Lemon Law: covers only wheelchairs when they are repaired three or more times or are out of service for 30 days or more for the same defect during a one-year warranty period.

Temporary Disability Benefits Law: employers are required to provide benefits, which may be offset by employee payroll deductions.

North Carolina

Uniform Veterans' Guardianship Act: adopted

North Dakota

Uniform Duties to Disabled Persons Act: adopted

Assistive Device Lemon Law: covers most assistive devices when they are repaired four or more times or are out of service for 30 days or more for the same defect during a one-year warranty period.

Ohio

Uniform Duties to Disabled Persons Act: adopted

Uniform Veterans' Guardianship Act: adopted

Assistive Device Lemon Law: covers most assistive devices when they are repaired three or more times or are out of service for 45 days or more for the same defect during a one-year warranty period.

Rights of the Disabled

Oklahoma

Uniform Duties to Disabled Persons Act: adopted
Uniform Veterans' Guardianship Act: adopted
Assistive Device Lemon Law: covers most assistive devices when they are repaired four or more times or are out of service for 30 days or more for the same defect during a one-year warranty period.

Oregon

Assistive Device Lemon Law: covers only wheelchairs, scooters, and similar devices when they are repaired four or more times or are out of service for 30 days or more for the same defect during a one-year warranty period.

Pennsylvania

Assistive Device Lemon Law: covers only wheelchairs when they are repaired four or more times or are out of service for 30 days or more for the same defect during a one-year warranty period.

Rhode Island

Uniform Veterans' Guardianship Act: adopted
Assistive Device Lemon Law: covers most assistive devices when they are repaired two or more times during a one-year warranty period, or are out of service for 30 days or more for the same defect during a two-year warranty period.
Temporary Disability Benefits Law: state benefits are funded through employee payroll deductions.

South Carolina

Assistive Device Lemon Law: covers most assistive devices when a reasonable number of attempts at repair have been made for the same defect during warranty period of at least one year.

South Dakota

Uniform Veterans' Guardianship Act: adopted
Assistive Device Lemon Law: covers most assistive devices when they are repaired two or more times or are out of service for 30 days or more for the same defect during a one-year warranty period.

Tennessee

Uniform Veterans' Guardianship Act: adopted

Texas

[no relevant state laws]

Utah

Assistive Device Lemon Law: covers assistive devices costing over $1,000 when they are repaired three or more times or are out of service for 30 days or more for the same defect during a one-year warranty period.

Vermont

Uniform Veterans' Guardianship Act: adopted
Assistive Device Lemon Law: covers most assistive devices when they are repaired three or more times or are out of service for 30 days or more for the same defect during a one-year warranty period.

Virginia

Assistive Device Lemon Law: covers most assistive devices when they are repaired three or more times or are out of service for 30 days or more for the same defect during a one-year warranty period.

Washington

Uniform Veterans' Guardianship Act: adopted
Assistive Device Lemon Law: covers only wheelchairs when they are repaired four or more times or are out of service for 30 days or more for the same defect during a one-year warranty period.

West Virginia

Assistive Device Lemon Law: covers most assistive devices when they are repaired three or more times or are out of service for 30 days or more for the same defect during a one-year warranty period.

Wisconsin

Uniform Veterans' Guardianship Act: adopted
Assistive Device Lemon Law: covers only wheelchairs when they are repaired four or more times or are out of service for 30 days or more for the same defect during a one-year warranty period.

Wyoming

[no relevant state laws]

COURT CASES

Disability rights are a concept that has been born out of federal legislation and then fought for in the federal courts. The judicial system has been the mechanism of interpreting disability rights issues, and thousands of cases have passed through the legal system. Most have involved rulings on the application of the Americans with Disabilities Act (ADA) or the Rehabilitation Act. The U.S. Supreme Court has been called upon numerous times to render verdicts on the ADA, often narrowing the definition of disability and causing disability rights activists to claim that the legal interpretation of the ADA no longer matches its legislative intent. Several key Supreme Court decisions are presented below as well as other significant federal court cases that have limited or expanded federal law.

BUCK V. BELL, 274 U.S. 200 (1927)

Background

Dr. Albert Priddy, superintendent of the Virginia State Colony for Epileptics and Feebleminded, applied in 1924 for permission to sterilize Carrie Buck, a 17-year-old patient at his institution who he claimed had a "mental age" of nine and an IQ of about 50. Carrie Buck's mother was also a patient at the colony and had been labeled "promiscuous" and "feebleminded" (a catch-all term used at the time for mental disabilities). Furthermore, Carrie Buck had an illegitimate infant daughter who was examined by experts and also found to be "below average" and "not quite normal." Because the traits of feeblemindedness and sexual promiscuity were thought by officials at the Virginia State Colony to be hereditary, they argued to sterilize Carrie Buck to prevent the production of other mentally defective offspring. A legal challenge to this procedure was mounted on Buck's behalf by her guardian, and while the case was making its way through the courts, Priddy died and his successor, Dr. James Bell, was named as defendant.

Legal Issues

Involuntary sterilization of individuals perceived to have mental disabilities was a result of the American eugenics movement of the early 20th century, a social effort that advocated the improvement of humanity through, among other strategies, elimination of undesirable hereditary traits. Virginia, like many other states, enacted a law in 1924 permitting state institutions to operate on individuals to prevent the conception of "genetically inferior" children. Carrie Buck was chosen as the first person to be sterilized under the new state law. Her lawyers argued that this procedure violated the Fourteenth Amendment to the U.S. Constitution, which prohibits the states from abridging the privileges of any citizen without due process, but a federal circuit court ordered the sterilization to proceed, and the Virginia Supreme Court upheld the order.

Decision

The U.S. Supreme Court affirmed the Virginia law. The justices decided that forced sterilization of people with disabilities was not a violation of their constitutional rights, on the grounds that the benefit to society of a "pure" gene pool outweighs the individuals' interest in their bodily integrity. Justice Oliver Wendell Holmes, Jr., delivered the 8-1 majority opinion:

> *We have seen more than once that the public welfare may call upon the best citizens for their lives. It would be strange if it could not call upon those who already sap the strength of the State for these lesser sacrifices, often not felt to be such by those concerned, in order to prevent our being swamped with incompetence. It is better for all the world, if instead of waiting to execute degenerate offspring for crime, or to let them starve for their imbecility, society can prevent those who are manifestly unfit from continuing their kind.*

The Court assumed that the offspring of feebleminded individuals would resort to a life of crime or be unable to care for themselves, and therefore, through the application of sterilization laws, society would be protecting them from this suffering. Holmes infamously concluded this line of reasoning with the statement: "Three generations of imbeciles are enough." Justice Pierce Butler, the sole dissenter in this case, declined to offer a written opinion.

Impact

Carrie Buck was given a salpingectomy (a form of tubal ligation) following this decision; she was told she was receiving an appendectomy. It was later discovered that her pregnancy had not been a result of "promiscuity" or "immorality" on her part, but rather she had been raped by a relative while in foster care and probably institutionalized to protect the family's reputation.

Buck v. Bell was used as justification for involuntary sterilization statutes passed in dozens of states. Most of these laws remained in effect until the 1960s, although most had fallen into disuse by the late 1940s, when the scientific reputation of eugenics declined in the wake of World War II. More than 8,000 other citizens were subjected to sterilization in Virginia alone, and the Virginia law was not repealed until 1974. In 2002, on the 75th anniversary of the decision, Virginia governor Mark R. Warner issued an apology for the state's participation in eugenics, calling the movement "a shameful effort in which state government never should have been involved."

PENNSYLVANIA ASSOCIATION FOR RETARDED CITIZENS (PARC) V. PENNSYLVANIA, 334 F. SUPP. 1257 (1971); 343 F. SUPP. 279 (1972)

Background

Until the second half of the 20th century, children with mental retardation could be legally excluded from public schools. These children were either placed in institutions or cared for at home. Like many other states, Pennsylvania's statutes specifically allowed public schools to deny services to children "who have not attained a mental age of five years" at the time they would ordinarily enroll in the first grade. A state association, the Pennsylvania Association for Retarded Citizens (PARC), and the parents of 13 children who had been classified as mentally retarded and excluded from public education joined together to challenge these and other similar state laws.

Legal Issues

PARC and the parents' group filed a class action lawsuit in federal district court in Pennsylvania, naming as plaintiffs all mentally retarded persons aged six to 21 and naming as defendants every school district in Pennsylvania. Invoking the Fourteenth Amendment to the U.S. Constitution, which promises equal protection of the laws to all citizens, the groups asserted that the state cannot deprive children with disabilities from receiving an education while providing a free education to children without disabilities.

Decision

The district court looked to the landmark 1954 civil rights case *Brown v. Board of Education* (347 U.S. 483) for applicable precedent. In *Brown*, the U.S. Supreme Court had ruled that schools owe students the equal protection of the law without discrimination on the basis of race, and the federal court applied that precedent to discrimination on the basis of disability. All children have the ability to learn, the court ruled, and all children have a constitutional right to a free and appropriate public education. As an outcome of this case, the state of Pennsylvania agreed to provide full access to education to children with mental retardation up to age 21. This case also established that every child has the right to an education appropriate to his or her learning capabilities and, as far as possible, that every child should be educated alongside his or her peers, with a preference toward placement in regular public school classes rather than special classes.

Impact

This case was one of two in the early 1970s that established the right to education for disabled students. In the other, *Mills v. Board of Education* (348 F. Supp. 866, 1972), a U.S. district court in Washington, D.C., reaffirmed the *PARC* decision but raised the question of how to pay for the specialized education that disabled children require, because Washington's city schools have to rely entirely on Congress for their funding. In response to these seminal cases, Congress began to examine the education of children with disabilities and passed the Education for All Handicapped Children Act (EAHCA) in 1975 (renamed the Individuals with Disabilities Education Act in 1990). These cases also inspired many other right-to-education lawsuits all over the country, when advocates for the disabled began to look to the courts as an avenue for the expansion of disability rights.

O'CONNOR V. DONALDSON, 422 U.S. 563 (1975)

Background

Kenneth Donaldson, a family man holding down a responsible position at a Florida defense plant, began to show signs of mental illness in the mid-1950s, claiming he was being poisoned. He had been treated for a psychotic episode once before, in 1943, and after a course of electroshock treatment he was released and had been living a seemingly well-adjusted life up until the recurrence of his symptoms. At his father's instigation, Donaldson was committed to Florida's Chattahoochee State Hospital in 1956, where he remained for the next 15 years.

During his confinement, Donaldson consistently denied that he was or ever had been mentally ill, and he maintained that he was not receiving any treatment for his supposed illness. A highly motivated, articulate, and educated individual, Donaldson made frequent requests for release, but all were denied by the hospital's staff. He also received repeated offers from outside institutions and individuals, including a Minnesota halfway house and a close college friend, to release him into their care, but hospital superintendent Dr. J. B. O'Connor refused, maintaining that Donaldson could only be released to his parents (although the parents supposedly were never informed of these offers). Finally, in February 1971, Donaldson brought suit against O'Connor and other staff members for intentionally and maliciously depriving him of his right to liberty. Before the trial, Donaldson was granted his release; soon thereafter, he again secured a responsible job in hotel administration.

Rights of the Disabled

Legal Issues

On the grounds of the Fourteenth Amendment to the U.S. Constitution, which prohibits states from depriving citizens of their liberty without due process of law, Donaldson alleged that the hospital kept him confined against his will for 15 years, even though he had never shown any signs of being a danger to himself or others. O'Connor maintained that Donaldson had been committed in accordance with state law, and that he was being kept in the hospital for simple custodial care because the staff believed that he would be unable to make a successful adjustment outside the institution. The federal district court considered the case as an examination of the right to treatment: the jury was instructed to rule for Davidson if, during his confinement in the hospital, he was not given a realistic opportunity to be cured or to improve his mental condition. The court returned a verdict for Davidson, and a federal appeals court affirmed the ruling. The case then moved to the U.S. Supreme Court.

Decision

In considering this case, the Supreme Court deliberately avoided examining the issue of right to treatment, an issue that the lower courts had already resolved. Instead, the Court addressed a single question regarding the constitutional right to liberty. In their unanimous decision, the justices upheld Davidson's release, asserting that the mere fact that someone has been found to be mentally ill offers no justification for locking up and confining that person indefinitely. If an individual is capable of surviving safely in freedom, with or without the help of willing and responsible family members or friends, then the state has no right to confine that individual against his or her will.

Impact

O'Connor v. Donaldson has been called the most important decision in law relating to psychiatric disabilities. Opponents of involuntary commitment (such as the American Civil Liberties Union) often use this case to argue that it is unconstitutional to commit people involuntarily who do not pose a threat to themselves or to others. Advocates of treatment argue, however, that it is too easy to generalize from a decision based solely on Kenneth Donaldson's individual situation, and that others who could be seen as surviving safely in freedom might be better off confined than living on the streets and scrounging their meals from garbage cans. By making it more difficult for the states to commit individuals with disabilities to institutions, this case helped lay the foundation for the controversial deinstitutionalization of psychiatric patients that followed in the late 1970s and early 1980s.

The Law and Disability Rights

SOUTHEASTERN COMMUNITY COLLEGE V. DAVIS, 442 U.S. 397 (1979)

Background

In 1974, Frances B. Davis applied for admission to the Associate Degree Nursing Program at North Carolina's Southeastern Community College that, she hoped, would lead to her qualification as a registered nurse. During the application process, the college asked Davis for a hearing evaluation because of her history of hearing disability. A qualified audiologist determined that with a change of hearing aid, Davis would be able to detect sounds almost as well as a person with normal hearing, but she still would not be able to discriminate among sounds well enough to understand normal speech, and she would have to continue to rely on her lipreading skills to communicate effectively.

Based on the audiologist's report, the college concluded that Davis's disability would make her unable to perform adequately either in training or in her desired profession, and thus denied her admittance to the nursing program. Davis contended that with certain program modifications—for example, if she were exempted from the requirement to take clinical courses and had a nursing supervisor assigned to her full-time to assist her—she could complete the program successfully. The college countered that doing so would require major program modifications and the lowering of standards, and thus continued to reject her admission. Davis filed suit against the college in federal district court under the provisions of Section 504 of the Rehabilitation Act of 1973.

Legal Issues

Because Southeastern Community College is a state institution receiving federal funds, Section 504 of the Rehabilitation Act of 1973 prevents any "otherwise qualified handicapped individual" from being excluded solely on the basis of his or her handicap from participation in any of the college's programs. Once it was determined that Davis did possess a hearing disability, the court had to determine whether or not she was also "otherwise qualified."

The college argued that no reasonable modification existed that would allow Davis to safely care for patients, given that she was dependent upon lipreading. For instance, all doctors and nurses in operating rooms wear surgical masks that make lipreading impossible. Thus, the court concluded that Davis's hearing impairment would prevent her from functioning adequately in Southeastern's nursing program, and therefore the decision to deny her admission was not discriminatory under Section 504.

A federal appeals court overturned this decision, however, finding that the district court had erroneously taken Davis's disability into account when determining whether she was "otherwise qualified" for the nursing program and that the college should have confined its inquiry to her academic and technical qualifications during the application process to comply with Section 504.

Decision

The U.S. Supreme Court decided unanimously in favor of the college. Section 504 does not prevent an educational institution from requiring reasonable physical qualifications for admission to a clinical training program, the Court found. The law does not obligate the college to dismiss the need for effective oral communication in the program, such as by giving Davis individual supervision when she attends patients or by eliminating certain program requirements; doing so, the Court argued, would impose an undue burden on the college. According to the Court, an "otherwise qualified" person is one who is able to meet all of a program's requirements in spite of, not except for, his or her disability.

Impact

In Davis, the U.S. Supreme Court interpreted Section 504 of the Rehabilitation Act for the first time, and the concept of "reasonable modification" generated by this case has become central in application of the law. In his opinion for the unanimous Court, Justice Lewis Powell noted that "the line between a lawful refusal to extend affirmative action and illegal discrimination against handicapped persons will not always be clear, and situations may arise where a refusal to modify an existing program to accommodate the needs of a disabled person amounts to discrimination against the handicapped," although this was not true in the specific case of Frances B. Davis. In fact, in the decades since this case, with ever-growing numbers of students with documented disabilities in higher education, courts and colleges have struggled in their efforts to identify reasonable accommodations and procedures that allow for nondiscrimination in admissions and program participation.

BOARD OF EDUCATION OF HENDRICK HUDSON CENTRAL SCHOOL DISTRICT V. ROWLEY, 458 U.S. 176 (1982)

Background

Amy Rowley, a student with minimal residual hearing but excellent lipreading skills, was attending elementary school in the Hendrick Hudson Central School District in Peekskill, New York. With her parents' approval, Amy had been placed into the regular classroom. The school administration had prepared an Individualized Education Program (IEP) for Amy, providing a wireless hearing aid in the classroom and several hours each week of speech therapy and tutoring for the deaf. With this support, Amy adapted well to the mainstream classroom, achieving high grades, making excellent social progress with her classmates and teachers, and moving easily from grade to grade. Her parents, however, requested a full-time sign language interpreter in all of Amy's academic classes, arguing that she was still only able to understand about half of what was spoken in her classes. The school administration concluded that such an interpreter was not necessary and turned down their request. The Rowleys filed suit in federal district court, contending that Amy would be unable to achieve her maximum potential without this support.

Legal Issues

Underlying this case was the interpretation of the federal Education for All Handicapped Children Act of 1975 (EAHCA, later amended and renamed the Individuals with Disabilities Education Act in 1990), which allots state educational agencies with federal funds to help them provide special educational services to disabled children attending school within their state borders. In order to qualify for these funds, the act specifies that these agencies must have in effect policies to ensure that all disabled children receive an education appropriate to their unique needs: Schools comply by designing an IEP for disabled children. The district court agreed with the Rowleys that Amy was not going to meet her potential through the IEP that had been designed for her, and a federal court of appeals later affirmed this ruling. The case was then brought before the U.S. Supreme Court.

Decision

In a 6-3 judgment, the Supreme Court decided against the Rowleys. The state of New York, the Court concluded, was in compliance with the EAHCA as long as each child was achieving a meaningful educational benefit, and as long as it followed the due process safeguards laid out in the act for designing the IEP and for handling complaints by parents. The intent of Congress in passing the act, however, was to provide an appropriate education, not the best possible education, to all children; therefore, New York was not required by the EAHCA to maximize the educational benefit to Amy Rowley.

Impact

The Rowley case was the first of many in which the Supreme Court was asked to rule on the EAHCA. At the time, many people feared that the newly passed legislation would overwhelm school systems with unmanageable requests for accommodation or even a flood of litigation from disabled students like Amy Rowley. The Court's ruling in this important case imposed significant limitations on both the services a school system could be required to provide to disabled students and the power the courts had to review those decisions when asked to by parents, in turn inspiring fears that the judiciary would severely limit the possibilities inherent in the EAHCA. Fortunately, however, in the intervening decades, these fears have proven to be largely unfounded.

SCHOOL BOARD OF NASSAU COUNTY, FLORIDA V. ARLINE, 480 U.S. 273 (1987)

Background

Elementary school teacher Gene Arline of Nassau County, Florida, was hospitalized with tuberculosis, a contagious disease, in 1957. The disease went into remission for the next 20 years, but Arline suffered two relapses in March and November 1978 and was suspended for the remainder of the school year after each one. At the end of the 1978–79 school year, the local school board dismissed Arline from her teaching position because of the continued recurrence of her illness. She appealed the dismissal in state administrative proceedings, but she was denied reinstatement. Afterwards, Arline filed suit in federal district court, claiming that her dismissal because of tuberculosis violated Section 504 of the Rehabilitation Act of 1973. The case eventually reached the U.S. Supreme Court, which tendered its ruling in 1987.

Legal Issues

It was not disputed in this case that Arline had been discharged solely on the basis of her illness; the central issue facing the district court was whether or not a person afflicted with a contagious disease should be considered a "handicapped individual" and would qualify for protection under the Rehabilitation Act, which defines such an individual as "any person who: (1) Has a physical or mental impairment which substantially limits one or more major life activities; (2) Has a record of such impairment; or (3) Is regarded as having such impairment."

The district court ruled that, although there was no question that Arline suffered a disability, she was nevertheless not a person with a disability under the statutory definition. The court found that her record of impairment was irrelevant in any case, since the school board had dismissed her not because of her diminished physical capabilities, but because of the threat that her relapses of tuberculosis posed to the health of others. The lower court also found it difficult to conceive that Congress had intended contagious diseases to be included within the definition of a "handicapped individual." Even assuming that the definition applied to a person with a contagious disease, the court decision went on to state that Arline was not "otherwise qualified" to teach elementary school.

Decision

The Supreme Court disagreed with the lower court, finding that a person afflicted with tuberculosis may be a "handicapped individual" within the meaning of Section 504. The fact that a person with a record of impairment is also contagious did not remove that person from Section 504's coverage. It would be unfair to allow an employer to distinguish between the perceived effects of a disease on others and the effects of a disease on a patient and to use that distinction to justify discriminatory treatment.

The Court was unable to resolve whether the risks of infection precluded Arline from being "otherwise qualified" for her job, however, and if so, whether it was possible to make some reasonable accommodation for her in that position or in some other position. The Court required more evidence concerning the duration and severity of her condition and the probability that she would transmit tuberculosis. Therefore, the case was remanded to the district court for further findings of fact.

Impact

Although this case did not involve Acquired Immune Deficiency Syndrome (AIDS), in the context of the growing AIDS epidemic in the late 1980s and widespread public concern about exposure to the virus that causes AIDS, this decision was considered a victory for victims of AIDS and others concerned about discrimination against them. Because the Supreme Court's decision clearly stated that fear of contagion was not a legal basis for terminating employment, this case set the precedent that AIDS-afflicted workers could not be dismissed from jobs in organizations subject to the Rehabilitation Act solely because of their medical history. The decision had ramifications beyond the sphere of employment as well; for instance, children excluded from public schools because of AIDS and the fear of infecting other students would also benefit.

ADAPT V. SKINNER, 881 F. 2ND 1184 (1989)

Background

Access to public transportation has long been a key issue for disability groups because many disabled individuals cannot drive or afford to purchase their own modified vehicles, and thus they tend to be disproportionately dependent on public transit. One such group, American Disabled for Accessible Public Transportation (ADAPT), was a national organization dedicated to using civil disobedience and similar nonviolent direct action tactics to enforce the civil rights of people with disabilities. In the early 1980s, for example, ADAPT began a national campaign for wheelchair lifts on buses, blocking buses in cities across the United States to demonstrate the need for better access. Another important action was ADAPT's lawsuit against U.S. Transportation Secretary Samuel Skinner over a succession of federal transit accessibility rules that had resulted in minimal service for the disabled.

Legal Issues

In 1978, the federal Department of Health, Education and Welfare (HEW) issued guidelines requiring all recipients of federal funds to make public transportation readily accessible to handicapped persons. In response, the Department of Transportation (DOT) issued regulations mandating retrofitting of buses to make them fully accessible to the disabled. These regulations were challenged by the American Public Transit Association as imposing onerous burdens on local transit programs and were subsequently invalidated in court in 1981. Rather than throw out the regulations it had drafted, the DOT established new interim regulations giving local transit programs plenty of flexibility in determining how to apply federal transit funds. Authorities could choose to install wheelchair lifts on mainline transit routes, to establish a paratransit system using lift-equipped vans separate from the mainline system, or to develop a mixture of the two, using paratransit for some parts of the system and lift-equipped buses on others. The final regulations issued in May 1986 established minimum service criteria requiring only that transit service for the disabled be comparable in hours, days of service, service area, and fares to service for the nondisabled. These regulations also established a "safe harbor" provision that stipulated that transit systems were not required to spend more than 3 percent of federal funds on service for the disabled, even if, as a result, they did not meet the minimum service criteria.

A coalition of seven disabled individuals and disability organizations joined ADAPT in filing suit in federal district court to contest these regulations, arguing that the flexibility they offered to the local authorities created a segregated and unequal transportation system for the disabled.

Decision

The U.S. Court of Appeals for the Third Circuit handed down a mixed decision in this case. The court disagreed with the plaintiffs that the law required "mainstreaming" (that is, making fixed-route buses and trains accessible to the disabled even in jurisdictions providing paratransit service);

the court determined that none of the relevant statutes or relevant case law supported this conclusion. However, the appellate court found that the 3 percent safe harbor was, in fact, an arbitrary and capricious provision, one that would enable cities to deny to the disabled the minimum quality of service mandated by Congress.

Impact

Although the court's decision was mixed, the attention focused on accessible transit by the ADAPT case resulted in many metropolitan transit systems making their buses accessible to the disabled. Furthermore, in 1990, the DOT presented new regulations that mandated all new buses had to be accessible. With the case decided, ADAPT refocused its efforts on lobbying for passage of the Americans with Disabilities Act, which contains stringent requirements for accessible transit in Title II. In August 1990, considering the transit issue a victory, ADAPT changed its name to American Disabled for Attendant Programs Today and now works to keep people with disabilities out of nursing homes and in the community.

SUTTON ET AL. V. UNITED AIR LINES, INC., 527 U.S. 471 (1999)

Background

In 1992, identical twin sisters Karen Sutton and Kimberly Hinton applied for jobs as airplane pilots with United Air Lines. Both sisters were well-qualified commercial pilots, having flown for several years with regional commuter airlines. They both also had poor vision. Although both sisters had perfect 20/20 vision when wearing glasses or contact lenses, they had only 20/200 vision without such aids, and this did not meet United Airline's standard of uncorrected 20/100 vision for its pilots. When the airline turned down their job applications, Sutton and Hinton filed suit against United in federal court, claiming that their poor vision constituted a disability protected under the Americans with Disabilities Act (ADA). They argued that in denying them positions for which they were otherwise qualified, United was discriminating against them on the basis of their disability. United countered that it did not regard the sisters as disabled, merely that, even when correctable, poor eyesight for pilots constituted an unacceptable safety risk.

Legal Issues

The federal court agreed with United and dismissed the case on the grounds that the sisters were not disabled under the ADA's definition of the term. In order to be considered disabled, the plaintiffs had to experience a substantial limitation of their life activities due to their impairment, but Sutton and Hinton were only barred from a particular job due to the regulations of a particular airline, not from pursuing an entire class of employment. A federal appeals court also affirmed the dismissal, but the judges found that the guidelines of the Equal Employment Opportunity Commission (EEOC) suggested that disabilities should be considered without regard to medications or assistive devices such as lenses. Because the language in the EEOC guidelines appeared to contradict the ADA, the Supreme Court was asked to review the case.

Decision

The Supreme Court also sided with United. The majority's interpretation was that in passing the ADA, Congress did not intend to classify millions of Americans with correctable conditions as disabled. The act was intended to help those whose impairments substantially limited one or more major life activities, not those whose conditions could, or might, do so if left untreated. The opinion of the two dissenting justices pointed out that the underlying issue in the case had become whether people were disabled as defined by the ADA, rather than whether they had experienced job discrimination due to a disability. These justices argued for a broader interpretation of the ADA, based on an individual's actual physical condition rather than an improved condition that could potentially be brought about through corrective therapy.

Impact

In addition to *Sutton,* two similar cases were decided by the Supreme Court on the same day: *Albertson's v. Kirkingburg* (527 U.S. 555, 1999), in which a truck driver was fired because his visual acuity had fallen below Department of Transportation standards, even though his condition did not impair his driving; and *Murphy v. United Parcel Service, Inc.* (527 U.S. 516, 1999), in which a truck driver was fired for having high blood pressure that could be corrected with medication. By siding with the employer in all three of these cases, the Supreme Court left a dramatic legacy in the law of disability discrimination in employment, stemming a potential tidal wave of lawsuits against employers under the ADA. Many disability advocates saw these three cases as a blow to the ADA because the Supreme Court had significantly limited the number of individuals protected by the legislation.

PGA TOUR, INC. V. MARTIN, 532 U.S. 661 (2001)

Background

The PGA Tour is a tax-exempt membership organization of professional golfers who compete for more than $250 million in prize money in three annual golf tournaments. The tour was affiliated with the Professional Golfers' Association of America (PGA), a membership organization for the nation's club professionals, until 1968, when the tournament players split from the main group to gain more control over their finances and schedule.

Players progress through several phases in order to gain entry into the championship tournament, and since 1997, golf carts have been permitted in all phases of the qualifying process except the last. Professional golfer Casey Martin of Eugene, Oregon, suffers from a congenital circulatory disorder in his legs that makes it very painful for him to walk long distances and forces him to use a golf cart to travel between shots on a golf course. In 1997, Martin asked the PGA Tour for permission to use a cart in official tournaments, but was turned down. Martin then sued the PGA Tour under the provisions of the Americans with Disabilities Act (ADA). While the case wound through the courts, a federal judge in Oregon issued an injunction permitting Martin to ride in a cart in the PGA Tour competitions; Martin continued to enjoy limited tournament success, winning a qualifying event in 1998.

Legal Issues

Title III of the ADA prohibits discrimination on the basis of disability in the full and equal enjoyment of the privileges of any public place of accommodation. Martin argued that if he were not allowed to ride in a golf cart, he would be prevented from competing in the golf tour, possibly even ending his professional golfing career, and thus the PGA Tour was required to make a modification of the tournament rules to accommodate him. Such a modification was reasonable according to Martin because walking is not fundamental to golf competition, and the tour itself allows carts in some of its tournaments.

The tour maintained that its prohibition against golf carts was intended to challenge the players, and to introduce an element of fatigue into the sport; if not required to walk, Martin would enjoy an unfair advantage over the other players. Furthermore, according to the tour, tournament players are providers of entertainment, similar to employees, and thus the tour was the only entity that should be deciding the rules of golf, not the courts. A federal district court and federal appeals court found in favor of Martin, and the PGA Tour appealed to the Supreme Court in 2000.

Decision

The Supreme Court ruled 7-2 that Title III of the ADA plainly prohibited the PGA Tour from denying Martin equal access to its tournaments on the basis of his disability. In fact, golf courses are included in the list of public accommodations that are specified in Title III. Allowing Martin to use a golf cart was not a modification that would fundamentally alter the nature of the PGA Tour, according to the majority opinion. The Court found that Martin's role in the tour was like that of a customer, not an employee, since thousands of individuals from the general public pay each year for the privilege of playing in the tour, thus making compliance with the ADA rules for public accommodations mandatory.

Impact

In this important case, the Supreme Court broadened the scope of the ADA to apply to at least one category of professional sports. However, the Court stressed that the decision was applicable to Casey Martin only and does not prohibit the walking requirement at all golf tournaments. The ruling tends to encourage other athletes with disabilities to approach professional sports organizations to seek modifications during competitions, and it signals future courts to consider individual circumstances when considering whether reasonable modifications are necessary under the ADA.

ATKINS V. VIRGINIA, 536 U.S. 304 (2002)

Background

After a day spent drinking alcohol and smoking marijuana in 1996, 18-year-old Daryl Atkins and another man drove at midnight to a convenience store in Virginia and abducted Eric Nesbitt, an airman from a nearby military base. Finding only a small amount of cash in his wallet, Atkins and his accomplice drove Nesbitt to an automatic teller machine (ATM) at a nearby bank and forced him to withdraw $200. Despite Nesbitt's pleas, the two then drove him to a remote field and shot him eight times, killing him. The surveillance camera at the ATM captured the killers on videotape, and they were quickly apprehended. Atkins's accomplice, who claimed convincingly that Atkins had pulled the trigger, negotiated life in prison in return for his testimony against Atkins.

Legal Issues

At trial, Atkins's defense argued that he has a mental disability, which they based on a test that he had taken years earlier that measured his IQ at 59, well below Virginia's standard for retardation. Nevertheless, he was convicted of murder and sentenced to death. On appeal, the Virginia Supreme Court ultimately upheld the conviction and sentence, taking into account the gruesomeness of the crime and Atkins's history of violent behavior and felony convictions. However, in light of the Eighth Amendment to the U.S. Constitution, which generally forbids cruel and unusual punishments, the U.S. Supreme Court agreed to review the case.

Decision

The U.S Supreme Court ruled that executing a mentally retarded individual is a violation of the Eighth Amendment. The goal of the death penalty is retribution and deterrence, the justices argued, but an individual with diminished mental capacity is less able to learn from experience, engage in logical reasoning, and understand the reactions of others, and therefore the execution of one mentally retarded individual would be less likely to deter other mentally retarded individuals from committing crimes. Imposing the death penalty on those with a limited capacity to understand why they are being executed also does not serve the goal of retribution.

The Court also relied on the judgment of the increasing numbers of state legislatures that had rejected the death penalty for mentally retarded offenders. When the Court last considered this issue, in *Penry v. Lynaugh* (492 U.S. 302, 1989), only two states, Maryland and Georgia, had outlawed such executions, and the Court majority cited the lack of national consensus in its decision that the Eighth Amendment did not prohibit them. Since that case, however, a total of 21 states plus the federal government have enacted laws against the execution of the mentally retarded, indicating changing standards of decency that mark the evolution of society. The Court did not specify the definition of mental retardation, leaving that to the individual states to determine.

Impact

This closely watched, symbolic case has caused stays of execution for many other death-row criminals with cognitive disabilities. Interestingly, however, Atkins's fate was not resolved after the Supreme Court decision. In 2005, prosecutors argued in state court that because of his reading, writing, and reasoning practice during trials and in prison, Atkins's IQ had increased sufficiently for imposition of a death sentence. This new sentence was later overturned again in the Virginia Supreme Court, but only because of a procedural irregularity.

Barden v. Sacramento, 292 F. 3rd 1073 (2002)

Background

Individuals with disabilities often face obstacles that threaten their safety when they need to navigate a city's pedestrian walkways. Utility lines, signposts, broken concrete, benches, or tree roots can block movement of a wheelchair over a sidewalk, forcing the wheelchair user into the street alongside the cars and trucks. Studies indicate that several hundred wheelchair users are struck and injured by motor vehicles every year, and about a dozen are killed. This situation compelled Joan Barden, a wheelchair user from Sacramento, California, and seven other residents with mobility and/or vision impairments to bring a class action lawsuit against Sacramento in 1999 to force the city to remove obstacles from sidewalks that impede the mobility of the disabled.

Legal Issues

Backed by the Berkeley, California–based Disability Rights Advocates, Barden and her fellow plaintiffs argued in federal district court that the city violated the Americans with Disabilities Act (ADA) by failing to install curb ramps in newly constructed or altered sidewalks and by failing to maintain existing sidewalks so as to ensure accessibility by removing other barriers, such as benches, sign posts, or protruding wires. The city settled the first part of the suit out of court by agreeing to increase the number of curb ramps it installs in new sidewalk construction every year. However, the lower court ruled that mid-block portions of sidewalks, that is, the parts between the curb ramps, were not covered by the ADA.

The plaintiffs then appealed the decision to the Ninth Circuit Court. Because Title II of the Americans with Disabilities Act (ADA) requires public entities to provide access to all of their "services, programs or activities," it became the circuit court's task to determine whether public sidewalks constitute such a service, program, or activity, and whether or not a federal law can dictate what a city does about them.

Representatives of the city of Sacramento argued strenuously that the ADA does not cover sidewalks. As one attorney pointed out, services can be received by the public, and the public can participate in programs or activities, whereas no one receives or participates in a sidewalk. Furthermore, if required to renovate existing walkways, the city argued, it would be saddled with staggering costs that it would be unable to pay. The case attracted nationwide attention, and more than 200 other cities and counties joined in filing briefs in support of Sacramento.

The judges found unanimously for the plaintiffs in June 2002, however, ruling that providing, constructing, and maintaining a system of sidewalks is an important government activity covered by Title II, and attempting to distinguish between public functions that are services, programs, or activities and those that are not would disintegrate into needless "hair-splitting arguments."

Decision

Sacramento appealed the circuit court decision to the U.S. Supreme Court. This move concerned many disability activists, who feared that if the high court took the case, it would result in further curtailment of the protections of the ADA. Because the parties in the lawsuit did reach an out-of-court settlement just a few days earlier, though, the U.S. Supreme Court rejected the appeal without comment on June 27, 2003.

The final settlement was approved January 22, 2004. Under the terms of this settlement, the city of Sacramento will allocate 20 percent of its transportation funds for up to 30 years to make the city's pedestrian rights of way accessible to persons with vision and/or mobility impairments. The city will also pay up to $795,000 in attorneys' fees as well as $10,000 to each of the eight plaintiffs.

Impact

This precedent-setting lawsuit has inspired more class-action litigation against local and state governments over equal access to the public right-of-way. Many of these lawsuits are still being decided, and meanwhile, municipalities are focusing new attention on ways to implement local and state access regulations that have been in effect for many years. In the long run, disability advocates hope that *Barden v. Sacramento* will make streets and sidewalks safer for everyone who uses them, not only in Sacramento, but across the country, giving all citizens, with or without disabilities, ways to access the employment, education, and recreational services that communities provide.

TENNESSEE V. LANE ET AL., 541 U.S. 509 (2004)

Background

In 1998, George Lane and Beverly Jones, two individuals with mobility impairments, brought suit against the State of Tennessee for failing to ensure that courthouses are accessible to individuals with disabilities. Both had experienced this inaccessibility first hand; Jones worked as a court reporter but could not reach all the floors of the court building because it lacked elevators. Lane was a defendant in a criminal case who could not access a courthouse that lacked ramps. He left his wheelchair and crawled up the courthouse steps to reach the courtroom on the morning of his trial date, but in the afternoon he refused to make the journey again and was arrested for failure to appear.

Legal Issues

Lane and Jones filed suit under Title II of the Americans with Disabilities Act (ADA), which prevents the government from denying people with disabilities the right to access services and facilities. The Tennessee attorney general asked a U.S. district court to dismiss the case on the grounds that the Eleventh Amendment protects states from federal lawsuits. The court denied the state's motion and ruled that the case could go forward. The Tennessee attorney general was subsequently denied when he tried to have the district court's decision appealed. The Tennessee attorney general then brought his appeal to the U.S. Supreme Court. At issue in the trial was the significant question of whether Congress has the authority to abridge state sovereignty. Congress has claimed such power in several cases prior to *Tennessee v. Lane*, but the Supreme Court has often ruled otherwise when these matters have been brought to court. In *Alabama v. Garrett* (2001), for example, the Supreme Court ruled that state employees could no longer sue states for monetary damages under Title I of the ADA.

Decision

In May 2004, the Supreme Court rendered its verdict. In a 5-4 ruling, the justices acknowledged that the Court had in some prior instances abrogated states' sovereignty when constitutional rights were at stake and had, at other times, protected the states from federal interference. Thus, legal precedent was not as much a factor in resolving the case as was examining the particulars of the case at hand.

The Court determined that Title II of the ADA does confirm that states are responsible for making needed accessibility modifications to accommodate people with disabilities. The Court, however, refused to extend this complaint to include all "the services, programs or activities of a public entity" as Title II dictates, meaning that plaintiffs would need to bring individual suit against public or state entities in piecemeal fashion to effect compliance.

More significantly, the Court affirmed that plaintiffs could sue the states for monetary damages under Title II because injunctive relief—that is, compelling states to simply promise to change their practices—was not a sufficient remedy for many individuals who had suffered discrimination. Because the Court did not choose to broaden its ruling to include all aspects of public entities, this monetary redress is currently confined to cases involving access to the court system.

Impact

The *Tennessee v. Lane* case has been heralded as a significant victory for the disabilities community. Giving plaintiffs the power to sue for damages is an incentive for states to make changes to comply with the ADA. Advocates expect that other suits against the states concerning different services, programs, and activities may bring similar results, giving people with disabilities a powerful weapon in forcing states to comply fully with the ADA.

CHAPTER 3

CHRONOLOGY

This chapter provides a chronology of important events in the history of disability rights in the United States. The focus of this timeline will be on the latter half of the 20th century, when various minority groups—including people with disabilities—fought for civil rights guarantees and protections.

1000 B.C.

- Under Hebrew Law, deaf people are denied the ability to own property.

355 B.C.

- The Greek philosopher Aristotle condemns people who are hearing impaired as "deaf and dumb," maintaining that people who are born deaf "become senseless and incapable of reason."

A.D. 354–430

- According to Christian theologian Saint Augustine, if parents sin, their sins will be reflected in the condition of their children. Therefore children with disabilities, or afflictions, are seen to be a manifestation of God's vengeance against sinning parents. In addition, while Augustine preached the importance of hearing to achieve faith and salvation, he did not totally discount the use of signs and gestures to communicate belief.

1501

- Italian physician Girolamo Cardano (1501–76) attacks the philosophies of Aristotle when he promotes the idea that hearing and reasoning are not inextricably tied. Cardano attests that individuals who have little or no ability to hear can still understand and communicate thoughts and feelings.

Rights of the Disabled

1510

- Two Dominican priests write *Malleus Maleficarum*, a treatise associating mental illness with witchcraft. The work leads to the execution of many individuals, some of whom probably suffered from mental disorders.

1575

- The deaf gain their first legal advocate when the Spanish lawyer Lasso argues that individuals who cannot hear should be granted the right to inherit property if they learn to speak.

1812

- Spurred by a desire to help his deaf daughter Alice, Dr. Mason Fitch Cogswell helps found the American Asylum for the Deaf and Dumb in Connecticut.

1817

- Thomas Hopkins Gallaudet founds the American School for the Deaf in Hartford, Connecticut, after visiting Europe and observing the methods of schools for the deaf located there. Opened with help from Louis-Laurent-Marie Clerc, a deaf teacher from l'Institut National des Sourds-Muets, this is the first school for individuals with a disability in the United States. Alice Cogswell is the first student.

1829

- The Perkins School for the Blind receives a charter from the Commonwealth of Massachusetts. Inaugural director Samuel Gridley Howe teaches classes from his home in Boston.
- Louis Braille, a Frenchman who lost his sight as a result of an accident when he was 3 years old, introduces the Braille alphabet in a well-received book.

1841

- After teaching a Sunday school class at the East Cambridge jail in Boston, Massachusetts, Dorothea Dix embarks on a crusade to improve the living conditions of the mentally ill in prisons and almshouses across the United States. Her efforts result in the founding of numerous mental hospitals, schools for individuals with disabilities, and institutions focused on training nurses to provide better care for the disabled.

1847

- The American School for the Deaf publishes the first issue of the *American Annals of the Deaf*, a scholarly journal promoting education and communication techniques to improve the lives of deaf individuals.

Chronology

1848

- The Perkins Institute, under the guidance of Samuel Gridley Howe, and with funding from the state of Massachusetts, opens its doors to mentally retarded students. Blind students at Perkins feel bitterness about the inclusion of the new students.

1860

- Dr. Simon Pollak introduces Braille at the Missouri School for the Blind, providing a practical system that allows the blind to both read and write.

1862

- The U.S. government approves legislation that creates the Civil War Pension Program. Soldiers with war-related disabilities as well as the widows and children of deceased soldiers are eligible for federal pensions.

1864

- President Abraham Lincoln signs a Congressional bill into law granting the Columbia Institution for the Deaf and Dumb and Blind the power to award college degrees. This school, which later evolves into Gallaudet College and then Gallaudet University, is the first college to provide a higher education specifically for disabled people.
- The Union Army grants Disability Pension payments to 36,000 veterans.

1869

- The U.S. Patent Office registers the first wheelchair patent.

1878

- Joel W. Smith, a blind piano teacher from the Perkins Institute, introduces Modified or American Braille to the American Association of Instructors of the Blind. In a divide known as the "War of the Dots," blind individuals advocate for the use of Smith's system, while sighted individuals promote the New York system. Without a standardized system, blind individuals must learn multiple codes and blind publishing houses print material in as many as three codes.

1880

- The National Association for the Deaf (NAD) is founded in August at the National Convention of Deaf-Mutes in Cincinnati, Ohio. Chairman Edwin Booth states, "We have interests peculiar to ourselves which can be taken care of by ourselves."

- At a September conference of the International Congress of Educators of the Deaf in Milan, Italy, oralism—a method of teaching deaf students to approximate speech sounds—is chosen as the preferred means of instructing deaf students, sign language is banned in the education field, and deaf teachers are fired. However, in the United States Gallaudet College continues to employ and teach sign language to its students.

1883

- Sir Francis Galton introduces his concept of eugenics, the idea that humanity can be improved through selective reproduction. As the United States embraces Galton's ideals, laws are enacted that prohibit individuals with disabilities from marrying, having children, and immigrating to the United States. Sterilization and institutionalization of disabled men, women, and children becomes commonplace.

1890

- The Progressive Era begins in the United States. Among the charities and rights organizations that come to the fore, many workers' rights activists begin a campaign to promote the establishment of state-funded Workers' Compensation programs for workmen disabled on the job.
- The Civil War Pension program is amended, and all disabled Civil War veterans are made eligible to receive federally funded benefits. Disabilities do not have to be resultant of military service to qualify an individual for the pension.

1892

- Frank H. Hall invents the portable Braille writer, giving blind individuals the ability to communicate more freely in a textual format.

1906

- The Vineland Training School, an institute specializing in the education of mentally retarded children, hires Henry H. Goddard to research the origins of mental retardation.

1908

- Clifford Beers exposes the deplorable conditions of state and private mental institutions in his autobiography *A Mind That Found Itself.* He subsequently founds the Connecticut Society for Mental Hygiene, the first organization dedicated to improving the quality of care in the mental health industry, preventing mental disorder and retardation, and providing accurate information concerning mental health.

1909

- Building on the principles of the Connecticut Society for Mental Hygiene, Clifford Beers leads the inauguration of the National Committee for Mental Hygiene which will in turn organize the National Association for Mental Health in 1950.
- After blind advocates call for the abandonment of the New York Point System, the New York public school system endorses the use of Modified Braille (also referred to as American Braille) in the education of blind children.

1911

- A federal commission is authorized, under a joint resolution from Congress, to begin investigating the need for workers' compensation programs and the extent of employer liability in compensating disabled workers. Wisconsin becomes the first state to institute a workers' compensation program, and by 1913 the number of states with workers' compensation programs rises to 23.

1912

- The eugenics movement remains strong and its principles reaffirmed in works such as Henry H. Goddard's best-selling *The Kallikak Family: A Study in the Heredity of Feeblemindedness*. After six years of research at the Vineland Training Institute, Goddard concludes that mental retardation is genetically inherited and results from the passing of a recessive gene from parent to child.

1915

- After refusing to perform surgery on a newborn baby with intestinal and rectal deformities, Dr. Harry Haiselden is tried for murder and found not guilty. Haiselden becomes a celebrity of the eugenics movement, and in 1917 plays himself in *The Black Stork*, a movie promoting eugenics. The movie plays commercially in theaters across the United States for over a decade. Helen Keller openly supports Dr. Haiselden's principles.

1918

- The Smith-Sears Veterans Vocational Rehabilitation Act provides disabled soldiers with federally funded vocational training. This act helps discharged, disabled soldiers transition from military service to civilian life by providing them with skills needed to find gainful employment.

1920

- *June:* President Woodrow Wilson makes federal vocational training available to disabled U.S. citizens who have not served in the military. Under the Smith-Fess Civilian Vocational Rehabilitation Act, any individual with a disability, either congenital or the result of injury or disease, is eligible for vocational training to aid in job placement.

1921

- Philanthropist M. C. Migel helps found the American Foundation for the Blind through outspoken support. Helen Keller provides recognition for the organization through her vigorous fund-raising campaigns.

1925

- Employees of vocational rehabilitation programs on both the state and federal levels found the National Rehabilitation Association. This organization will provide a strong voice for individuals with disabilities throughout the following century.

1927

- Supreme Court Justice Oliver Wendell Holmes, Jr., states, "Three generations of imbeciles are enough" when ruling on the Supreme Court case *Buck v. Bell.* In this landmark decision, the Court upholds previous rulings of Virginia state courts and finds that forced sterilization of individuals deemed mentally disabled to be constitutional. As many as 60,000 disabled individuals will be sterilized in the United States over the next 50 years.
- Henry H. Goddard retracts earlier opinions on the mentally retarded, stating that they should be allowed to have children if they want to and should not be isolated from society in segregated communities.

1929

- Dorothy Harrison Eustis and Morris Frank found Seeing Eye in Nashville, Tennessee. The organization, which later moves to Morristown, New Jersey, becomes the first to train and match guide dogs with blind individuals in the United States.

1932

- Members of the American Association of Workers for the Blind (AAWB) and the American Association of Instructors of the Blind (AAIB) meet with members of similar British organizations and sign the "Treaty of London." Under its mandate, Standard English Braille is established and the codes of American and English Braille become more standardized.

- Congress grants a charter to the Disabled American Veterans (DAV), making it the official representative organization of disabled veterans in the federal government. This nonprofit group, made up of veterans who are disabled during wartime, serves disabled veterans and their families by providing counseling, job placement, and health care assistance.

1933

- Franklin Delano Roosevelt is sworn into office as the 32nd President of the United States. Even though he is the first severely disabled individual to head a world government, his physical disabilities are often overlooked due to his great leadership abilities.
- Using long-playing phonograph records, the American Foundation for the Blind creates Talking Books.

1934

- Sixteen blind and 13 sighted individuals join together to create the California Council for the Blind. Dr. Newell Perry, a blind mathematician, serves as the organization's first president. This organization serves as the model for the National Federation for the Blind that will be founded six years later.

1935

- *May:* After being denied a meeting with the director of the Emergency Relief Bureau, six disabled individuals stage a sit-in at the New York City offices to demand work opportunities for people with disabilities. These individuals form the nucleus for what will become the League of the Physically Handicapped, an organization that will continue to protest and demonstrate through the remainder of the 1930s.
- *August:* Congress approves the Social Security Act, and it is signed into law by President Roosevelt. This act provides federally funded social insurance benefits, including income support and vocational training for people with disabilities.

1938

- The Fair Labor Standards Act is passed with the goal of bettering conditions for workers in the United States. Working conditions and wages improve for all individuals except those in blind workshop programs. These programs increase production, continue to compensate workers with less than minimum wage, and provide unsuitable working conditions.

1940

- At the first convention of the National Federation of the Blind, founder Jacobus tenBroek states, "Individually, we are scattered, ineffective and inarticulate. Collectively, we are the masters of our own future and the successful guardian of our own common interests." The organization encourages blind citizens to take a more active role in shaping the governmental decisions and legislation that most directly affects them.
- Paul Strachan founds the American Federation for the Physically Handicapped. The organization lobbies on behalf of individuals with varying types and degrees of disabilities, making it the first organization of its kind in the United States. From its inception, the federation focuses on ending job discrimination against the disabled.

1943

- With the passage of the Vocational Rehabilitation Amendments of 1943, federal funding for vocational rehabilitation is expanded to include physical rehabilitation. These amendments, known as the LaFollette-Barden Act, also provide services for individuals with mental retardation and illness.

1944

- Dr. Howard Rusk pioneers the field of rehabilitation medicine at the U.S. Army Air Force Convalescent Center in Pawling, New York. He begins to treat disabled air force veterans using a comprehensive program that focuses not only on the disability or injury, but also on the individual's emotional, psychological, and social needs.

1945

- With the signing of Public Law 176, President Harry Truman authorizes the creation of National Employ the Handicapped Week. The commemorative week, to be held annually, is intended to encourage employers to hire individuals with physical disabilities.

1946

- Parents of children with cerebral palsy join together and found a fundraising support group known as the Cerebral Palsy Society of New York City. This organization seeks to increase awareness of the problems facing individuals with cerebral palsy and provide alternative services that do not include institutionalization. Two years later, the United Cerebral Palsy Association of America is founded, expanding the group's reach nationwide.

- The National Mental Health Act passes with a clause allowing for the creation of the National Institute of Mental Health in 1949. Funds appropriated by this legislation allow for research into the causes, prevention, and treatment of mental illness, as well as investigations of current conditions in mental health institutions.

1947

- Following the return of thousands of paralyzed veterans from the battlefields of World War II, delegates from Veterans Administration hospitals nationwide found the Paralyzed Veterans of America (PVA). The organization becomes a leading force in ensuring that paralyzed veterans receive needed health care and civil rights protections.
- Following the first meeting of the President's Committee on National Employ the Physically Handicapped Week, federal, state, and local governments begin a cooperative effort to encourage the employment of physically handicapped individuals. Movie trailers, billboards, and radio and television ads all emphasize the ability of handicapped individuals and promote the benefits of hiring the physically disabled.

1948

- In an effort to provide services to civilians with spinal cord injury, members of the Paralyzed Veterans of America found the National Paraplegia Foundation, which will later become the National Spinal Cord Injury Association. The new organization works to raise disability awareness nationwide with local branches campaigning on a grassroots level for disability rights.
- The University of Illinois at Galesburg introduces a Rehabilitation Program for disabled students in response to the large number of disabled World War II veterans seeking educational opportunities. Timothy Nugent, the first director, establishes a program that will serve as the model for other rehabilitation and independent living programs.
- Psychiatric patients at the Rockland State Hospital in New York found We Are Not Alone (WANA), a self-help group for mental patients. The organization also establishes the Fountain House, a club in which individuals released from mental hospitals can seek support from other recently released patients to ease the transition from institutional life to integrated community living.

1949

- Timothy Nugent serves as Tournament Director for the first National Wheelchair Basketball Tournament at the University of Illinois campus at Galesburg. The National Wheelchair Basketball Association (NWBA) is founded, providing the needed central organizing body to spur the exponential growth of disability sports.

1950

- President Truman signs into law the Social Security Amendments of 1950, which create the Aid to the Permanently and Totally Disabled (APTD) program. Under the APTD, federal funding is provided for the creation of state assistance programs for the disabled.
- Parents of mentally retarded children join together to form the National Association of Parents and Friends of Mentally Retarded Children. Later the organization is renamed the National Association for Retarded Children, and changes again to "the Arc" in the 1990s.

1951

- After his success with disabled air force veterans, Howard Rusk founds the Institute of Rehabilitation Medicine at New York University Medical Center. The new center allows Rusk to integrate innovative treatments into a complete rehabilitation program and to establish a protocol for treating the entire individual, not just the disability.

1952

- After witnessing the difficulty disabled individuals faced when searching for jobs, Henry Viscardi establishes Abilities, Inc. From its inception, the organization aids individuals with disabilities in job training and placement and contracts with defense corporations, providing manufacturing positions for many disabled World War II veterans.

1954

- Congress passes amendments to the Vocational Rehabilitation Act, under which federal funds are allotted to state governments in an effort to encourage the creation of new programs to aid in vocational rehabilitation for the disabled. Universities and colleges are also allotted funds to expand their disability training programs.

1956

- The Social Security Amendments of 1956 provide new, monthly, disability-based benefits. Under the Social Security Disability Insurance Program, workers ages 50–65 who are unable to work as a result of disability are eligible to receive monthly insurance payments to sustain them during their period of unemployment.

- The National Wheelchair Athletic Association is founded to expand the variety of wheelchair sports available to disabled athletes. In 1994, the organization is renamed Wheelchair Sports, USA.

1958

- Gini Laurie begins publication of the *Toomeyville Jr. Gazette*. The publication connects the severely disabled community and serves as a forum where polio survivors can share their stories of how they live with their disabilities in their homes, not in institutions. The paper also provides a platform for disability rights advocacy.
- Following a conference in Grand Rapids, Michigan, the American Federation of the Physically Handicapped is replaced with the new organization The National Association of the Physically Handicapped, Inc.

1960

- Four hundred disabled athletes from 23 countries participate in the inaugural Paralympic Games in Rome, Italy. This event continues to be held every four years, coinciding with the Olympic Games. Since 1988 the games have even been held at the same venues as the Olympics.
- Morton Birnbaum, an attorney and physician, publishes the article, "The Right to Treatment," that will serve as the basis for the 1971 court decision in *Wyatt v. Stickney*. In it, Birnbaum advocates for the legal rights of mental patients, focusing on the right of each individual to receive specialized treatment and freedom to leave an institution by one's own free will.

1961

- Disbanding of the Braille Free Press Association leads to the formation of the American Council of the Blind.
- The President's Panel on Mental Retardation forms in October following a presidential order by John F. Kennedy. Twenty-six experts, including doctors, scientists, teachers, lawyers, psychologists, and social scientists, convene to discuss and report on the current situation for mentally retarded citizens in the United States.
- In both the private and public sectors, organizations begin using *American Standard Specifications for Making Buildings Accessible to, and Usable by, the Physically Handicapped* as a guide for constructing and renovating buildings. This manual, published by the American National Standards Institute, Inc., is the first publication to provide ground rules for making buildings accessible to the physically disabled.

Rights of the Disabled

1962

- Under President Kennedy, the President's Committee on Employment of the Physically Handicapped begins addressing employment discrimination toward the mentally handicapped as well as the physically handicapped. The committee changes its name to the President's Committee on Employment of the Handicapped.
- Edward V. Roberts enrolls in and begins classes at the University of California, Berkeley. He is the first severely disabled student to attend the school.

1963

- President Kennedy calls for deinstitutionalization of mentally disabled and ill citizens nationwide, and promotes a new policy of integrating these individuals into the society as a whole. Additionally, increased government funding is allotted for the purpose of constructing non-profit public and private mental health centers with the passage of the Mental Retardation Facilities and Community Mental Health Centers Construction Act.
- The Rolling Quads student disability advocacy group forms at University of California, Berkeley, as more disabled students are admitted to the university.

1964

- Robert H. Weitbrecht enables deaf people to communicate over the telephone with the invention of the "acoustic coupler." This device allows individuals to send typed messages over telephone lines using a teletypewriter (TTDs, later renamed TTYs).

1965

- The Social Security Amendments of 1965 create the federally funded health care programs Medicare and Medicaid. Both the elderly and disabled are eligible to receive benefits.
- The Vocation Rehabilitation Act Amendments of 1965 expand the definition of disabled to include individuals with a history of substance abuse as well as those with social handicaps; economic need is removed as a condition for eligibility. In addition, these amendments call for the creation of the National Commission on Architectural Barriers to Rehabilitation of the Handicapped, and increased federal funding is provided to build and expand rehabilitation centers nationwide.
- Publication of *A Dictionary of American Sign Language on Linguistic Principles*, by William C. Stokoe, Carl Croneberg, and Dorothy Casterline,

legitimizes American Sign Language as a valid language and code system. Oralism begins to lose prominence as the preferred method for teaching the deaf.

- Bernard Rimland founds the Autism Society of America (ASA), following the publication of his book *Infantile Autism: The Syndrome and Its Implications for a Neural Theory of Behavior* in 1964. The ASA works to change the stereotypes of children with autism, to increase the services available to the children and their families, and to combat the generally accepted diagnosis of poor parenting as the cause of autism.
- President Lyndon Johnson creates the President's Committee on Mental Retardation. The committee seeks methods of prevention, recognition, and treatment. It also works to ensure that both legal and human rights of the mentally retarded are upheld. Increasing public awareness becomes a committee goal and is considered essential for completing the other tasks.
- Following half a decade of workshops for the vocational rehabilitation of the deaf, the Professional Rehabilitation Workers with the Adult Deaf (PRWAD) is founded. The organization, later renamed the American Deaf Advocacy Rehabilitation Association (ADARA), works as an advocacy organization on behalf of deaf people.

1966

- The Fair Labor Standards Act (FLSA) Amendments of 1966 set the minimum wage for disabled individuals, in workshops and private industry, equal to or more than 50 percent of the minimum wage under the FLSA. Disabled workers often receive only the minimum of half what nondisabled workers are paid.

1968

- Congress passes the Architectural Barriers Act (ABA), necessitating accessibility for physically handicapped individuals in all buildings using federal funds for design, construction, alteration, or rent. However, compliance with the ABA is not ensured until the creation of the U.S. Architectural and Transportation Compliance Board in 1973.

1969

- Normalization, first introduced in the United States by Dane Niels Erik Bank-Mikkelsen and Swede Bengt Nirje, provides the practical framework to carry out deinstitutionalization across the United States. This concept emphasizes the need for mentally disabled individuals to live and participate in a full community, not isolated in institutions.

Rights of the Disabled

1970

- Ex-mental hospital patients join together to form the support and advocacy group, the Insane Liberation Front in Portland, Oregon. This is the first of multiple ex-patient organizations that form in the early years of the decade.
- Congress adds the Disabilities Services and Facilities Construction Amendments to the Mental Retardation Facilities and Community Mental Health Centers Construction Act of 1963. These amendments are the first to employ a legal definition of developmental disabilities that includes mental retardation, cerebral palsy, epilepsy, and other neurological conditions that result in significant disability. State Developmental Disability Councils, or "DD Councils," are created to provide a governmental voice advocating for the developmentally disabled and grants are provided to construct rehabilitation facilities in association with universities.
- Paraquad, an independent living organization, is conceived by Max Starkloff, who is quadriplegic and living at the St. Joseph Hill Infirmary in St. Louis, Missouri.
- Following her employment discrimination suit against the New York City Board of Education, Judy Heumann and others at Long Island University, Brooklyn, found Disabled In Action (DIA), a civil rights organization that demonstrates and advocates on behalf of the disabled.
- Ed Roberts, John Hessler, Hale Zukas, and other disabled University of California, Berkeley, students strengthen the push for university support of on-campus, independent living. With a grant from the U.S. Department of Health, Education and Welfare, they organize the Physically Disabled Students' Program.
- Federal funds are earmarked for the improvement of urban mass transportation systems after the passage of the Urban Mass Transportation Assistance Act. Additionally, the legislation mandates that public transportation be made available to the elderly and disabled.

1971

- In the ruling of *Wyatt v. Stickney*, proper education and appropriate, individual treatment are deemed constitutional rights to be granted every patient in either a state school or institution. Custodial institutions, where patients are locked away without the provision of adequate treatment or education, are deemed unsuitable for accommodating disabled individuals.
- At WGBH Public Television in Boston, the Caption Center, the first captioning agency in the world, produces its first captioned programs for deaf or hard of hearing viewers.

- Under the Fair Labor Standards Act Amendments of 1971, individuals with disabilities other than blindness qualify for inclusion in the sheltered workshop programs. Sheltered workshop programs for individuals with developmental and mental disabilities increase yearly.

1972

- Two landmark federal court cases uphold the right of disabled children to attend public school, providing the groundwork for the Education for All Handicapped Children Act of 1975. In *Mills v. Board of Education*, the ruling states that disabled children cannot be denied enrollment in publicly funded schools on the basis of their disability. In *PARC v. Pennsylvania*, state laws cited to keep disabled children out of public schools are ruled unconstitutional.
- The Physically Disabled Students' Program at University of California, Berkeley, founds the Center for Independent Living (CIL). Independent living centers worldwide are created following the CIL model.
- The Supplemental Security Income (SSI) program is instituted following the passage of the Social Security Amendments of 1972. This program provides assistance to the aged, blind, and disabled, as well as to their families, helping to alleviate these individuals' financial burdens.
- Wolf Wolfensberger's seminal work *The Principle of Normalization in Human Services* calls on communities to take responsibility for care of the mentally retarded. With the success of this book, deinstitutionalization finds a broader audience than ever before and begins to take firm root in American society.
- The concept of deinstitutionalization is given a human face with the lawsuit *New York ARC v. Rockefeller* and the ABC television exposé "Willowbrook, the Last Great Disgrace." Parents of individuals confined at the Willowbrook State School in Staten Island, fed up with the abusive treatment their children received, file the lawsuit in an attempt to end the cruelty. Outrage over the television report leads to intensified advocacy and pressure, resulting in the removal of thousands of individuals from the institution and relocation into community-based centers.
- Disabled In Action (DIA) leads protests in Washington, D.C., following the veto of the Rehabilitation Act by President Richard Nixon. Tactics include occupying the Nixon election headquarters on two separate occasions in the days leading up to the presidential election.

1973

- Washington, D.C., becomes the first city to issue special parking permits for individuals with disabilities, allowing them to park in designated spots.

- The Mental Patients' Liberation Project and a psychology professor at the University of Detroit cosponsor the Conference on Human Rights and Psychiatric Oppression. This meeting is the first large-scale gathering of the ex-patients movement and provides an opportunity for those in attendance to outline ways in which the movement should proceed to achieve patient liberation.
- A provision in the Federal-Aid Highway Act of 1973 calls for mandatory curb cuts, allowing for wheelchair accessibility, in all federally funded sidewalk projects.
- After being vetoed by President Nixon one year prior, the Rehabilitation Act of 1973 becomes law. This act provides the most significant anti-discrimination protection for individuals with disabilities in the United States to this point. The entire legislation states that no individual shall be refused federally funded services or employment as a result of his or her disability.
- The Consortium for Citizens with Disabilities provides the combined lobbying power of consumer groups, service providers, and professional organizations to the disability rights movement. The efforts of the consortium help lead to the passage of the Developmentally Disabled Assistance and Bill of Rights Act of 1975 and the Education for All Handicapped Children Act of 1975.
- The disability access code of Ronald Mace, architect and founder of Barrier Free Environments, is adopted in North Carolina.
- The continued advocacy of Barrier Free Environments results in the codification of buildings nationwide.

1974

- Filing of the *Halderman v. Pennhurst State School and Hospital* suit leads to a series of appeals that will last until the Supreme Court makes a ruling on the case in 1981. In the final decision, the school is ordered to close as a result of its subhuman living standards and poor treatment of residents; residents are transferred to improved living and educational situations.

1975

- As part of the Community Services Act of 1974 (signed into law in 1975), the Head Start program is established to offer community services to low-income families. In order to ensure that all families and their children receive equal access, one out of every 10 spots in the program is reserved for a disabled child.
- With the passage of the Developmentally Disabled Assistance and Bill of Rights Act, grant money becomes available to states under the condition that their governments set up protection and advocacy systems

(P&A systems) for individuals with developmental disabilities. Autism and dyslexia are defined as developmental disabilities, and guidelines are established to ensure that individuals receive specialized treatment that best addresses their disabilities.

- President Gerald Ford signs into law the Education for All Handicapped Children Act (EAHCA, Public Law 94-142). This law seeks to ensure that all disabled children receive free, public education that specifically addresses their individual needs. Federal funds are earmarked for the creation of these educational programs at the state and local levels. This legislation results in an exponential increase in the number of disabled individuals who receive public education.
- Professionals studying methods for educating individuals with physical and developmental disabilities found The Association of Persons with Severe Handicap (TASH). They use this organization as a platform to highlight the negative impact and horrific nature of techniques, such as electric shock and physical restraint, used in many residential institutions.
- Disabled young adults and nursing home staff found the Atlantis Community in Denver, Colorado. This independent living community provides individuals with the opportunity to live outside of a nursing home and become an active member of the community.
- In *O'Connor v. Donaldson*, the U.S. Supreme Court states that any individual who is "capable of surviving safely in freedom" cannot be committed to and held in an institution against his or her will.
- The first issue of *Mainstream: Magazine of the Able-Disabled* is published in San Diego. This magazine, written by, for, and about individuals with disabilities, ceases print publication in 1999 but continues Internet publication.
- Edward Roberts, former University of California, Berkeley, student, is appointed director of the California Department of Rehabilitation. Roberts works to open nine independent living centers statewide; worldwide popularity of this model follows.

1976

- Colleges are required to accommodate physically disabled students in compliance with an amendment to the Higher Education Act of 1972.
- Disabled In Action (DIA) continue their advocacy aimed at redefining disability by protesting at both the 1976 and 1977 United Cerebral Palsy telethons. DIA disapproves of these and similar shows (such as the Muscular Dystrophy Association "Jerry Lewis" telethons) because they are seen as paternalistic and focusing on disability to evoke pity.
- Ralph Nader's Center for the Study of Responsive Law sponsors the creation of the Disability Rights Center in Washington, D.C. This

organization serves the disabled by protecting and advocating for their consumer rights.

- The United Nations declares that 1981 will be the International Year of Disabled Persons. Goals of the year include promotion of full equality and participation for individuals with disabilities, and creating a better understanding of the abilities of individuals with disability on the national, regional, and international level.

1977

- Across the United States, disabled individuals begin protesting the lack of action by the Jimmy Carter administration in passing measures that would lead to stricter enforcement of Section 504 of the Rehabilitation Act of 1973. In ten cities, protestors stage sit-ins at their local Department of Health, Education and Welfare (HEW) offices. The longest and most publicized protests occur at the San Francisco HEW office, where demonstrators remain for almost 30 days until new regulations are signed and approved.
- With the inaugural White House Conference on Handicapped Individuals, thousands of disabled individuals convene in Washington, D.C. The conference agenda allows for these individuals to voice their opinions about the needed federal legislation and leads to the creation of local organizations that continue to lobby on behalf of disabled people.

1978

- Wade Blank leads 19 disability rights activists from the Atlantis Community in a protest against the Denver Regional Transit Authority. The protestors take a bus hostage, demanding that wheelchair lifts be added to all the public buses. This demonstration leads to a national fight for wheelchair accessibility in public transportation vehicles.
- Under Title VII of the Rehabilitation Act Amendments of 1978, federal funding is provided for the establishment of independent living centers, and individuals with disabilities are given central roles in the creation and maintenance of these facilities. Additionally, the National Council on the Handicapped is created as an agency operating within the Department of Education.

1979

- In *Southeastern Community College v. Davis*, the U.S. Supreme Court hands down the first ruling concerning Section 504 of the Rehabilitation Act of 1973. The Court finds that federally funded public programs are required to make moderate modifications to their admittance qualifications in order to accommodate disabled individuals; however, the decision does not specify the extent of modifications required. Admittance to a program can be denied if an individual's disability could interfere with his or her ability to perform needed tasks.

- Adults with disabilities and parents of children with disabilities join together to form the Disability Rights Education and Defense Fund (DREDF) in the tradition of civil rights advocacy organizations such as the NAACP Legal Defense and Educational Fund.
- The National Alliance on Mental Illness (NAMI) is founded and begins work on behalf of individuals with mental illness. NAMI seeks cures as well as improved quality of life for those individuals with mental illnesses.
- Howard E. "Rocky" Stone founds Self Help for Hard of Hearing People, Inc. (SHHH), a membership organization dedicated to raising awareness and aiding individuals who are deaf or hard of hearing. In 2005, the organization is renamed the Hearing Loss Association of America.

1980

- *January:* The *Disability Rag* begins publication, presenting a forum for the debate of political issues concerning the disability community and providing a voice for disability rights. In 1997, the publication changes its name to the *Ragged Edge* and launches its web site.
- *May 23:* The rights of individuals in government institutions become federally recognized and protected when President Jimmy Carter signs the Civil Rights of Institutionalized Persons Act of 1980 into law. Those protected under the law include individuals with disabilities, elderly people in nursing homes run by the government, and prisoners in jails.
- *June:* The 250 individuals with disabilities in attendance at the World Congress of Rehabilitation in Winnipeg, Canada, feel shut out of the decision-making process by the able-bodied members of the organization. Eighteen months later, they formally charter Disabled Peoples' International (DPI) to provide an international voice for individuals with disabilities, especially those in developing countries.
- *June 9:* The Social Security Amendments of 1980 alter the availability of benefits for workers with disabilities. Periodic reviews are instituted to determine each individual's continuing eligibility for Social Security Disability Insurance and Supplemental Security Income. Under the new system, many people are found ineligible and their services are reduced.

1982

- *January 3:* With the passage of the Telecommunications for the Disabled Act of 1982, public service buildings are required to install telephones that are accessible to individuals who are deaf or hard of hearing.

Additionally, the act states that all pay phones must be made accessible for individuals using hearing aids by January 1, 1985.

- *April 9:* "Baby Doe" is born in Bloomington, Indiana, with a connection between the trachea and esophagus that prevents food from reaching the stomach. The newborn's parents, with advice from their doctors, refuse surgical treatment for their child and opt instead to allow the baby to starve to death. This event, combined with a similar instance occurring two years later, leads to the passage of the Child Abuse Prevention and Treatment Act Amendments of 1984, which outlaw medical infanticide.
- *July:* Irving Kenneth Zola assumes publication duties for the *Disability and Chronic Disease Newsletter*. Zola also helps found the Section for the Study of Chronic Illness, Impairment, and Disability (SSCIID), a scholarly society that investigates disability rights issues. In 1986, it is renamed the Society for Disability Studies (SDS), and the *Disability and Chronic Disease Newsletter* becomes *Disability Studies Quarterly*, the official newsletter of the SDS.
- *December 3:* At the conclusion of the International Year of Disabled Persons, the United Nations General Assembly extends the program by inaugurating the International Decade of Disabled Persons. In accordance, the UN offers suggestions to international governments concerning employment and education of individuals with disabilities, as well as the improved treatment of individuals with mental illness.

1983

- *October:* Building on the protests staged in 1978, the Atlantis Community in Denver establishes American Disabled for Accessible Public Transit (ADAPT) to protest at the American Public Transit Association's national convention. Over the following seven years, ADAPT will forcibly prevent public buses from running their normal routes in major U.S. cities and stage other protests calling for the creation of legislation mandating accessible transportation.

1984

- *February 22:* The National Council on the Handicapped becomes an independent agency of the U.S. federal government, charged with providing continual review of the status of individuals with disabilities. Reports published by the agency, such as the *National Policy for Persons with Disabilities* report and *Toward Independence*, offer suggestions for reform and call for legislation to ensure individuals with disabilities are afforded the same rights as other citizens.
- *July 5:* The U.S. Supreme Court hands down its ruling in *Irving Independent School District v. Tatro*, a suit concerning the school district's refusal

to provide special services to a student with spina bifida. The Court reaffirms that under the Education for All Handicapped Children Act of 1975, a school receiving federal funds must provide support services necessary for a child to receive a free public education.

- *October 9:* President Ronald Reagan signs the Social Security Disability Benefits Reform Act of 1984 into law. This legislation curbs the frequency and stringent standards of the continuing disability reviews and reinstates coverage for many whose benefits had been taken away. Additionally, a new appeal process is outlined for individuals to dispute the termination of their benefits.
- *September 28:* The Voting Accessibility for the Elderly and Handicapped Act is passed by Congress. Under this act, polling places nationwide must make accommodations for physically handicapped and elderly individuals to ensure their ability to vote in federal elections. If accessibility cannot be achieved, an alternative method of voting must be available.

1985

- *April 29:* In *Burlington School Committee v. Department of Education*, the U.S. Supreme Court finds that parents of a child with disabilities are eligible for reimbursement of private school fees if that school, not a public school, provides the child with the best opportunity to receive an appropriate education as defined by the Education for All Handicapped Children Act of 1975.

1986

- *October 2:* President Reagan signs the Air Carrier Access Act, which mandates that both domestic and international airlines provide flights that are accessible for individuals with physical or mental disabilities at no additional cost to the individual.
- *October 21:* Under the Rehabilitation Act Amendments of 1986, individuals with severe disabilities can be placed into integrated, competitive employment with the necessary support services as part of their rehabilitation. This law is designed to offer alternatives to segregated, sheltered workshop programs.
- *November 10:* President Reagan signs the Employment Opportunities for Disabled Americans Act into law. Under this legislation, workers with disabilities who are out of work and receiving Supplemental Security Income and Social Security Disability Insurance remain eligible for benefits even after returning to employment. The act aims to create incentives for individuals with disabilities to join or rejoin the workforce.

Rights of the Disabled

1987

- *March 3:* The U.S. Supreme Court hands down its decision in *School Board of Nassau County v. Arline*. The Court finds that an individual with a contagious disease can be defined as disabled under Section 504 of the Rehabilitation Act of 1973 and is provided protection from wrongful dismissal. The Court further concludes an employer cannot fire an individual based solely on the unfounded perception that the person with the disease will be a threat to the health of others.
- *June 30:* The Federal Disability Determination Services (FDDS) is formed by the Social Security Administration. The FDDS serves as the office for all disability issues related to Social Security, including reviews of potential disability benefit reform and the processing of Continuing Disability Reviews.

1988

- *January 20:* According to the U.S. Supreme Court ruling in the *Honig v. Doe* case, school officials do not have the authority to remove children with disabilities from the classroom, even following instances of dangerous or disruptive behavior. Only upon the conclusion of a hearing evaluating the appropriate method of education for the child can the student be assigned to a new class setting or expelled from the current class setting.
- *January 29:* The National Council on the Handicapped presents its report *On the Threshold of Independence*. Included in this report is the first draft of the Americans with Disabilities Act (ADA). Following its release, individuals in the disability community begin strong lobbying efforts that result in the first presentation of the ADA to the Congress and Senate in April, by Representative Tony Coelho and Senator Lowell Weicker.
- *March 13:* I. King Jordan is appointed president of Gallaudet University, making him the first deaf president of this prestigious academy for the deaf. The university's Board of Trustees select Jordan in response to student protests of the board's appointment of the seventh nondeaf president since the university's establishment in 1864.
- *March 22:* President Reagan's veto of the Civil Rights Restoration Act of 1987 is nullified with a congressional vote in favor of making the act law. Passage of this act mandates that if any program within an organization receives federal funds, the entire organization is required to abide by antidiscrimination practices, even if the funding is only applied within one specific program.
- *August 19:* President Reagan signs the Technology-Related Assistance for Individuals with Disabilities Act of 1988. Increased federal funds are

allotted to state governments to facilitate a greater availability of assistive technology for individuals with disabilities.

- *September 13:* The Fair Housing Amendments Act (FHAA) becomes law, extending civil rights protections to individuals with disabilities who are seeking to purchase, rent, or finance a home. Additionally, the legislation outlines the types and conditions of reasonable structural and policy modifications.
- *November 7:* The National Council on the Handicapped is renamed the National Council on Disability.

1989

- *May:* A redrafted version of the Americans with Disabilities Act is presented to Congress. Disability rights organizations nationwide unite to lobby for the passage of the act. The Senate passes an amended version of this act on September 7, with the House version following suit on May 22, 1990. The two versions are reconciled and sent to President George H. W. Bush.
- *May 10:* With an executive order, President Bush changes the name of the President's Committee on the Employment of the Handicapped to the President's Committee on Employment of People with Disabilities.
- *November:* The Georgia Supreme Court grants Larry James McAfee, who became a quadriplegic following a motorcycle accident, the right to turn off his own respirator and have a doctor administer pain relieving drugs while he ends his own life. Following the court case, disability rights activists dissuade McAfee from killing himself and use McAfee's change of heart to support the ban on assisted suicide.

1990

- *March 12:* American Disabled for Accessible Public Transit (ADAPT) coordinates the Wheels of Justice protests in Washington, D.C., to show unity and support for the Americans with Disabilities Act. Over 200 activists leave their wheelchairs, crawl up the steps of the U.S. Capitol Building, and remain there overnight. Many are arrested when they refuse to move from the steps.
- *July:* The first issue of *Mouth: The Voice of Disability Rights* is published, encouraging individuals with disabilities to get involved in the disability rights movement. The bi-monthly magazine focuses on telling the real stories of individuals with disabilities and questions mainstream disability rights advocacy and activism.
- *July 26:* President George H. W. Bush signs the Americans with Disabilities Act (ADA) into law. Under this legislation, individuals with disabilities receive full governmental protection from discrimination, and

accessibility becomes the law. The act specifically addresses employment, public services and transportation, public accommodations and facilities, and telecommunications.

- *July:* After passage of the Americans with Disabilities Act (ADA) legally guarantees accessibility in public transit, American Disabled for Accessible Public Transit (ADAPT) shifts their advocacy efforts to addressing availability of attendant services. The organization renames itself American Disabled for Attendant Programs Today (also ADAPT) and begins a campaign to promote "community based attendant services."
- *October 30:* Individuals with Disabilities Education Act (IDEA) becomes the new title for the Education for All Handicapped Children Act (EAHCA). The legislation continues to mandate a free, appropriate public education for all children along with the development of Individualized Education Programs (IEPs) to address each child's specific educational needs.
- *December 14:* In a Missouri court, a judge rules that the parents of Nancy Cruzan, a patient in a vegetative state, have the right to remove her life support systems. Earlier that year, the U.S. Supreme Court held that the feeding tubes could not be removed because no one had given compelling evidence that Cruzan would have wanted to die. But later testimony from her friends convinces the courts otherwise.

1991

- *September:* Activists Cris Matthews and Mike Ervin perform their first annual protest of the Jerry Lewis Muscular Dystrophy Association Telethon. They name themselves Jerry's Orphans to reject the "Jerry's Kids" appellation that they acquired as former poster children for the telethon. In Denver, another former Jerry's Kid, Laura Hershey, organizes her own protest of the telethon, which she dubs "Tune Jerry Out."

1993

- *May 20:* President Bill Clinton signs the National Voter Registration Act into law in order to aid individuals with disabilities in exercising their right to vote. Programs that receive state funding to serve the disabled are given the responsibility of providing the disabled community with voter registration forms and ensuring that the forms are filled out properly and sent to the appropriate offices.

1994

- *January 24:* The ruling in the federal court case *Holland v. Sacramento City Unified School District* finds that a mentally disabled elementary school student would receive the most appropriate education within classes among children without disabilities.

1995

- *February 2:* In *Helen L. v. DiDario*, the U.S. Court of Appeals for the Third Circuit finds that, in accordance with the ADA, a nursing home resident must be discharged and provided integrated care in his or her own home if a program for such care is available.
- *February 8:* The first e-mail of the Justice For All (JFA) e-mail network is sent out. Justin Dart, Jr., Mark Smith, Fred Fay, and Becky Ogle begin the service to increase communication within the disability rights community and facilitate grass roots advocacy.
- *May 23:* PBS airs the film *When Billy Broke His Head . . . and Other Tales*, in which Billy Golfus documents his life after the car accident that left him with severe brain damage. The documentary presents a humorous and honest look at the daily life of individuals with disabilities and the ongoing activism of the disability rights movement.
- *May 27:* Film actor Christopher Reeve is paralyzed as a result of an equine sports injury that causes severe spinal cord damage. Reeve becomes a spokesperson in the disability community, donating money and creating funds to research cures for spinal cord injuries. Many disability activists, however, see Reeve's emphasis on finding a cure as overshadowing the need for social change that favors acceptance of people with disabilities.
- *July 25:* Individuals with disabilities gather together under the leadership of Justin Dart, Dr. Sylvia Walker, Pal Hearne, John D. Kemp, and I. King Jordan to found the American Association of People with Disabilities. The organization works to promote inclusion of all Americans with any type of disability into U.S. society.

1996

- *January 23:* Sandra Jensen becomes the first patient with Down syndrome to receive a heart-lung transplant. Hospitals at both Stanford University and University of California at San Diego refused to place Sandra Jensen on the waiting list for a transplant, based on the belief that Jensen's disability would prevent her from complying with the needed follow-up regimen of drugs and care. Jensen performs the neccessary follow-up, but dies 16 months later due to complications with the anti-rejection drugs.
- *February 8:* The Telecommunications Act of 1996 becomes law, amending the earlier Communications Act of 1934. The new amendments specifically address the accessibility of telephone services and equipment,

mandating that both landline telephones and cell phones be made available to individuals with disabilities.

- *April 27:* Following the legal acquittal of Jack Kevorkian for assisting in the suicide deaths of patients who wanted to die, Diane Coleman founds Not Dead Yet, an organization dedicated to fighting the legalization of assisted suicide. The organization's protests and activism help lead to the conviction of Jack Kevorkian in 1999.
- *August 22:* The enactment of the Personal Responsibility and Work Opportunity Reconciliation Act of 1996 provides revised guidelines to determine whether a child qualifies for SSI disability benefits. Specifically, clauses such as the "comparable severity standard" and "maladaptive behavior" will no longer be used to define a child's eligibility.

1997

- *June 26:* In two landmark U.S. Supreme Court Cases, *Washington v. Glucksberg* and *Vacco v. Quill*, the "right to die" is not deemed a constitutional right. States, however, are given dominion over the legalization of assisted suicide.

1998

- *June 25:* The U.S. Supreme Court rules in *Bragdon v. Abbott* that the condition of HIV/AIDS—in this case—falls under the definition of disability as defined by the ADA because having the virus "substantially limits" the "major life activity" of reproduction. The ruling in the case gives medical professionals the authority to assess the risk of treating an individual with a potentially threatening health condition and make decisions about the method of treatment based on this assessment.
- *October:* Congress passes the Crime Victims with Disabilities Awareness Act in order to highlight the often ignored problem of crimes against individuals with disabilities. In accordance with the legislation, statistics are collected nationwide to assess the magnitude of the problem and raise awareness.
- *November 13:* President Bill Clinton signs the Assistive Technology Act (ATA) into law. The ATA, an updated version of the Technology-Related Assistance for Individuals with Disabilities Act of 1988, provides federal funds for state use to increase the scope and availability of assistive technology for qualified residents.

1999

- *August 23:* Project Civic Access reaches its first civil access settlement with the city of Toledo, Ohio. The initiative works with communities nationwide to ensure that public services such as accessible voting are available to individuals with disabilities in all states. Some 150 settlement agreements will be made by 2007.

- *December 17:* President Bill Clinton signs the Ticket to Work and Work Incentives Improvement Act of 1999 (TWWIIA). This legislation increases employment options for individuals with disabilities while still allowing them to have access to federal health care programs. In accordance, the Social Security Administration (SSA) is charged with providing job training and placement services.

2000

- *September 29:* Film actor and director Clint Eastwood is found guilty of two infringements of the ADA following a suit against one of his ranches, and he is not required to pay damages totaling over half a million dollars to the plaintiff. These violations were remedied before the verdict of the case was handed down, and Eastwood begins a campaign asking Congress to give businesses 90 days to address alleged violations before being taken to court.
- *October:* In the updated Violence Against Women Act, a clause is added to authorize funds for programs to increase the protection of women with disabilities against violent crimes.
- *November:* Disability rights advocates claim that people with disabilities were severely underrepresented in the presidential election polls because many polling stations lacked accessibility and only 12 counties in the entire nation utilized the easy-to-access touch-screen voting machines.
- *December:* Congress authorizes the creation of the Office of Disability Employment Policy (ODEP) in its appropriations bill for Fiscal Year 2001. ODEP, an agency within the U.S. Department of Labor, is charged with the task of ensuring that individuals with disabilities have the opportunity to obtain gainful employment and receive all the protections assured by the Americans with Disabilities Act.

2001

- *February 1:* President George W. Bush establishes the New Freedom Initiative in order to promote community integration for individuals with disabilities by increasing opportunities for education, homeownership, employment, and transit. Additionally, emphasis is placed on making accessible technologies available to all individuals in need.
- *May:* The U.S. Paralympic Committee is established as a division of the U.S. Olympic Committee with the purpose of creating new, competitive, Olympic opportunities for athletes with disabilities through increased funding and outreach.

- *June 18:* President Bush issues an Executive Order titled Community Based Alternatives for Individuals with Disabilities, which calls for the widespread promotion and utilization of community-based services to aid individuals with disabilities and their integration into community life.

2002

- *April 18:* In *Access Now, Inc. v. Southwest Airlines, Co.*, a U.S. District Court in Florida finds that web sites, and the Internet in general, are not covered by the accessibility mandates of the ADA because they are not included in the definition of "places of public accommodation."
- *April 29:* President George W. Bush orders the creation of the President's New Freedom Commission on Mental Health. This committee, made up of individuals who are both consumers and providers within the field of mental health, is charged with conducting a review of the current state of mental health care in the United States and recommending program alterations to create improved services and community integration.
- *October 29:* After its passage in both the House and the Senate, President Bush signs the Help America Vote Act of 2002 (HAVA) into law. Under this act, new voting regulations are passed, and funds are allocated to help states update and improve voting systems that do not provide equal accessibility.

2003

- *July 25:* The President's Committee on Mental Retardation is renamed the President's Committee for People with Intellectual Disabilities.

2004

- *July 22:* President George W. Bush signs an Executive Order entitled Individuals with Disabilities in Emergency Preparedness. Within the Department of Homeland Security, a council is created to evaluate the consideration given to these individuals in current emergency preparedness plans and suggest reform where needed.

2005

- *January 19:* Not Dead Yet and other disability rights advocates picket the Chicago Film Critics Association to protest critics' overwhelming support of the Clint Eastwood movie *Million Dollar Baby*. Not Dead Yet and other organizations such as the National Spinal Cord Injury Association are vocally critical of the film, in which a female pro boxer receives assistance in committing suicide after a boxing accident leaves her quadriplegic.

- **March 18:** A U.S. circuit court rules that Terri Schiavo's life support systems are to be removed, allowing her to die from dehydration and starvation. Schiavo, a woman whose heart failure 15 years prior left her with brain damage and in a vegetative state, became the center of national controversy. Right to life groups like Not Dead Yet see her death as the highest form of discrimination against a disabled person.

- **July:** The documentary film *Murder Ball* is released, providing a look at the sport of competitive wheelchair rugby. The film documents the U.S. team's journey to the 2006 Paralympic games in Athens, Greece, as well as the daily lives of wheelchair-bound players. *Murder Ball* wins numerous awards at independent film festivals nationwide and receives an Oscar nomination for Best Documentary.

- **September:** After Jarek Molski has filed hundreds of lawsuits against California businesses under the ADA accessibility strictures, a Superior Court judge labels Molski, a wheelchair user, a "vexatious litigant" and bans him from filing any more suits in California without first obtaining a judge's permission.

2006

- **March 27:** The Disability Service Improvement Initiative of the Social Security Administration is completed. This initiative provides new guidelines, offices, and positions to improve the process of applying for Social Security disability benefits. Changes include a streamlined method of determining disability when an individual's disability is apparent; the creation of the position of Federal Reviewing Official to assess the decisions of state agencies when a claim is made to the federal office; and the creation of the Decision Review Board, which will serve as a regulatory body, examining and revising determinations as well as evaluating and enforcing consistent rulings.

2007

- **March 30:** Eighty member countries of the United Nations (UN) ratify the UN Convention on the Rights of Persons with Disabilities. The United States declines to sign or adopt the convention, which promotes and protects the rights of people with disabilities, because the George W. Bush administration maintains that pursuing national, not international, policy is the correct method for ensuring civil rights.

- **May:** After the George W. Bush administration resolved in 2006 to remove funding for the Survey of Income and Program Participation (SIPP) from its 2008 budget, the president reverses his decision. Under some pressure from policy advisors, President Bush reinstates this Census Bureau polling project that assesses the effects of government programs related to poverty, health insurance, and disability.

2008

■ *January:* The House Education and Labor Committee holds the first congressional hearing on the ADA Restoration Act (H.R. 3195), a bill introduced in 2007 by Representatives Steny Hoyer (D-MD) and James Sensenbrenner (R-WI). The bill proposes to eliminate the "substantial limitation" on a "major life activity"—wording from the ADA so that the protections of the law can reach a broader range of disabled Americans. The bill also seeks to use more defining terms such as *mental impairment* and *physical impairment* in the language of the law and to curtail court's prerogative to consider mitigating measures when assessing a claimant's disability during litigation.

CHAPTER 4

BIOGRAPHICAL LISTING

This chapter profiles significant individuals who are part of the history of the disability rights movement in the United States. This controversial subject has touched many sectors of the American public, and therefore the list includes prominent politicians, spokespersons, authors, and activists. Given the focus of disability rights, the individual sketches are purposefully brief and are not meant to provide a comprehensive biography.

Adrienne Asch, psychotherapist. A disability rights scholar and activist, Asch is currently the Henry R. Luce Professor in Biology, Ethics and the Politics of Human Reproduction at Wellesley College in Massachusetts. In addition to her groundbreaking 1988 book, *Women with Disabilities: Essays in Psychology, Culture, and Politics*, she has written numerous articles and book chapters on disability rights issues. Asch, who is blind, serves on the board of the American Society for Bioethics and Humanities, and the Ethical, Legal, and Social Implications Policy Planning Group of the National Human Genome Research Institute.

Michael W. Auberger, cofounder of American Disabled for Attendant Programs Today (ADAPT). A proponent of nonviolent disobedience as a means for attaining civil rights for the disabled, Auberger helped establish ADAPT in 1978 by demonstrating against Regional Transit District bus services in Denver. Since the passage of the Americans with Disabilities Act, Auberger has fought for personal assistance services (PAS) for the disabled and against the incarceration of people with disabilities in nursing homes.

Gerald Baptiste, Sr., African-American activist for ethnic minorities with disabilities. Working to raise awareness of the concerns of black Americans with disabilities, Baptiste, who is blind, has broadened the scope of the disability rights movement. In 1986, he cofounded the Multicultural Committee of the National Council of Independent Living (CIL), and later he became Deputy Director of the CIL in Berkeley, California.

Elmer Bartels, cofounder of the Boston Center for Independent Living. When Bartels, a paraplegic, was appointed commissioner of the Massachusetts Rehabilitation Commission in 1977, he became the first disabled person to hold an executive position in a state rehabilitation agency. He has also been involved in the National Paraplegia Foundation, the Massachusetts Association of Paraplegics, the U.S. Sports and Fitness Center for the Disabled, and other organizations.

Clifford Whittingham Beers, disability rights movement pioneer. An early 20th-century mental patient, Beers was subjected to poor living conditions and brutal mistreatment at the hands of mental institution attendants. He wrote about his experiences in his autobiographical account *A Mind that Found Itself* in 1908 and devoted the rest of his life to ending institutional abuse of people with mental disabilities. In 1909, he cofounded The National Committee for Mental Hygiene, which later provided psychiatric care to World War I veterans, created children's community mental health clinics, and helped pass the National Mental Health Act in 1946, increasing funding for mental health programs. In 1950, the National Mental Health Foundation and the Psychiatric Foundation joined forces to become the National Association for Mental Health.

Alexander Graham Bell, inventor. As a tutor for the deaf, Bell dismissed the use of American Sign Language and instead became a well-known advocate for oralism, the teaching of speech and lipreading skills to the deaf. Bell fought for the integration of deaf children into the hearing community, but he also argued against deaf people marrying each other in order to prevent the propagation of deaf offspring.

Wade Blank, founding member of American Disabled for Attendant Programs Today (ADAPT). A vocal disability rights activist in the 1980s and 1990s, Blank worked to help disabled people unnecessarily admitted to nursing homes live more free and independent lives in their own private residences. He also organized nationwide lawsuits and nonviolent protests against mass transit systems in an effort to make public transportation more accessible to the disabled.

Elizabeth Monroe Boggs, founding member and eventual president of the Association of Retarded Children. The mother of a retarded child, Boggs became a full-time advocate for the rights of retarded children when her own son and other mentally handicapped children were denied equal access to public education. Boggs lobbied for the passage of numerous legislative acts that benefited the developmentally disabled, including the Mental Retardation Facilities and Community Health Centers Construction Act of 1963 and the Developmentally Disabled Assistance and Bill of Rights Act of 1975.

Biographical Listing

Frank G. Bowe, former executive director of the American Coalition of Citizens with Disabilities. Deaf from a young age, Bowe became an educator and a proponent of telecommunications access for the disabled. His influential book *Handicapping America* surveyed the social, architectural, and legal obstacles faced by Americans with disabilities in the 1970s. Bowe demonstrated for federal regulations that would enforce public adherence to Section 504 of the Rehabilitation Act of 1973. In addition to authoring numerous books and articles on people with disabilities, Bowe joined Hofstra University in Long Island, New York, as a professor in the counseling, special education and rehabilitation department in 1989.

Mary Lou Breslin, president of the Disability Rights Education and Defense Fund (DREDF) from 1988 to 1991. A national leader in the disability rights movement, Breslin, a polio survivor, applied her knowledge of the law to oversee a variety of important disability rights cases. She testified in support of legal enforcement of Section 504 of the Rehabilitation Act in 1984, which led to the Civil Rights Restoration Act of 1987.

Marca Bristo, former president of the National Council on Independent Living (NCIL) from 1986 to 1989. A victim of spinal cord injury, Bristo founded Access Living in Chicago, the first independent living program in that city, and she was later appointed by President Bill Clinton to chair the National Council on Disability in 1994. Also in the 1990s, Bristo served on the Executive Steering Committee of the United Nations International Decade of Disabled Persons and as executive director of the President's Committee on Employment of People with Disabilities.

William Bronston, founder of the World Independence Fund. A proponent for the rights of people with cognitive and developmental disorders, Bronston helped pass the Civil Rights of Institutionalized Persons Act of 1980 (CRIPA). He later became the director of Project Interdependence, a program promoting the integration of high school students with cognitive disabilities into mainstream high schools.

Robert L. Burgdorf, Jr., attorney and author of the Americans with Disabilities Act of 1990 (ADA). A polio survivor, Burgdorf helped establish the National Center for Law and the Handicapped while he was still in law school. He later became codirector of the Developmental Disabilities Law Project, Inc., at the University of Maryland Law School in Baltimore. As an attorney and research specialist for the National Council on the Handicapped, Burgdorf later drafted the initial legislation that became the ADA.

Christopher Joseph Burke, actor. Best known as "Corky" on the television drama *Life Goes On* in the 1990s, Burke helped shatter the stereotypes surrounding people with Down syndrome, a condition he has. In addition to acting, Burke has worked as an advocate and spokesperson for the National Down Syndrome Society, and he has fought for greater employment opportunities for people with disabilities.

George H. W. Bush, 41st president of the United States. The Bush administration was one of the first to court the political power of people with disabilities, and Bush favored the passage of—and subsequently signed into law—the landmark Americans with Disabilities Act in 1990. Some biographers attribute the former president's sympathetic attitude toward disability rights to the fact that several members of his own family had disabilities.

George W. Bush, 43rd president of the United States. Like his father, George W. Bush has publicly committed to ensuring the rights of people with disabilities. In 2001, he launched the New Freedom Initiative to increase government support for assistive technologies, accessible transportation, and home ownership for the disabled. Some in the disabilities community, however, have criticized Bush's Medicare plans and his cuts to veterans' programs, insisting that his disability policies have not translated into positive actions.

John H. Catlin, architect known for his barrier-free designs. Acknowledged for his skill in creating accessible, design-friendly spaces for people with disabilities, Catlin, who is deaf, was appointed by President Bill Clinton to serve on the U.S. Architectural and Transportation Barriers Compliance Board in 1994. He also provided input for drafts of the Americans with Disabilities Act Architectural Guidelines (ADAG), mandating equal access to government facilities.

Louis-Laurent-Marie Clerc, cofounder of deaf education in the United States. Partnered with Thomas Hopkins Gallaudet, Clerc was influential in developing American Deaf culture and American Sign Language (ASL). He helped found the American School for the Deaf in Hartford, Connecticut, in 1817 and became president of the New England Gallaudet Association of the Deaf in 1854, America's first national organization run entirely by deaf people.

Tony Coelho, former U.S. congressman from California. Discriminated against for having epilepsy since age 15, Coelho faced further prejudice in the political arena when an opponent questioned his ability to serve Congress with this condition. Coelho nonetheless won a seat in Congress in 1978 as the California representative from the San Joaquin Valley. By 1986, he held a powerful position in the House Democratic Leadership as majority whip. He was instrumental in introducing an early draft of the Americans with Disabilities Act to Congress in 1988. After leaving Congress in 1990, Coelho became involved with the National Foundation for Affordable Housing Solutions and other disability rights organizations.

Diane Coleman, founding member of Not Dead Yet. A staunch opponent of assisted suicide, Coleman founded Not Dead Yet in response to the work of Dr. Jack Kevorkian and other right-to-die proponents. Having a neuromuscular disability since birth, she has written extensively on disability rights issues and has served on a number of disability-related organizations, including the State Advisory Committee to the U.S. Civil Rights Commission, the Statewide Independent Living Council, and the Center for Independent Living in Nashville, Tennessee.

Timothy Cook, attorney. Cook was instrumental in the struggle for accessible public transportation for the disabled. He developed the Disability Rights Litigation Project at the Legal Aid Society of New York City, which brought education- and employment-related class action suits to trial on behalf of disabled Americans. He later served as counsel for numerous landmark disability rights cases such as *Bowen v. American Hospital Association*, fighting for the right of disabled infants to receive medical care. He died at age 38 after contracting AIDS from a blood transfusion meant to treat his hemophilia.

Barry Corbet, independent filmmaker. A former filmmaker for the National Geographic Society, Corbet suffered a spinal cord injury in a helicopter crash in 1966. Since then, he has devoted part of his film career to the production of films concerning disability and rehabilitation, including *Outside: Spinal Cord Injury and the Future* (1980). He is also the editor of *New Mobility*, a lifestyle magazine for the disabled.

George A. Covington, former cochair of the Universal Design Task Force of the President's Committee on Employment of People with Disabilities. Legally blind, Covington has received national attention for his photography and for using his art as a means to help others with visual impairments explore their surroundings. He has advised the government on the use of technology for disabled workers and on making Washington, D.C., more accessible to disabled tourists. He is a founding member of the National Council of Citizens with Low Vision and is involved in the American Council of the Blind.

Justin Dart, principal author of the Americans with Disabilities Act (ADA). A polio survivor, Dart became involved with disability rights issues in the 1980s when he chaired the Texas Governor's Committee for Persons with Disabilities. In 1982, he was appointed vice-chair to the National Council on the Handicapped, where he became an advocate for a single civil rights act for people with disabilities, what later became the ADA. Dart organized support for the legislation throughout the United States as cochair of the Congressional Task Force on the Rights and Empowerment of Americans with Disabilities. In 1995, Dart organized the fifth year anniversary celebration of the ADA at the National Press Club in Washington, D.C. He remained an active proponent for disability rights, participating in international lectures and demonstrations until his death in 2002. A number of annual awards have also been named in Dart's honor, including the Justin Dart Award of the President's Committee on Employment of People with Disabilities.

Robert Joseph Dole, former U.S. senator. Partially paralyzed in World War II, Bob Dole is recognized as an influential public figure in the fight for disability rights. He founded the Dole Foundation in 1984, a foundation championing competitive employment opportunities for people with disabilities in the United States. In 1986, he headed a bipartisan coalition to enact the Air Carrier Access Act, legislation which prevents airlines from discriminating against people with disabilities.

Clint Eastwood, film actor and director. After one of his tourist resorts was cited in 1997 for alleged accessibility violations under the Americans with Disabilities Act (ADA), Eastwood advocated before Congress that the ADA should be altered so that businesses would be allowed a 90-day grace period to remedy ADA noncompliance complaints before suffering legal suit. No such amendment passed. Eastwood's Oscar-winning 2005 film *Million Dollar Baby* also incurred criticism from some in the disabilities community for its supposed promotion of assisted suicide as a preferable remedy to living a disabled life.

Frederick Fay, national leader in the disability rights movement. A quadriplegic since 1961, Fay is recognized as a pioneer in the independent living movement and for his innovative ideas in computer technologies for people with disabilities. His inventions include devices enabling people with disabilities to control lights, thermostats, phones, and computers from their wheelchairs. In 1967, he served as the first president of the Washington chapter of the National Spinal Cord Injury Association and cofounded the Boston Center for Independent Living in 1974. In 1995, Fay cofounded Justice for All with Justin Dart and Becky Ogle, an organization created to address attacks on disability legislation.

Eunice Fiorito, first president of the American Coalition of Citizens with Disabilities (ACCD). Fiorito, who is blind, has worked as the director for Psychiatric Social Work and Rehabilitation at the Bellevue Medical Center at New York University and the nation's first Mayor's Office for the Handicapped in New York. In 1978, she founded the League of Disabled Voters and since then has also served as a special assistant to the commissioner of Rehabilitation Services in the U.S. Department of Education.

Andrew G. Fleming, advocate for disabled sports and athletic programs. After losing both legs in a train accident at age 24, Fleming became a wheelchair athlete and continues to encourage the recognition of disabled people through athletic competition. In 1982, he became the first executive director of the National Wheelchair Athletic Association and a member of the U.S. Olympic Subcommittee on Programs for Athletes with Disabilities.

Biographical Listing

LaDonna Fowler, project director for the American Indian Disability Legislation Project (AIDL). Fowler is a leading advocate for disability rights for Native Americans. She is a member of the National Council on Independent Living Multicultural Committee and of the Personal Assistant Services Advisory Council of the World Institute on Disability.

Lex Frieden, former executive director of the National Council on the Handicapped. Internationally recognized as a key figure in the disability rights movement, Frieden, a quadriplegic, helped draft the Americans with Disabilities Act and is an authority on independent living and rehabilitation. In 1990, he became assistant national secretary of the U.S. Council on International Rehabilitation, and later, a clinical associate professor in the department of community medicine at Baylor University.

Robert Funk, cofounder and first executive director of the Disability Rights Education and Defense Fund (DREDF). Funk has argued for public recognition of people with disabilities as a specific class of citizens whose civil rights are protected under law. In 1990, he was appointed chief of staff of the U.S. Equal Employment Opportunity Commission, and, in 1993, he joined Evan Kemp Associates, Inc., in Washington, D.C., a consulting firm specializing in disability rights.

Hugh Gregory Gallagher, researcher and author. Gallagher is well known for his research and writings about the Nazi extermination programs waged against people with disabilities during World War II and about disability in the life of President Franklin Roosevelt. He also authored the Architectural Barriers Act of 1968, the first federal disability rights law, which paved the way for future disability rights legislation. In 1995, Gallagher received the Henry B. Betts Award for improving the lives of people with disabilities.

Edward Miner Gallaudet, founder and first president of Gallaudet University in Washington, D.C. Gallaudet's father founded the American School for the Deaf, where Edward, who was fluent in sign language, began teaching in 1855. In 1864, he became superintendent of the Columbia Institution for the Deaf and Dumb and Blind in Washington, D.C. Here, he was a proponent of combined methods of teaching the deaf, encouraging the use of sign language, lipreading, and speech. Gallaudet helped raise the school to the status of a fully functioning college, the National College for the Deaf. It was later renamed Gallaudet College, in honor of his father, in 1894.

Thomas Hopkins Gallaudet, cofounder of the American School for the Deaf in Hartford, Connecticut. Gallaudet studied methods for teaching the deaf in Europe and was inspired most by French methods at the Royal Institution for the Deaf in Paris. With Laurent Clerc, a deaf instructor at the school in Paris, Gallaudet returned to America to found his own school. Like his son after him, Gallaudet was a staunch proponent of American Sign Language.

Donald Galloway, former vice president of the National Association of Minorities with Disabilities. Galloway, who is blind, has worked specifically to include African Americans with disabilities in the disabilities rights movement. In addition to directing Peace Corps programs and directing the District of Columbia Center for Independent Living, Galloway founded Visually Impaired Persons of Color. This group later merged with the National Federation of the Blind in 1991.

Jack Randle Gannon, historian. Acknowledged as a preeminent historian of Deaf America, Gannon is the author of such works as *Deaf Heritage: A Narrative History of Deaf America* and *The Week the World Heard Gallaudet*, a historical account of Gallaudet University students' fight for a deaf president at the college in the 1980s. He received an honorary doctorate from Gallaudet University in 1988 for his career of service to the Deaf community.

Rosemarie Garland-Thomson, associate professor of women's studies at Emory University. Through her scholarly work, Rosemarie Garland-Thomson has been most responsible for opening up the field of disability studies in the humanities. Her critically acclaimed works include *Extraordinary Bodies: Figuring Physical Disability in American Literature and Culture* and *Freakery: Cultural Spectacles of the Extraordinary Body*.

Howard Geld, founder of the Mental Patients Liberation Project. Institutionalized in a mental hospital at age 13, Geld suffered a number of indignities that would later inspire him to advocate for the civil rights of the mentally disabled. He argued for the patients' rights to view their own records, refuse medication and shock treatments, and decline to work inside mental institutions without fair compensation for their efforts.

John Hessler, first director of the Physically Disabled Students' Program at the University of California, Berkeley. In the late 1960s, Hessler, a quadriplegic, was the second severely handicapped student admitted to UC Berkeley. Here, he organized other disabled students to advocate for their rights on campus. He later cofounded the Center for Independent Living in Berkeley and was instrumental in creating momentum for the independent living movement throughout the United States.

Judith E. Heumann, independent living movement pioneer. Discriminated against in the public school system after becoming disabled by polio at a young age, Heumann became a determined advocate for disability rights. Winning an employment discrimination lawsuit in 1970, she became the first public school teacher in the New York City Public School system to use a wheelchair. That year she also founded Disabled In Action (DIA), a group known for agitating politically for disability rights. In 1983, she cofounded the World Institute on Disability (WID), and in 1993, President Clinton appointed her assistant secretary for Special Education and Rehabilitative Services at the U.S. Department of Education.

Robert Benjamin Irwin, early leader of the American Foundation for the Blind. After doing postgraduate research at Harvard on the administration of schools for the blind in 1909, Irwin accepted a position from the Cleveland Board of Education to create that city's first classes for blind children. While in this position, Irwin's innovations included advocating for large-print books for children with poor vision. Later, he founded Howe Publishing Company, which produces books in Braille for adults.

Mary Johnson, editor. In 1980, Johnson cofounded and became the first editor of *The Disability Rag & Resource*, a disability rights bimonthly magazine. The journal became a mouthpiece for the disability community and has since been renamed the *Ragged Edge*. In addition to her work in magazine publishing, Johnson's own writing on disability rights issues has appeared in the *New York Times*, the *Nation*, and elsewhere.

Irving King Jordan, first deaf president of Gallaudet University. Jordan began his career at Gallaudet University in 1973 as an assistant professor of psychology, and he later became chair of the Department of Psychology in 1983. Jordan was elected as the university's first deaf president in 1988, after student strikes and demonstrations erupted on campus when a hearing candidate was first selected for the post.

Helen Keller, disability rights advocate. One of America's most recognizable disabled figures, Helen Keller became both blind and deaf as a child through illness in the late 1880s. An intelligent child, she quickly learned to communicate through finger-spelling and to read lips with her fingers. After graduating from Radcliffe College in 1904, she became an advocate for the blind, fighting for equal rights to education and employment. However, she also supported some eugenics practices such as allowing doctors to withhold lifesaving treatment from severely disabled newborns. Keller's 1902 autobiography, *The Story of My Life*, was a popular success when it was serialized in the *Ladies' Home Journal*. Keller continued to write books and articles throughout her life, and her story inspired the 1957 Broadway play and subsequent 1962 film *The Miracle Worker*.

Simi Linton, psychologist. A long-time disability rights scholar and activist, Simi Linton taught at Hunter College in the Department of Educational Foundations and Counseling Programs until 1998. She was founder and the first chairperson of the National Coalition on Sexuality and Disability, and in 1995 she was a recipient of a Switzer Distinguished Fellowship from the U.S. Department of Education's National Institute on Disability and Rehabilitation Research. Her published works include *Claiming Disability: Knowledge and Identity* and *My Body Politic*, a memoir.

Paul K. Longmore, author. Through his writings about the "hidden history" of disabilities in American culture, Longmore has become a key player in the disability rights movement. His work provides a theoretical guide for the movement as he dissects the social history of people with disabilities in the United States. Longmore is an associate professor of history at San Francisco State University and contributing editor of *Disability Studies Quarterly*.

Ronald L. Mace, architect. As a polio survivor, Mace has used a wheelchair since age nine. Interested in creating wheelchair accessible environments, he became an architect, in part to design and advocate for widespread accessible architecture. Mace's drafting of the Handicapped Section of the North Carolina Building Code became a model for building code legislation in other states. Mace frequently testifies before Congress, providing expertise on accessibility issues on behalf of disability rights legislation.

Arlene Mayerson, lawyer. A leading expert in disability rights law, Mayerson is an attorney for the Disability Rights Education and Defense Fund (DREDF). Her work as a lawyer is best known for cases that have established federal precedents in disability rights such as the Handicapped Children's Protection Act, the Civil Rights Restoration Act, the Fair Housing Amendments Act, and the Americans with Disabilities Act.

David T. Mitchell, director of the doctoral program in disability studies at the University of Illinois, Chicago, and associate professor in the Department of Disability and Human Development. Mitchell is a former president of the Society for Disability Studies and a founding member of the Modern Language Association Committee on Disability Issues. He is coeditor of the book *The Body and Physical Difference: Discourses of Disability* and codirector and producer of the film *Vital Signs*, which won documentary awards including the Grand Prize at Rehabilitation International 1996.

Timothy Nugent, founder of the disabled students' program at the University of Illinois, Galesburg campus. In 1948, Nugent's founding of the disabled students' program was the first effort of its kind in America. His program strove to incorporate disabled students into all aspects of campus life, including housing, sports, and social life. Nugent also founded the National Wheelchair Basketball Association in 1949, and in 1959 he became the first director of research and development of the American National Standards Institute Project A117. This project established the basis for architectural access legislation and regulation nationwide.

Mary Jane Owen, author and activist. As an active protestor for disability rights and the author of more than 600 articles on disability-related issues, Owen has been regarded as an important figure within the disability rights movement since the early 1970s when she began working as a paralegal for the Center for Independent Living's Disability Rights Center in Berkeley. In 1984, she became the executive director and president of

Disability Focus, Inc. Since the 1990s, Owen has been an outspoken opponent against euthanasia, protesting the actions of Dr. Jack Kevorkian and other right-to-die activists.

David Pfeiffer, professor of public administration. Pfeiffer is credited with bringing disability studies to the attention of academia. A polio survivor, he has served as the chair and director of the masters of public administration program at Suffolk University, which offers a concentration in disability studies. In 1986, he helped found the influential Society for Disability Studies (SDS), and he later became editor of that organization's publication *Disability Studies Quarterly* in 1995.

Christopher Reeve, actor. World renowned for his film portrayals of Superman, Reeve moved into the disability rights movement's spotlight after a horseback-riding accident in 1995 left him paralyzed. Before his death in 2004, Reeve became an outspoken advocate for increased federal funding for finding a cure for spinal injuries. Many disability rights activists, however, were disappointed that Reeve, as such a visible and much loved public figure, did not use the media spotlight to advocate more for disability rights.

Edward Roberts, independent living movement pioneer. Disabled by polio as a child and unable to breathe without the help of either a respirator or an iron lung, Roberts fought for the right to attend the University of California at Berkeley in 1962. While there, he was instrumental in founding the university's Physically Disabled Students' Program, and he was the first director of the Center for Independent Living in Berkeley in 1972.

Franklin Delano Roosevelt, 32nd president of the United States. Roosevelt was stricken with polio at age 39 and spent much of his life trying to regain the use of his legs. He succeeded in having an active political career, both as governor of New York and later as president of the United States, despite his disability, which he chose to keep hidden from the public when he could. Roosevelt established a rehabilitation center at Warm Springs, Georgia, to help other polio survivors and to manage his own rehabilitation regimen.

Harilyn Rousso, psychotherapist and educator. Rousso is the founder of the Networking Project for Disabled Women and Girls of the Young Women's Christian Association of New York City. In addition to advocating for disabled rights for women and adolescent girls, she is the executive director of Disabilities Unlimited Consulting Services, an organization that offers disability rights advocacy services to all disabled people and their families.

Marsha Saxton, activist and author. Saxton, who writes from the perspective of someone with spina bifida, has written numerous articles on disability rights and women's health issues. She is the founder and director of the Project on Women and Disability in Boston.

Frederick Schreiber, first executive director of the National Association of the Deaf (NAD). Under Schreiber's directorship (which lasted from 1964 until his death in 1979), NAD began to play a more important role in advocating for the rights of deaf people. Schreiber was also the founder of the American Coalition of Citizens with Disabilities.

Jean Stewart, author. Stewart's 1989 novel, *The Body's Memory*, focuses on the realistic disability experiences of the main character and explores such disability rights-related issues as independent living and the misconceptions able-bodied people have about people with disabilities. Stewart is also the founder of the Disabled Prisoners' Justice Fund, an organization that advocates for rights of prisoners with disabilities.

Mary Elizabeth Switzer, former director of the federal government's Office of Vocational Rehabilitation (OVR). As director of the OVR in the 1950s, Switzer focused on assisting people with disabilities to become self-sufficient. With her influential power over federal funding, she helped create university-based rehabilitation-related training programs for people with physical and mental disabilities.

Jacobus tenBroek, founder and president of the National Federation of the Blind (NFB). As the founder of the NFB in 1940, tenBroek headed the largest political organization in the United States made up of the blind and the visually impaired. Dr. tenBroek and the NFB worked to dispel stereotypes about the blind and advocated for their full participation in American society.

Henry Viscardi, Jr., author. Born without legs, Viscardi suffered discrimination throughout his life because of his disability. During World War II, Viscardi, who had learned to walk with the aid of prostheses, volunteered with the Red Cross to help teach disabled veterans how to adjust to their own prostheses and to rehabilitate them back into normal life activities. After the war, Viscardi cofounded Just One Break (JOB), an organization that helped find jobs for disabled workers. He is also known as an author of eight books, including his popular autobiography *A Man's Stature*.

Barbara Faye Waxman, advocate for sexual and reproductive rights of people with disabilities. A former director of the Americans with Disabilities Act Training and Technical Assistance Project of the California Family Planning Council, Waxman is best known for her speeches and writings on reproductive rights and sexual issues relating to disabilities. She was an outspoken critic of the use of genetic screening for the selective abortion of fetuses with disabilities, and a staunch opponent of assisted suicide.

Boyce Robert Williams, rehabilitation specialist. Williams is credited for expanding educational and employment opportunities for the deaf and hard of hearing. Working with Mary Switzer through the Office of Vocational Rehabilitation, Williams helped create innovative programs for the deaf, such as the National Theatre of the Deaf, the Registry of Interpreters for the Deaf, and Captioned Films for the Deaf.

Robert Williams, commissioner of the Administration on Developmental Disabilities at the U.S. Department of Health and Human Services. A poet and writer with cerebral palsy, Williams advocates primarily for people with disabilities that affect their speech. Before being appointed to his Health and Human Services position, Williams served as president of Hear Our Voices, an advocacy group for people who rely on augmentive devices for communication. He also served as vice president of The Association for Persons with Severe Handicaps (TASH).

Irving Kenneth Zola, sociologist, professor, and author. Irving Zola is a well-respected author within the disability rights movement for his prolific work, which foregrounds the disability experience. Zola served as chair of the Department of Sociology at Brandeis University, and he also founded the Society for Disability Studies (SDS). Through the SDS, Zola also founded and edited *Disability Studies Quarterly*. Zola's best known book is his 1982 autobiographical work *Missing Pieces: A Chronicle of Living with a Disability*.

CHAPTER 5

GLOSSARY

This chapter presents definitions of many of the most prominent terms that might appear in any discussion of the social, legal, and political dimensions of disability rights. Some of the entries are obsolete but are nonetheless included to show how terminology has changed with society's evolving conception of disability and the growing acceptance of people with disabilities as a minority with guaranteed rights and protections.

ableism   A negatively biased perception of people with disabilities. Like racists and sexists, ableists discriminate against the disabled due only to the fact that they have disabilities and believe in the superior nature and abilities of nondisabled people. Ableism often implies a connection between disability and abnormality.

accessibility   One of the main causes of the disability movement, accessibility concerns more than just physical access to buildings and vehicles for transportation. Accessibility issues arise from the belief that individuals with disabilities should be afforded the same opportunities as other members of society. For this reason, accessibility includes technological access to devices such as telephones and computers and participatory access to programs and services such as Social Security. Disability advocates fight for accessibility to promote full community integration for people with disabilities.

acoustic coupler   A forerunner of the modern modem that allows typewritten communication over telephone lines. Though now obsolete, the acoustic coupler permitted teletype machines to connect and transmit messages, revolutionizing communications opportunities for the hearing impaired in the early 1960s and into the 1970s.

adapted athletics   The term used to describe sports programs established for and played by individuals with some type of physical or mental disability. The earliest, nationwide adaptive athletic program was developed for the sport of wheelchair basketball. Since then, adapted athletics continually expand and now include sports such as downhill skiing, track and field, soccer, ice sledge hockey, and equestrian events.

Glossary

American Sign Language (ASL) A system of visual signs, performed mainly with the hands, to communicate without the use of spoken words. While ASL was developed in the United States, it is not just a visual representation of English. ASL employs specific grammatical rules in a manner most appropriate to conveying ideas through the use of manual signs. Different standardized forms of sign language exist worldwide just as spoken languages vary from country to country. ASL has its own alphabet as well as specific gestures corresponding with distinct and complex ideas and emotions.

assistive listening devices Technological inventions used to enhance the ability of hearing impaired individuals to better perceive specific sounds. Unlike hearing aids, which increase the volume of all sounds in an environment, assistive listening devices are employed to emphasize one particular sound, such as a professor at the front of a large lecture hall or a television in a crowded room. When using these devices, a microphone is placed near the sound the individual wishes to hear and then that sound is magnified so it can be heard over the other sounds in the setting.

assistive technologies Technological devices or applications employed by individuals with disabilities to ease or make possible the performance of activities that would otherwise be limited or prohibited. One early assistive technology was the **teletypewriter (TTY)**, which made communication over telephone lines possible for deaf people. As technologies have evolved, the computer industry has continued to create innovative assistive technologies designed to facilitate computer use for individuals with disabilities. For example, new software allows alternative methods of data entry so that individuals can navigate the world of personal computers using voice commands rather than a mouse and keyboard. Another new technology is the Braille computer screen reader that provides blind people the opportunity to read displayed text. These are only a few examples of the assistive technologies that have been developed to provide equal access and opportunity for individuals with disabilities.

autism A developmental disability characterized by an individual's inability to communicate and interact with others. When autism was first clinically defined, its cause was often attributed to poor parenting and, more specifically, to a mother's inept child rearing. As time has progressed and studies continue, autism has been widely recognized as a neurological disorder.

Braille A codified system of dot cells with six dots arranged in different patterns to create text that can be read by touch with the fingertips. Braille dots can be arranged in as many as 63 combinations, representing individual letters as well as contractions. This system enables people with visual impairments to read and write. The system was invented by Louis Braille, a blind Frenchman, in 1821.

cerebral palsy   The term given to neurological disorders characterized by a lack of muscle control resulting from the brain's inability to properly direct muscle movement. Cerebral palsy is most likely to strike infants and children under three years of age, with the severity of the muscle impairment remaining consistent over time.

closed captioning/captioning   Textual descriptions of on-screen audio information that include spoken dialogue as well as musical cues, audience reactions, and background sounds. Closed captions are codes embedded in television signals that are decoded by devices installed in all televisions. In accordance with Federal Communications Commission (FCC) guidelines, all televisions manufactured since 1993 are equipped with such decoding devices.

cochlear implant   A device surgically installed within the ear to improve hearing ability. Unlike hearing aids that magnify the sounds of the environment to enable processing by the damaged portions of the ear, cochlear implants provide signals directly to auditory nerves, completely bypassing damaged sections. An individual who is fitted with one of these implants must relearn how to interpret the auditory signals as they do not restore or imitate regular hearing.

crippled   An outdated, politically incorrect term used to describe individuals with physical disabilities. The word has taken on a derogatory connotation that implies otherness and inability to perform tasks easily accomplished by the nondisabled.

curb-cut   A ramped portion of a street curb that allows for an easier pedestrian movement from the sidewalk to the street, thus avoiding the vertical drop of up to six inches off uncut curb edges. Curb-cuts create improved access for individuals in wheelchairs and other people with mobility impairments, as well as for the rest of the general public. After years of lobbying by disability rights groups, curb-cuts in sidewalks became mandatory with the passage of the Americans with Disabilities Act in 1990.

Deaf movement   An organized group of people who share the conviction that deafness is not a disability but a distinct minority culture with its own language, **American Sign Language (ASL)**. The term "Deaf," therefore, applies to those who see themselves as part of this minority culture, while the lowercase "deaf" refers to anyone with a severe hearing impairment.

deinstitutionalization   The policy of moving individuals with disabilities out of segregated, confining residential homes to community living centers that emphasize participation in the broader community. A specific trend to deinstitutionalize people with mental illness began in the mid 1950s with the introduction of antipsychotic drugs. Many of the institutions housing these individuals were closed upon their release, leaving some to blame the policy for increased homelessness and increased crime rates in surrounding locales.

Glossary

developmental disability The term describing chronic conditions that impair an individual in either a physical or mental capacity, and manifest before age 22. Developmental disabilities often make it difficult for individuals to speak with other individuals, to learn, to control body movements, and to live independently. Autism, cerebral palsy, hearing loss, mental retardation, and vision impairment all fall under the categorization of developmental disability according to the U.S. Centers for Disease Control and Prevention.

disability A term describing a condition that significantly limits an individual's ability to partake in a major life activity, such as obtaining employment, communicating, or living independently.

eugenics [movement] The name given to a science popularized in the early 20th century that asserted that humanity would be best served if individuals who possessed the most desirable traits were encouraged to breed while those with the least desirable characteristics were weeded out of the population. In the United States, the eugenics movement held enough sway to convince state authorities to routinely sterilize "feeble-minded" or other disabled individuals so that they could not procreate and pass on their tainted genes. The eugenics philosophy attained its notorious apogee in Nazi Germany where all undesirables—including Jews, gypsies, and people with disabilities—were slaughtered in the name of promoting a master race.

euthanasia Greek term for "good death," euthanasia refers to the deliberate killing of individuals in order to relieve suffering. At times referred to as mercy killing or assisted suicide, euthanasia has been employed throughout history to end the lives of individuals with disabilities, resulting from the misperception that individuals with disabilities do not lead happy or productive lives. Many disability rights advocates oppose the practice, fearing it will reinforce the notion that a disabled life is a life not worth living.

handicapped An outdated term used to describe individuals with disabilities. The term is now obsolete due to its connotations of helplessness and inability, and many disability rights activists oppose its use because it places emphasis on the disability and not the individual. Many enduring government and private organizations that once employed the term "handicapped" in their title have since changed names to dispense with its negative associations.

hidden disabilities A category of conditions that have an impairing impact on an individual's life but are not obvious to others upon observation. Diabetes, some learning disabilities, epilepsy, allergies, cancer, and heart disease are all classified as hidden disabilities. Individuals with hidden disabilities are afforded the same protections under the Americans with Disabilities Act as individuals with visible disabilities.

Rights of the Disabled

HIV/AIDS Acquired immunodeficiency syndrome (AIDS) is a disease in which an individual's immune system is severely weakened following contraction of the human immunodeficiency virus (HIV). An individual with AIDS (or its precursor syndrome) can receive protection under the Americans with Disabilities Act.

Human Centered Design See **Universal Design.**

independent living The ability of a person with a disability to live in an integrated community setting and actively participate in that community through employment and social interaction. The promotion of independent living began in the 1960s and 1970s with the opening of independent living centers nationwide that provided the needed support to aid individuals in the transition from institutional living to integrated community life.

individualized education programs (IEPs) Written plans formulated by the educators, parents, and school staff for an individual with a disability, to ensure the best possible educational results for that student. Often, even the student is present when the IEP is created so that he or she can participate in setting educational goals and deciding what methods best aid his or her individual learning process. IEPs were mandated with the passage of the Individuals with Disabilities Education Act (IDEA).

institutionalization The confining of individuals with physical or mental disabilities at residence centers, effectively segregating them from the rest of society. Institutionalization was the preferred method of handling individuals with disabilities until the mid-20th century when the appalling conditions of some facilities were exposed and new, more effective models of treatment were popularized.

integration The process of moving individuals with disabilities into living situations where they can participate in a diverse community experience. The Independent Living Movement aided many disabled individuals who had lived most of their lives isolated in institutions, in moving to new community settings where they lived and worked alongside individuals without disabilities. Schools were similarly integrated through the enactment of the Individuals with Disabilities Education Act (IDEA).

mainstreaming A term originally used in the 1970s to refer to the policy of blending children with disabilities into school programs with nondisabled peers. In accordance with the Individuals with Disabilities Education Act (IDEA), many children with minor and moderate disabilities were placed into regular classroom settings with nondisabled children, and even children with more severe disabilities—who had to receive special education classes—were assumed to benefit with interaction with nondisabled peers in hallways and lunchrooms. The term has since been broadened to refer to the moving of all disabled people from segregated environments into the "mainstream" where they could live and interact with the general public.

manual method/manualism A theory of educating children who are deaf or hard of hearing that is based on the belief that sign language is the natural language of deaf people. In the 1860s, Edward Miner Gallaudet advocated for the incorporation of this method into all education programs for the deaf, where it was to be used in combination with the **oral method** so that each individual could find the best way to communicate. After sign language was standardized and became internationally recognized as a unique language, manualism began to gain popularity over **oralism**.

medical model of disability A paradigm that assumes that a disability is a medical problem that needs to be solved. This mode of thinking places emphasis on the expert opinion of doctors or physicians, who strive to offer the best potential treatments in hopes that the individual with the disability can function "normally" in society. Disability activists argue that the influence of the medical model has perpetuated damaging myths that people with disabilities are less capable than their nondisabled peers and therefore deserve pity because of their limitations. The medical model is the antithesis of the **social model of disability**.

Medicare and Medicaid Two federally funded insurance programs run by the U.S. Social Security Administration designed to cover the high cost of medical care. Each program offers benefits to qualifying individuals with disabilities based on the type of disability, work status, and income level. Medicare is disbursed by the federal government, while Medicaid is administered by individual states. Some individuals are eligible to receive benefits from both programs.

mental retardation A condition characterized by below average intellectual abilities. Causes for this type of developmental disability range from congenital defects to brain injury or disease. Symptoms may include difficulty with communication, learning, and socialization.

normalization A policy of encouraging mentally disabled individuals to live in an environment as similar as possible to that shared by all other members of society. The policy was popularized in the United States in the 1970s, and although it originally applied strictly to the "normalized" education of people with mental disabilities, it quickly broadened to promote the idea that people with mental disabilities should be removed from institutions and given the opportunity and assistance to live independent lives.

oral method/oralism A method of teaching individuals who are deaf or hard of hearing through lipreading and the imitation of speech sounds. Oralism became popular in the United States in the 19th century and gained support by such prominent figures as inventor Alexander

Graham Bell and Bernard Engelsman, the first to establish an oral education program in America. Oral schools discouraged the use of sign language because it was thought to hinder an individual's capacity to learn to speak. In the early 20th century, oralism garnered many critics who argued the method tried to paint deafness as a problem that could be overcome. From then on it began to lose favor as the benefits of teaching through combined methods, including **manualism**, became apparent.

Paralympics An international, competitive sports competition for athletes with disabilities. Held every four years in conjunction with and at the same site as the Olympic Games, the Paralympics offer athletes the opportunity to compete in a variety of adapted sporting contests.

paraplegia Paralysis from the waist down or paralysis of both legs. Paraplegia is often caused by spinal cord injury or disease.

paratransit Transportation services, available by reservation, for individuals with disabilities. Often run by independent, nonprofit groups, paratransit services cater mainly to individuals who do not have access to other forms of transportation. Passage of the ADA required state and local governments to make paratransit services available in areas where public transportation is inaccessible and to make the services complimentary or available at a comparable fee to other public transit options. Typical paratransit vehicles include accessible vans, taxis, and minibuses that can be scheduled for use at a specific time.

personal assistance services (PAS) The aiding of individuals with disabilities in the accomplishment of necessary, daily tasks such as eating, dressing, bathing, and toileting. People who provide PAS can also provide help with tasks such as handling money or communicating with others. These services can also extend to the workplace, where an individual is aided with the specific duties he or she must perform to be successful at that job. Most PAS programs are government funded, but these are commonly devoted to disabled individuals with low incomes and those over 60 years old. Disability advocates argue that millions more people are in need of these services, thus making the issue a focal point of recent disability rights activism.

physical disability Any condition that impairs an individual's ability to perform tasks because of limited or incomplete bodily control. Often this type of disability is characterized by restricted mobility. However, individuals who experience difficulty in utilizing objects that individuals without disability employ easily can be said to have a physical disability. Physical disabilities can be brought on by injury, disease, or genetic disorder.

quadriplegia Paralysis from the neck down or paralysis of all four limbs. Spinal cord injury or disease is often the cause of the condition.

Glossary

rehabilitative medicine A medical field aiding individuals with disabilities in learning to perform essential daily tasks independently and acquiring skills that reduce the limitations a disability could potentially impose. This field was pioneered by physicians aiding disabled veterans in learning how to live with their disabilities after returning home during and following World War II.

reproductive rights A crucial platform of the disability rights movement, focusing on the right of women with disabilities to have children. This right was denied from many in the United States when legalized, forced sterilization of disabled people was the norm. State-sponsored sterilization began in the 1900s with the widespread influence of the **eugenics** movement and continued through the 1970s. An estimated 60,000 Americans were denied the ability to procreate through sterilization programs. The disability rights movement has continually fought to ensure that individuals with disabilities are afforded the same opportunity to start a family and provided with the same level of prenatal and postnatal care as an individual without a disability.

sheltered workshops Segregated workhouses that employ workers who have disabilities. Begun in the 1830s, sheltered workshops were initially conceived of as places where disabled workers could receive vocational training before finding gainful employment in mainstream businesses. However, because many businesses refused to hire people with disabilities, the workshops became permanent industries. Sheltered workshops for people with disabilities—especially those with mental disabilities—have remained active in the United States since their inception. Defenders of the system claim it is the only opportunity for many disabled people to find employment; critics charge that segregation reinforces social biases and counteracts the benefits of community integration.

social model of disability (sociopolitical model of disability) The conception of disability as a social concern that focuses on the barriers that impede a disabled individual's ability to participate equally in society. This model is championed by individuals with disabilities in order to shift emphasis away from the **medical model of disability** that views the person as the source of disability. Instead of promoting individual remedies and rehabilitation, the social model looks for ways to cure society of the biases that exacerbate medical-model thinking. Thus, the social model advocates that discrimination against individuals with disabilities will lessen when societal prejudice subsides.

special education Teaching programs developed to meet the needs of individuals with disabilities affecting their ability to learn. Often, special education classes are separated from the regular classrooms, generating great debate as to whether individuals with disabilities actually receive an equitable education when isolated in specifically designed programs.

The Individuals with Disabilities Act (IDEA) encourages programs that allow individuals with disabilities to remain in an integrated classroom setting, leaving the classroom only as needed to effectively gain a complete education.

sterilization   A surgical procedure that leaves an individual unable to procreate. Policies making sterilization of individuals with disabilities compulsory were common across the United States beginning in the 1900s and continuing through the 1970s. By some estimates, more than 60,000 individuals were denied their reproductive rights before the practice was outlawed.

super crip   A stereotype perpetuated in stories of people with disabilities who persevere and overcome the limitations of their disability to reach a level of social success that inspires others. Most disability rights activists consider the stereotype damaging because it creates undue admiration stemming from a sense of pity and reinforces the belief that successful people with disabilities are endowed with inordinate willpower and capabilities not shared by the rest of the disabilities community. Super crip stories also emphasize personal achievement, downplaying the history of collective action that has made some elements of individual success possible.

talking books   The first audio books that used long playing records to contain the text of popular fiction and nonfiction works. The process was developed by the American Foundation for the Blind in 1933 and later served the needs of people with other types of disabilities. The Library of Congress and individual states run talking book programs and have since embraced newer recording technologies to store texts of many varieties.

telecommunications device for the deaf (TDD)   An **assistive technology** device used by deaf people that uses phone lines to send and receive messages. First appearing in the 1970s, TDDs were cheaper and less bulky than **teletypewriters (TTYs)** and came to be the preferred communication machines for the hearing impaired. The acronym TDD was phased out in the 1990s, however, in part because the machines were being used by more than just the deaf, and all telecommunications devices for the hearing impaired are regularly referred to as TTYs.

telethon   A televised fund raiser that solicits donations from viewers for a specific charity or cause. Though popular television fare, programs such as the Jerry Lewis Telethon for Muscular Dystrophy and the United Cerebral Palsy Telethon have become the targets of harsh criticism and protest from the disability rights community. Groups such as Jerry's Orphans argue that telethons are paternalistic and encourage pity toward individuals with disabilities because these programs tend to portray disabled people as helpless victims. Telethons have also been accused of funding only efforts to develop cures for disabilities while ignoring the reality that people with disabilities need more practical assistance and would benefit from promoting social acceptance rather than emphasizing medical remedies.

teletypewriter (TTY)   An **assistive technology** device used by deaf people to transmit text-written messages over phone lines. Teletypewriters were supplemented by **telecommunications devices for the deaf (TDDs)** in the 1970s, but in the 1990s, all such devices were more commonly referred to as TTYs.

universal design   An architectural and consumer design theory advocating the creation of spaces and objects that can be easily utilized by individuals of all ages and abilities. Universal design principles apply to structural properties, such as wide doorways and hallways in homes, and to utilitarian practicalities, such as loop handles replacing door knobs and drawer pulls because they require no twisting or gripping. These concepts were pioneered by Ronald Mace in the 1960s and 1970s at North Carolina State University. In 1973, his ideas helped North Carolina's government draft the first state building code in America.

vocational rehabilitation   Assistance programs that aid people with disabilities to develop skills to find gainful employment. Services provided by these programs include job training, placement, and career counseling. Vocational rehabilitation programs aim at giving individuals the opportunity to live independently while remaining contributory members of society.

PART II

GUIDE TO FURTHER RESEARCH

CHAPTER 6

HOW TO RESEARCH DISABILITY RIGHTS ISSUES

Researching disability rights would at first seem a less daunting task than, for example, studying other civil rights movements in America. After all, the disability rights movement began only seven decades ago, and its heyday arose in the last 40 years and culminated in the passage of an act that is less than half as old. And because of its advent in the modern age, there would seem to be plenty of written accounts of its germination and growth. However, as many disability advocates have pointed out, the movement has not been as well detailed as, for example, the fight for women's rights or African-American civil rights.

Many critics maintain that the lack of attention is yet another example of how people with disabilities are willfully overlooked and ignored in society. This is not to suggest, however, that there is a paucity of information on the subject: Books, magazines, and web sites are devoted to the topic. Comparatively, though, the subject is underrepresented among other minority rights research issues. Indeed, much of the history of disability rights is still being filled in, and the relative newness of the field of disability studies underscores the fact that more research on the subject has been prepared in the last 10 years than has been conducted since the movement's inception. This chapter is designed to provide those who are interested in researching disability rights with the tools necessary to locate resources in order to approach the topic effectively.

BOOK SOURCES

While much of the controversy concerning issues of disability rights is best captured in timely periodical articles, newspaper editorials, and up-to-the-minute Internet newswire services, the background and historical context that informs such pieces has been more thoroughly expounded in books. However, the number of books contending with the general history of disability and the disability rights movement in America is relatively small. James Charlton's *Nothing about Us without Us: Disability Oppression and Empowerment* (1998), Doris Zames Fleischer and Frieda Zames's *The Disability Rights Movement: From Charity to Confrontation* (2001), Paul T. Jaeger and Cynthia Ann Bowman's *Understanding Disability: Inclusion, Access, Diversity, and Civil Rights* (2005), Joseph Shapiro's *No Pity: People with Disabilities Forging a New Civil Rights Movement* (1993), and Jacqueline Vaughn Switzer's *Disabled Rights: American Disability Policy and the Fight for Equality* (2003) stand out as the more comprehensive volumes on disability history (see chapter 7 for bibliographic citations). Yet only three of these works were published in the 21st century, leaving a good deal of recent events unattended.

Because much of disability rights history views the passage of the Americans with Disabilities Act (ADA) of 1990 as a high-water mark, the fight for this piece of legislation and its resulting impact have been the subject of a number of books. A few have been histories of the act and its passage; more have dealt with the policies of its implementation. Other issues of public policy, such as health concerns, accessibility, and housing, have also been covered in a variety of books and anthologies. Much recent scholarship, however, has been turned to the burgeoning field of disability studies. This area elaborates on the social construction of disability and traces its influence in sociology and the humanities. This research tends to be collected in specialized anthologies, and though much of it would be tangential to inquiries on specific rights and legal matters concerning disability, some of these unique perspectives speak to the way in which disability has been codified as weakness, as otherness, in society.

Researchers delving into books on the topic of disability rights—especially because it has not been covered thoroughly—should be aware of two factors that will impact the way in which the information can be utilized. First, like all media, book authors have a point of view—a bias—that will affect what sources they consult for their data and how they arrange that data in order to draw their conclusions. In the case of disability rights literature, it is worth pointing out that most works come from those involved in the movement, and there are no book-length criticisms of the movement to date. Researchers should, therefore, seek out independent reviews or critiques of the books they read to find out how other scholars have appraised the work. Reviews and critiques of recently published book sources are often available on book merchant web sites such as Amazon.com and Barnes&Noble.com (bn.com). If the book is older or has not been reviewed on merchant sites, appraisals can often be found by simple typing the book's name into an Internet search engine.

The second factor that will impact a book's usefulness is its publication date. The information within a book is never contemporaneous with the date that it was published. A book printed in 2004 may have research extending only until 2001, depending on the time it took the author to write the book and secure a publisher to release it. This has been a noticeable problem in disability rights historical scholarship because so few books are published on the subject each year, and some of the most important occurrences—such as the resolution of court cases that have impacted the implementation of the ADA—have timely consequences that change faster than books can be published. Such factors do not make historical overviews obsolete, since book authors still provide excellent analyses of events of the recent past, and they often make insightful conjectures about future trends. However, researchers should extend and even test an author's analysis by bringing the topic up-to-date through more contemporary periodicals and Internet resources that address the same subject.

Books on the topic of disability rights may be available at local libraries, though many smaller community libraries often have limited storage capacity and therefore tend to sell off or dispense with older, damaged, or unpopular titles. Researchers are more apt to find the book resources they need at university libraries. There, whole shelves are commonly devoted to disability studies, public policy, history, and health topics, for example, and any book resource unavailable can usually be requested from other university libraries in the area. Students and instructors have the broadest privileges at university libraries (especially in terms of how many books can be checked out over extended periods), but most university libraries currently permit nonstudents in the community to purchase or otherwise acquire library cards to check out materials from the general stacks. Materials that cannot be found in libraries might be available online from various merchant web sites, and those sites—such as half.com—that deal with older and obsolete titles are also valuable repositories for disability titles.

PERIODICAL AND NEWSPAPER DATABASES

Besides acting as a storehouse of useful books, libraries typically provide patrons with access to periodical and newspaper databases. In researching the topic of disability rights, these databases are essential reference tools. Both university and public libraries commonly subscribe to a database service such as InfoTrac or EBSCO that indexes articles from various periodical and newspaper resources (both national and international). By typing in key search terms (such as disability rights, disability studies, and even disability) one can pull up an array of article entries that match the search terms. Some of the entries that result from a search will link to computerized reproductions of the articles as they appear in their original print sources; other entries are merely abstracts that give a hint of what topics the original articles cover. These latter entries will require the researcher to track down the hardcopy originals. Libraries will often store hardbound volumes or microfilm versions of original print sources for those publications that do not provide full text reproductions on the periodical databases. A reference librarian can help one determine how to obtain these stored periodicals.

Many of the publications available on periodical databases will have articles from the most recent print-source copies as well as archives of articles from previous issues. Depending on the periodical, the archives may extend two decades into the past. A researcher should take the time to ascertain the scope of the archive for each relevant periodical. Additionally, periodical and newspaper databases give their users the ability to limit searches by time period. Thus, one can choose to pull up articles that were published in a specific year or between a span of years. This power to limit searches is an excellent means to find articles on the ADA, for example, or editorials on the influence of the ADA on business interests in the more recent year.

Since articles written prior to the 1980s will not typically show up on periodical databases, students of the subject may have to be more creative in locating information pertaining to earlier decades. One useful method is to examine the bibliographies of books on disability issues. Many times the authors of well-researched books will provide citations for (and, sometimes, summaries of the content of) pertinent periodical resources published prior to the time periods covered by magazine and newspaper databases.

While library databases offer the convenience of collecting scattered articles into one easy-to-examine format, those researching disability rights (or any topic) should be aware that individual databases draw from a limited number of periodical sources. That is, even though a database may have hundreds of journals, newspapers, and magazines within its archive, not all extant print sources will be referenced. Furthermore, each database commonly draws from a different pool of resources, so conducting searches on more than one database is a good way of ensuring broader coverage of print resources.

Even by casting this larger net, some useful publications may not fall within the purview of database search engines. Some of these publications have simply not licensed their content to be used or accessed by any database. For example, *Disability Studies Quarterly*, a foremost publication in the field, is not available on cataloged databases. Tracking down articles on disability rights in these overlooked print resources can be more challenging. If one is looking for a specific journal or newspaper that is not represented in a database, then it may be possible to track down the periodical through the Internet. Several publications—from academic journals to local newspapers—have their own web sites, and some offer archives of previously published articles. By typing in a known author, article title, or even subject (such as disability rights) into the search field commonly provided on these web sites, one may be able to locate the full text of a desired article. Researchers should be aware, however, that while some publications provide access to their archives free of charge, others do not. A few of the latter offer the lead-in text of an article and charge a fee to view the full text, and others require a subscription rate be paid up front for unlimited access. *Disability Studies Quarterly*, for instance, has its content available on the Society for Disability Studies web site (http://www.dsq-sds.org), where it can be accessed only through a membership subscription.

It is also worth noting that some major disability journals have changed their names over time. The United Kingdom publication *Disability & Society*, for example, was printed under the title of *Disability, Handicap & Society* until the term "handicap" fell out of favor with the disabilities community, and the title changed in 1999. Similarly, *The Disability Rag* print magazine began publication in 1980 and was available for 17 years before becoming an Internet magazine entitled *The Ragged Edge*. Thanks to archiving, the entire original run of *The Disability Rag* is available for purchase on CD-Rom from *The Ragged Edge* site (http://www.raggededgemagazine.com).

INTERNET RESOURCES

As *The Ragged Edge* archives reveal, the Internet is a vast storehouse of information waiting to be tapped by computer users. For those interested in the topic of disability rights, the World Wide Web is probably the best place to start research because of the variety of resources that can be found there. In addition to housing the web pages of specific magazines or newspapers that may cover disability news, the Internet offers informational sites with editorials on disability issues, government disability legislation, legal issues pertaining to disability rights, and personal reflections on living with disabilities. Such sites generally provide news, analysis, and opinions on disability issues, and they often contain gateways, or links, to other sites that might be of further use.

Navigating and accessing the wealth of information from the various web sites that contend with disability rights is the first challenge to Internet researchers. Some research information may be readily accessed in the most basic search of the web; other topics of interest may take time to locate by following a complex chain of links. Thus, patience and determination are the bywords of the most fruitful Internet searches. And once useful web sites are found, bookmarking each site and cataloging the information there will facilitate researchers in retrieving that data for future reference. Knowing how to conduct efficient searches and store the found information, then, are the two keys to using the Web to research rights of the disabled.

Rights of the Disabled

USING SEARCH ENGINES

To help glean information from the World Wide Web, there are many search engines and web directories available. Search engines are specific web sites that specialize in scouring the Internet for information and then indexing that information for a user. A search engine operates via keywords, or search terms, that tell the engine what information to look for and retrieve. For example, a researcher looking for information on the ADA might enter that title in the search field on a search engine web page. After pressing the "search" key near the search field, the engine will pull up and organize a list of web sites and web documents that contain the given terms. The list, or index, will be structured in a hierarchy of relevance. That is, the retrieved documents that contain all the words "Americans," "disabilities," and "act" will be listed at the top, and the documents that contain only some of the words will be arranged toward the bottom of the list. Sometimes it can be fruitful to search in this unrestricted manner, because occasionally sites that contain only a few of the terms—such as "disabilities" and "act," for example—might be unexpectedly useful. However, if only sites and documents on the ADA are desired, then it is more efficient to enclose the search terms in quotation marks. Thus, a search for "Americans with Disabilities Act" will limit a search engine to pull up only those sites that have text in which all four words appear, grouped in that order.

The use of search engines is typically very straightforward and relies almost exclusively on entering the keyword search terms. Each search engine may have its own quirks, but any problems or queries that arise can usually be answered by the "help" link provided on each engine's Internet home page. This link may also give users more specific guidelines on how to limit or expand their searches to produce the desired results in a more efficient manner. Fortunately for researchers, the operating instructions for search engines are nearly identical, and therefore the manner in which searches can be narrowed or broadened in scope are nearly universal. The following is a list of some of the most general methods by which search field keywords can be manipulated:

- To conduct broad searches, enter a few general terms that convey the desired topic. Simply typing "disability," for example, will result in a list of any document or site that includes the word *disability* somewhere in its text. This is an ineffective approach, since the index will include all web documents that use the word in any context—not necessarily in relation to disability rights. Typing such keywords as "disability rights," "disability legislation," or "people with disabilities," for example, will be more limiting since the first resources listed in the index should contain both terms (though not necessarily as a single phrase unless the user remembers to enclose them in quotation marks).

- To perform narrow searches on specific topics, add as many relevant terms to the search field as possible. Thus, entering "New York disability law" (without quotations) will prompt a search engine to first list those sites that have text that matches all four terms. Adding quotes to a specific phrase will instruct the engine to find sites where all four words are aligned as a single phrase. In this way, very specific search prompts can cut through the millions of entries on somewhat related topics to bring forth those sites that match specifically the terms entered. Obviously, though, this operation has the drawback of excluding potentially useful sites that may not contain the exact wording of the search terms. To conduct a more thorough research, then, may require multiple searches using different keywords and, perhaps, the implementation of Boolean limiters (explained hereafter).

- To further limit searches, use the Boolean term "AND" between two or more desired terms in the search field. For example, typing "California AND accessibility" (without quotes) will instruct a search engine to find documents and web pages that contain both terms. A plus sign can also be used to indicate an AND limiter. Thus, "California" +"accessibility" +"law" will yield an index that contains documents having all three terms, though not necessarily grouped together.

- To limit searches by excluding unwanted results, utilize the Boolean term "NOT" before undesired terms in a search field. "Center +independent +living NOT Berkeley" (no quotes), for instance, will mainly bring up web sites and documents that focus on centers for independent living (CILs) around the world, while excluding sites that mention the original CIL in Berkeley, California. A minus sign (-) can also be used in place of the NOT term to achieve the same results.

- To broaden a search, use the Boolean "OR" term between two or more search terms. For example, typing "disability OR disabilities" (no quotes) will result in a massive index of entries that contain either term (used in any context). The OR function is, perhaps, the least useful of the Boolean terms since the lists generated will likely be exceedingly long and unfocused. It is typically more beneficial to conduct multiple focused searches rather than blanket searches on broad topics.

Currently there are many search engines available on the Internet, most of which are managed by distinct companies. While each may have its own method of searching and ranking results, the indexes generated by one engine will be similar to those generated by any other. Among the most popular search engines on the Internet are:

- Alta Vista (http://www.altavista.com)
- Excite (http://www.excite.com)

- Google (http://www.google.com)
- HotBot (http://www.hotbot.com)
- Lycos (http://www.lycos.com)
- WebCrawler (http://www.webcrawler.com)

Because search engines are designed with specific subject orientations and ranking criteria, each does however have its own strengths and weaknesses. In an effort to compensate for this, some companies have created metasearch engines that plug search field queries into several of the web's search engines at once and then compile the results into a single index. Many Internet researchers find these metasearch sites useful because they cast a wide net and therefore provide an excellent place to begin a thorough examination of a topic. Some of the most commonly used metasearch sites are:

- Ask (http://www.ask.com)
- Dogpile (http://www.dogpile.com)
- Metacrawler (http://www.metacrawler.com)
- Search (http://www.search.com)

USING WEB DIRECTORIES

Since search engines begin scanning the Internet from the ground up (that is, by looking for keyword search terms wherever they may exist in web site names, web documents, and other web-related text), researchers may find it more useful to approach the topic of disability rights from the top down by utilizing a web directory. Like search engines, web directories provide entries that link to specific sites and documents of interest, but instead of randomly ranging through the billions of sites on the Internet, web directories use preset categories that lead users to the most popular sites that relate to a given topic.

One of the most popular web directories is available from Yahoo!, an indexing web site that offers both directory and search engine capabilities. On the site's home page (http://www.yahoo.com) is a section for its web directory. By following the link, a user can pull up a categorical list of popular subject areas (such as Business & Economy, Entertainment, Science, and Arts & Humanities). Disabilities information falls under the "Society and Culture" heading, and the subject title "Disabilities" will appear in a subsidiary list of topics when that initial "Society and Culture" link is selected. Following the "Disabilities" link will lead to site listings for specific topics such as "Independent Living," "Personal Experiences," and "Therapy and Rehabilitation." Most of these site links will connect a user to an organizational or personal web site that is related to the specific topic. Following the "Independent Living" category link, for example, will lead one to the topic "Centers for Independent Living." That link, in turn, connects to a list of independent living centers worldwide that have a web presence.

Because web services like Yahoo! have done some of the research work and created lists of what they consider the more valuable resources on a topic, users often feel secure in the belief that the information on these sites is more credible than that on unlisted sites. While this may be true to a degree—since the resource sites typically listed in a web directory include the web sites of major organizations and government agencies—not all useful web resources are represented. Web documents from scholarly journals and common periodicals are usually excluded from web directories. More thorough searching using a search engine is advisable. Still, the organizations that are accessible through web directories are commonly the preeminent sites that relate to a specific field of research. To begin Internet research on the topic of disability rights, one can do no better than to start with the main organizations and government agencies that are already grouped for convenience in a web directory.

USEFUL DISABILITY RIGHTS WEB SITES

Many of the disability rights web sites that are accessible through web directory catalogs are those of prominent advocacy organizations and government regulatory bureaus (all of which are listed in chapter 8 of this book). These sites are extremely useful not only for self-help information, government policy, and current political action, but also for general history and contemporary disability issues. A few of the most helpful Internet sites include:

- **Americans with Disabilities Act Home Page** (http://www.ada.gov) is the U.S. Department of Justice's web resource for all issues related to the definition and application of this groundbreaking piece of legislation. The site offers explanations of the various titles within the ADA and their application to businesses, state and federal transit systems, and new and remodeled construction projects. The ADA site also provides information on other disability rights laws and the general enforcement of all disability rights legislation. Separate archives are also maintained for official speeches and testimony regarding the ADA and its implementation, and there are catalogs of ADA-related publications including the Disability Rights Online News.

- **Cornucopia of Disability Information** (http://codi.buffalo.edu) is operated through the Center for Assistive Technology, University at Buffalo (New York), and bills itself as a "community resource for consumers and professionals." The web site is divided into directories that house articles and web links pertaining to topics such as computing, legal issues, mobility, and traveling. The articles stored on the site extend back to the 1990s, and some are available only through the site.

- **Disability Resources Monthly Guide to Disability Resources on the Internet** (http://www.disabilityresources.org) is a clearinghouse for disability information. It is managed by Disability Resources, Inc., which gathers and archives useful web resources, and provides some description of what can be found on each resource site. The site also includes a step-by-step guide to finding and evaluating disability resources. Of particular interest are the links to web sites devoted to disability history.

- **Disability Rights and Independent Living Movement Oral Histories/Archives** (http://bancroft.berkeley.edu/collections/drilm/) is a University of California collection of digital resources pertaining to the disability rights and independent living movements. A major part of the collection is a repository of oral histories of people involved in the birth of these movements as well as narratives on the intersection of disability and education, gender, race, technology, culture, and other topics.

- **A Guide to Disability Rights Laws** (http://www.usdoj.gov/crt/ada/cguide.htm#anchor65610) is a U.S. Department of Justice web page that provides brief descriptions of the federal laws concerning disability rights. Besides the brief explanations, the site provides government contacts for further inquiry or legal complaints.

- **Internet Law Library's Handicapped Individuals and the Law** (http://www.lawguru.com/ilawlib/102.htm) is part of a popular legal web site that categorizes laws pertaining to various issues. The page on disability rights provides links to various federal and state regulatory agencies and the laws they monitor. The list of links also includes some explanatory documents about U.S. disability laws as well as links to a few foreign web sites (primarily from Canada and the United Kingdom).

FINDING ORGANIZATIONS AND INDIVIDUALS ON THE WEB

Poring through articles and web documents may lead students of disability rights to seek out more information on specific individuals or relevant organizations that are referenced in these sources. Many web directories can provide links to prominent and popular organizations. Chapter 8 of this book also contains a fairly thorough catalog of government agencies and independent advocacy groups, but neither of these resource lists is exhaustive. If web contact information for a disability organization does not appear in this book or in web directories, then Internet users should try typing the name of the desired organization into a search engine.

While it may be tempting to simply insert an organization's name into a web address and see if the right web site responds to a query command, it is more productive to enter the full name of the organization into a search field of a search engine. This is because some organizations' web addresses utilize abbreviated forms of their official names. For example, the home page of the American Society for Deaf Children is located on the web at http://www.deafchildren.org, while the U.S. Department of Justice home page for the ADA relies on the act's initials and can be found at http://www.ada.gov. Entering the entire name of the organization into a search engine should result in the organization's official web site and web address ranking among the first listings in the index created and will thereby eliminate the guesswork of randomly typing in hypothetical addresses.

Furthermore, as these two examples above indicate, organizations on the Web use different address suffixes to delineate what type of site they are. Governmental departments use the ".gov" suffix, educational institutions employ the ".edu" suffix, most (but not all) advocacy groups favor the ".org" suffix to distinguish themselves as organizations, and corporate as well as some personal web sites rely on the ubiquitous ".com" suffix. Again, by merely typing an organization's name into a search engine, one can avoid guessing which suffix applies.

Finally, when searching for individuals on the Internet, the same strategies apply. Typing a person's name into a search engine (leaving out any middle initial unless more than one individual is likely to have the same name) should lead to any web pages and documents that mention that individual. Some individuals have personal web pages or faculty web pages with contact information. Others may be organization spokespeople or staff writers for specific periodicals, and their contact information will probably reside on the web site of the respective organization or news source. In addition, the names (and sometimes e-mail addresses) of journalists, commentators, and researchers will often accompany articles that they have written. Therefore, those looking for more information on disability rights may be able to use a search engine to pull up several topical articles written by the same individual.

CONDUCTING LEGAL RESEARCH ONLINE

While disability rights and their application in the United States is the subject of public debate, its name attests that it is also a matter of legislative and judicial concern. The concept of disability rights has only been around since the mid-20th century, and most laws surfaced in the last 30 years of that century. All of these laws have been well documented in books and in online resources. In addition, judicial interpretation of the ADA and other federal laws has become a key aspect of the disability rights debate, and many of the decisions have been the subject of extensive analysis and commentary.

Rights of the Disabled

With the wealth of information on these laws and court cases, finding appropriate resources is not difficult. The Internet, in fact, has made it unnecessary to pore through voluminous law books to find the statutes and legal cases that have come to define disability rights. Locating and navigating the web's legal resources, however, is not always a straightforward task for those unaccustomed to legal research.

Finding Laws

There are several web sites on the Internet that lay out the text of state and federal disability laws. The U.S. Code (the compilation of all federal laws), for example, can be reached through the House of Representatives Office of the Law Revision Council web site (http://uscode.house.gov). This database can be searched by code title, section number, or even subject. Thus, the public law that was adopted as the Education for All Handicapped Children Act of 1975 (EAHCA) can be found by typing in the name of the act into the web site's keyword search field. That will lead to a list that includes the entry "Table of Popular Names," which if followed will link to a brief note that says to see 20 U.S.C. 1400. Returning to the search field and typing in this info in the title (20) and section (1400) fields will bring one to the text of the act (and a note that indicates the act has since been changed to the Individuals with Disabilities Education Act). Alternatively, a second entry in the initial keyword result list is the heading "20 USC Chapter 33 – Education of Individuals with Disabilities," which if followed will also lead to the same information.

The federal code can also be searched through a Cornell Law School web site (http://www4.law.cornell.edu/uscode/). Cornell's site is, perhaps, more user-friendly since it provides a master list of the U.S. Code that can be navigated with ease. For example, one can look up the ADA in the "Table of Popular Names" to find that the law is "Pub. L. 101-336, July 26, 1990, 104 Stat. 327 (42 U.S.C. 12101 et seq.)," which can be followed by hyperlink "Pub. L. 101-336." That link will lead to a table that provides researchers with access to the text of the law, the sponsors of the original bill, amendments, congressional actions pertaining to the law, and other information regarding the ADA legislation.

Both of these databases are extremely useful for researching and documenting disability rights law. They may best be used in conjunction with the U.S. Department of Justice's "A Guide to Disability Rights Laws" (http://www.usdoj.gov/crt/ada/cguide.htm#anchor65610) listed previously in this chapter. That database provides the popular names of disability laws, which can then be used to search the House of Representatives web site or the Cornell archives to find more detailed information on the specific legislation.

How to Research Disability Rights Issues

Keeping Up with Legislation

The U.S. Congress regularly addresses disability issues that are proposed in new bills and amendments by one or more of its members. Some of these bills pass one chamber of Congress while failing or stalling in the second. Keeping abreast of the progress of legislation can be a daunting task. News services may keep readers current on the status of topical bills, but the Library of Congress maintains the most comprehensive list of all legislation that has been proposed, voted upon, and signed into law.

Accessing the legal resources of the Library of Congress requires logging into its THOMAS database (http://thomas.loc.gov). This web catalog can be used in many ways, but there are two features that are most helpful in researching legislation that relates to disability rights.

First, the records of the current session of Congress can be searched by specific bill numbers or by keywords (such as "disability"). Each session of Congress is designated by a number that changes consecutively every two years (the 109th Congress, for example, was in session from 2005 through 2006; the 110th Congress will be in session from 2007 through 2008). By searching for "disability" in the current session's records, a user will be able to pull up a list of all the legislative action that relates to that term. At the beginning of March 2007, for example, 98 bills referencing "disability" were before Congress, the majority of which pertained to the allocation of disability benefits to various civil and military organizations.

The second helpful function available on the THOMAS site is the ability to search the Bill Summary & Status catalog (under the "Bills, Resolutions" link on the THOMAS home page) of both current and past congressional sessions (reaching as far back as the 93rd session). Users can choose a session of Congress and search its records by means of keywords, bill numbers, bill sponsors, relevant committees, and other focused criteria. Conducting such a search will yield brief entries, each of which will include a bill number, its sponsors and cosponsors (if any), the committees it has been referred to, and any action that Congress has taken on the bill. Following the link given for the bill number will lead to another list through which users can access the exact text of the legislation.

Although all federal legislation is available in one convenient database, the same is not true for bills addressed in state legislatures. Unfortunately, there is no single site that offers a thorough account of the legislative actions in all 50 states. However, each state typically has its own legal database that is accessible through its government web site. For example, the home page for the government of Alabama (http://www.alabama.gov) has links that will eventually connect interested visitors to its ALISON (Alabama Legislative Information System Online) web site. Such sites can then be examined and manipulated in much the same way as the federal government's THOMAS site.

Rights of the Disabled

Finding Court Decisions

Legislative databases are excellent resources for locating specific bills and noting how they have been amended over time. These databases, however, do not cover the ways in which the legislation has been utilized or challenged after being signed into law. This facet of the legal process is partially documented on judicial databases, where researchers can learn how various courts have interpreted laws, ruled on cases that involve infractions of laws, and even upheld or abolished the very legal authority of specific laws.

The most far-reaching legal cases are commonly those that garner the attention of the U.S. Supreme Court, the highest authority of judicial review and decision-making in America. Many cases involving the rights of the disabled have come before this august body (several of the most significant are detailed in chapter 2 of this book). To seek out the arguments before and the judicial decisions of the Supreme Court, researchers should consult the Cornell Law School Legal Information Institute web site (http://www.law.cornell.edu). This legal resource has records of all Supreme Court decisions rendered since 1990. The site also maintains an archive of 600 other influential Supreme Court decisions that predate the contemporary record.

Some federal lower court decisions can be found on the Legal Information Institute site (of primary interest are the listings for the federal court of appeals), but these records often don't extend very far back in time. A better resource for a variety of federal lower court records (including circuit and appellate court decisions) is the Washburn School of Law web site (http://www.washlaw.edu).

Both the Cornell and Washburn web sites also have listings for state court cases. These listings are actually links that lead to the government web sites of each individual state. Every state's archive of court cases, though, varies in scope and detail.

Searching through the legal documents found on the above sites (or any other web site) can be a daunting task. Legal citation is a language all its own, and navigating the host of briefs, cases, decisions, and opinions requires a rudimentary understanding of legal terminology. The first aspect of legal citation that researchers should become familiar with is the way in which cases are titled.

In most newspaper or magazine articles, the titles of court cases are often abbreviated to the names of the plaintiff and the defendant. Thus, the first case to test the ADA is commonly referred to as *Bragdon v. Abbott*. The full citation of this case, however, reads *Bragdon v. Abbott et al.* 524 U.S. 624 (1998). This citation first spells out the plaintiff and defendant and then notes that the case can be found in volume 524 of the U.S. Supreme Court Reports, beginning on page 624. It also indicates that the case was decided in 1998. The citation for a lower court case will replace the "U.S." marker in a Supreme Court reference with another notation that indicates the district or circuit in which the given case was heard.

Beyond the unique titling of court cases, the jargon within the formal complaints and the judicial decisions can also be somewhat inscrutable. While a close reading of the relevant court documents should convey the basic progress and conclusion of a case, any confusing language can be cleared up by consulting legal resources. Both the Legal Information Institute and the Washburn web sites, for example, have helpful pages devoted to clarifying difficult terminology for users who are not legal scholars.

BOOKMARKING ONLINE SOURCES

Searching through the endless amount of online data can be made easier by following the aforementioned strategies, but once relevant web sources are located, another task of the researcher is to organize the useful material so it can be handily recalled. Unlike hardbound reference materials, Internet resources can not be picked up from a pile of resources and scanned when pertinent information is needed. Instead, the key to effectively utilizing web sites and web documents for reference is to create a virtual "folder" in which these resources are stored.

Web browsers (such as Netscape and Microsoft's Internet Explorer) as well as Internet service providers (such as America Online) commonly provide users with a "Favorites" or "Bookmarks" menu among their Internet tools. This menu allows users to create and name folders where, with the click of a button, web site addresses can be "bookmarked" or cataloged. The process for compiling these folders is nearly identical from one browser to the next. Typically, researchers who find a useful web page can open their Favorites menu from the browser toolbar and then select the function "Add Top Window to Favorites" (or a similar phrase). The name and web address of the given site should then be accessible when the Favorites menu is reopened. Users need only click on the web site name (which can be manually altered for convenience) in the menu listing to have the browser locate and open that site.

Students of disability rights will likely have sites for government networks such as DisabilityInfo.gov, organizations such as the Disability Resources, Inc., and disability issues news services such as *Disability Studies Quarterly* "bookmarked" in the Favorites folder. If the list of these resources remains manageable, keeping them all within one Favorites folder should be sufficient. If the number of sites becomes unwieldy, however, then a researcher may wish to create separate Favorites folders for advocacy groups, government agencies, news groups, and the like.

The bookmarking and storage features of web browsers, coupled with the versatility of search engines, will make the vast resources of the Internet into an extremely useful asset for those researching the subject of disability rights. By following some of the tips in this chapter, one should be able to put together a valuable and up-to-date library of reference materials on disability rights that will benefit any investigation of the topic.

CHAPTER 7

ANNOTATED BIBLIOGRAPHY

This chapter provides a representative bibliography of works relating to the topic of disability rights in America. The collection of references includes books, periodicals, Internet documents, and other media resources—most of which have been published after 1990 and therefore touch on the impact of the Americans with Disabilities Act (ADA) on public policy and the expansion or retrenchment of disability rights. In addition to works that contend with the history of the disability rights movement, this bibliography includes works in the field of disability studies, many of which analyze the social conditions that attend the evolving treatment of people with disabilities in America.

ACCESSIBILITY

BOOKS

Johnson, Mary, and Barrett Shaw, eds. *To Ride the Public's Buses: The Fight that Built a Movement*. Louisville, Ky.: Advocado, 2001. Culled from the pages of Johnson's *Disability Rag*, this book collects various articles covering the American Disabled for Accessible Public Transportation's (ADAPT) fight to make public transportation accessible. These insightful pieces show how ADAPT built and maintained a grassroots movement over several years in the 1980s as it held protests and bus-blocking demonstrations in several major U.S. cities.

Mueller, John. *Accessibility for Everybody: Understanding the Section 508 Accessibility Requirements*. New York: Springer-Verlag, 2003. A book aimed at software developers, this volume tries to translate government accessibility policy into readable instructions for making Windows and Internet programs accessible. While not specifically contending with rights issues, the work is interesting for demonstrating how legislation is being brought up to date in its application to ever-changing technology.

Rights of the Disabled

PERIODICALS

Altom, Tim. "Is Designing for Blind Worth the Trouble and Cost?" *Indianapolis Business Journal*, vol. 27, no. 38, November 27, 2006, p. 42A. Web accessibility issues prompt an editorial that argues the world is divided between those who know and understand the needs of the disabled and those who do not.

Boliek, Brooks. "AMC to Alter Wheelchair Seating: Also Will Pay $200,000 in Damages to Settle DOJ suit." *Hollywood Reporter*, vol. 392, no. 35, January 13, 2006, p. 8. Boliek reports on the outcome of a suit against the AMC movie theater chain. After being slapped with a lawsuit claiming patrons with disabilities had line of sight problems in viewing movies because of lack of accessible seating, the AMC movie theater chain agreed to make costly changes.

Borcover, Alfred. "Access at Sea: What about Land Excursions?" *Chicago Tribune*, August 1, 2005, p. 3A. This article presents a U.S. Supreme Court ruling that foreign ships are required to adhere to accessibility laws when in American waters. Borcover reports that the Court, however, did not say what improvements ships should make, nor did it make any pronouncement about shore excursions from ships.

Duffy, Shannon P. "Amtrak Wins Battle over Accommodations for Disabled Groups." *Legal Intelligencer*, June 22, 2005, p. 1. This article reports on a U.S. district court ruling that Amtrak was not violating the ADA when it informed a large group of wheelchair users that they would have to pay an extra charge to compensate for the necessary removal of seats to accommodate such a large party that wished to travel together.

Egelko, Bob. "Disabled Sue Caltrans over Alleged Hazards on State's Sidewalks: Wheelchair Users Sometimes Must Veer into Traffic." *San Francisco Chronicle*, August 24, 2006, p. B2. According to this article, disabled activists are suing the California Department of Transportation (Caltrans), claiming state sidewalks are sometimes broken, blocked, or have faulty curb ramps.

Jeter, Lynne. "Intergenerational Travel Poses Challenges, Offers Rewards." *Mississippi Business Journal*, vol. 27, no. 22, May 30, 2005, p. 36. Mount Vernon, George Washington's former home, is one example of a national tourist attraction that is still inaccessible or unaccommodating to the disabled and the elderly. Jeter reports on how savvy tourist destinations are making changes to cater to the disabilities community.

Scheck, Justin. "Court Throws Life Preserver in Suit against Cruise Line." *Recorder*, June 7, 2005, p. 1. In one publicized case, the U.S. Supreme Court ruled that an American cruise line must make accommodations for passengers with disabilities. Scheck reports on this and another case working its way through the court system that has not reached that verdict because the cruise line in question is owned by foreign interests.

Thiruvengadam, Meena. "Stadium-Style Seating at Theaters Violates Disability Rights Laws, Court Rules." *San Antonio Express-News*, June 29, 2004, p. 5. This article reports on the U.S. Supreme Court ruling that steeply tiered stadium seating in movie theaters violates the ADA.

"Understanding the True Impact of Handicap and Disability Regulations." *Nation's Restaurant News*, vol. 40, no. 39, September 25, 2006, p. 72. Complying with the ADA and other business codes means that both existing and newly constructed restaurants have to adhere to accessibility guidelines. According to this article, some of these guidelines are obvious; some involve detailed knowledge of the law.

Weilkel, Dan. "Getting There Is None of the Fun." *Los Angeles Times*, November 13, 2006, p. B1. This article reports that, frustrated by lack of access and disability provisions on public sidewalks, wheelchair activists are filing lawsuits against state and local governments to force improvements.

INTERNET DOCUMENTS

Parker, Laura. "National Federation of the Blind Files Target Lawsuit." Council for Disability Rights (Chicago, Ill.) web site. Available online. URL: http://www.disabilityrights.org/1106.htm#national. Posted November 2006. This article details the lawsuit of a blind man against the Target department store chain because of the lack of accessibility on the store's web site. The author presents opinions of experts who predict that the case will have broad ramifications if other Internet retailers are called upon to make accessibility improvements.

Ryan, Jean. "Disability Discrimination—Alive and Well in NYC." Ragged Edge Online. Available online. URL: http://www.raggededgemagazine.com/departments/reflections/000910.html. Posted April 17, 2006. The vice president of Disabled In Action attests to how difficult it is for people with disabilities to find accessible transport in New York City. She laments the fact that able-bodied transit passengers often blame people with disabilities for delays and other problems experienced when transit drivers do not know how to accommodate disabled riders.

ACTIVISM AND ADVOCACY

BOOKS

Crewe, Nancy M., and Irving Kenneth Zola, eds. *Independent Living for Physically Disabled People*. Lincoln, Neb.: iUniverse, 2001. Originally published in the 1980s, this anthology has become a cornerstone of independent living history and research. The authors examine the course of the movement, its philosophical tenets, and the practical policies and services of independent living centers. The essays relate the movement to the broader civil rights struggle and the self-help and consumerist aspects of independent living.

Little, Jan. *If It Weren't for the Honor—I'd Rather Have Walked: Previously Untold Tales of the Journey to the ADA*. Cambridge, Mass.: Brookline, 1996. Using personal narrative and interviews, Little portrays the disabilities activists who pushed for legislation in the 1980s and 1990s as heroes who brought about much needed change in public policy.

Longmore, Paul K. *Why I Burned My Book and Other Essays on Disability*. Philadelphia: Temple University Press, 2003. Well-known disability critic Longmore writes various essays about the intersection of disability and social activism. He covers many topics from the evolution of the disability rights movement to the assisted suicide debate, arguing that redressing decades of entrenched discrimination requires that people with disabilities take a stand. If they do not, he warns, they are likely to remain shut out of the opportunities afforded to the nondisabled world.

Matson, Floyd. *Walking Alone and Marching Together: A History of the Organized Blind Movement in the United States, 1940–1990*. Baltimore: National Federation of the Blind, 1990. Matson tells the story of the formation of the National Federation of the Blind, its philosophies, and its advocacy accomplishments. He uses many excerpts from speeches and magazine articles to demonstrate the intensity and passion of those involved in lifting the blind out of segregated workhouses into social participation. He also emphasizes that collective action has had the greatest impact on social change, not just for the blind but for all civil rights movements.

PERIODICALS

Adler, Jane. "Projects for Disabled Aim to Encourage Independence." *Chicago Tribune*, February 19, 2006, p. 1. Adler reports that Access Living continues to push for allowing people with disabilities to live wherever they like, not merely in segregated housing. The group supports a government voucher system to help the disabled pay for housing in any affordable community.

Berube, Michael. "Citizenship and Disability." *Dissent*, vol. 50, no. 2, spring 2003, p. 52. The father of a child with disabilities, Berube argues for the rights of the disabled and insists that all Americans have a stake in fighting for these rights.

Burson, Pat. "Paving the Way for Social Change: Civil Rights Movement Inspires Other Groups in Their Struggles against Discrimination."

Newsday (Melville, N.Y.), April 23, 2006, p. 8. Burson presents testimonies from disability activists about how they have embraced the accomplishments of the black Civil Rights movement as inspirational to the continuation of their own fight for equality. These activists also share their belief that the victories of the black Civil Rights movement have led other civil rights interests to expect nothing less than full participation in society.

"Disability Advocates Are Taken Aback by Consumer and Staff Attitudes." *Report on Disability Programs*, vol. 27, no. 18, September 2, 2004, p. 140. According to this article, after conducting voter registration drives, disability advocates were shocked to find that many disabled people thought their conditions made them ineligible to vote. The article also reports that these advocates found that caregiving centers routinely discouraged people with disabilities from voting.

"Disabled Voters Have Options for Assistance at Polling Place." *Post and Courier* (Charleston, S.C.), October 27, 2004, p. B7. Results of a survey that found that more than one-fifth of disabled people of voting age would be unable to vote in the 2004 election due to transportation or polling place accessibility issues are presented in this article. One activist suggests ways to overcome the difficulties.

Wappett, Matthew T. "Self-determination and Disability Rights: Lessons from the Women's Movement." *Journal of Disability Policy Studies*, vol. 13, no. 2, fall 2002, p. 119. According to this article, the women's rights movement proved that a unifying theory, activism at the grassroots and government levels, and consciousness-raising helped open doors to increased economic, political, and social participation. Wappett argues that the disability rights movement could utilize this model to move forward.

INTERNET DOCUMENTS

Biondi, Larry. "Field Report: ADAPT Nashville Action." Ragged Edge Online. Available online. URL: http://www.raggededgemagazine.com/departments/closerlook/000860.html. Posted March 27, 2006. This article chronicles recent demonstrations staged by American Disabled for Attendant Programs Today (ADAPT) in Nashville, Tennessee, to protest state policies that favor institutionalization of people with disabilities. Biondi reports that ADAPT blocked downtown traffic in hopes of convincing the governor to support community living assistance.

"Group Adopts '60's Style Freedom Ride to Tell Officials People 'Want to Live at Home.'" Ragged Edge Online. Available online. URL: http://www.raggededgemagazine.com/departments/closerlook/000489.html. Posted October 16, 2005. This article details the actions of a group of 30 disability advocates and their friends who set out on a "freedom ride" through Illinois—which has a high rate of disability-based institutionalization—to convince communities that the elderly and the disabled are better off if they live in their own homes rather than being shut away in private institutions and nursing homes.

OTHER MEDIA

Advocating Change Together. *Self-Advocacy: Freedom, Equality, and Justice for All* (1996). Program Development Associates, DVD, 1996. This video is a primer for self-advocacy in the disabilities movement. Strategies for becoming an advocate are discussed as well as the history of self-advocacy within the movement.

Golfus, Billy, and David E. Simpson. *When Billy Broke His Head . . . and Other Tales of Wonder* (1994). Fanlight Productions, VHS/DVD, 1994. This documentary follows the growing political awareness of Billy Golfus, a radio journalist who suffered brain injury after a scooter accident. Joining the ranks of people with disabilities, Golfus tours the country and meets activists who have a commitment to justice for the disabled.

AMERICANS WITH DISABILITIES ACT (ADA)

BOOKS

Anderson, Robert Carl, ed. *A Look Back: The Birth of the Americans with Disabilities Act.* New York: Haworth Pastoral, 1996. This anthology looks at key individuals and events surrounding the push for and passage of the ADA. Many chapters are devoted to the connection between the fight for disability rights and the religious community.

Colker, Ruth. *The Disability Pendulum: The First Decade of the Americans with Disabilities Act.* New York: New York University Press, 2005. Colker argues that the high expectations placed on the ADA have not been met in its first decade of service. She maintains that presidential disregard and, more significantly, court rulings have limited the power of the act, leaving most plaintiffs unable to successfully claim its promised protection.

Francis, Leslie Pickering, and Anita Silvers, eds. *Americans with Disabilities: Exploring Implications of the Law for Individuals and Institutions.* New York: Routledge, 2000. Collecting essays from legal scholars, academics, and other commentators, this volume provides a comprehensive study of the ADA and its impact on people with disabilities and society. Select pieces examine how comprehensive the ADA is, how it has been limited in the courts, and how it has affected the medical profession, the workplace, and other venues. The authors also address the backlash against the ADA, and what the implications of noncompliance have been for the business world.

Hablutzel, Nancy, and Brian McMahon, eds. *Americans with Disabilities Act: Access and Accommodations.* Orlando, Fla.: Paul M. Deutsch, 1992. This anthology culls expert opinion to define employers' and employees' rights regarding the implementation of the ADA. Access issues as well as special needs requirements are covered.

Johnson, William G., ed. *The Americans with Disabilities Act: Social Contract or Special Privilege?* Thousand Oaks, Calif.: Sage, 1997. Part of the Annals of the American Academy of Political and Social Science, this anthology examines post-ADA America. Authors examine whether the ADA has been successful and the future of disability policy in the wake of the ADA. Other essays address who is included in ADA protection and how people with disabilities have fared in the workplace and other social venues under these protections.

Jones, Timothy L. *The Americans with Disabilities Act: A Review of Best Practices.* New York: AMA Membership Publications Division, 1993. Attempting to overcome the fear many business managers have in implementing the ADA, Jones provides simple ways of viewing the ADA as a beneficial corporate tool, one that respects the intentions of the law and allays concerns over increased costs of accommodation and unfounded worries about poor performance from disabled employees.

Krieger, Linda Hamilton, ed. *Backlash against the ADA: Reinterpreting Disability Rights.* Ann Arbor: University of Michigan Press, 2003. A collection of essays, this anthology explores how judicial opinion, media criticism, and public apathy have limited the effectiveness of the ADA. The authors ultimately try to define the connection between the law and social change in order to explain what forces slowed the progress of the disability rights movement after the passage of the ADA and how they might be mitigated.

Mezey, Susan Gluck. *Disabling Interpretations: The Americans with Disabilities Act in Federal Court.* Pittsburgh: University of Pittsburgh Press, 2005. According to this book, the ADA has not proved resilient in the court system, and many cases—including significant U.S. Supreme Court cases—have failed to deliver on the promise of ADA protections. Mezey argues that this is because the ADA was designed by Congress with specific, unstated intentions, and the courts have not followed the spirit of the intentions but instead have focused on the letter of the law.

Null, Roberta, with Kenneth F. Cherry. *Universal Design: Creative Solutions for ADA Compliance.* Belmont, Calif.: Professional Publications, 1998. Written mainly for interior designers, Null's work describes how to make buildings—and notably, workplaces—function while adhering to the strictures of the ADA.

Rights of the Disabled

Spechler, Jay W. *Reasonable Accommodation: Profitable Compliance with the Americans with Disabilities Act.* Delray Beach, Fla.: St. Lucie, 1996. Written for corporations facing modifications to accommodate employees with disabilities, this interesting volume discusses, among other things, the implications of many lawsuits involving high-profile companies and how the lessons of these noncompliance examples can be translated to businesses seeking to make accommodations to stay compliant and profitable while creating a positive work environment.

West, Jane, ed. *Implementing the Americans with Disabilities Act.* Cambridge, Mass.: Blackwell, 1996. Ten articles address employment, transportation, and personal assistance issues relating to the implementation—and failed implementation—of the ADA.

PERIODICALS

Bagenstos, Samuel R. "The Americans with Disabilities Act as Welfare Reform." *William and Mary Law Review*, vol. 44, no. 3, February 2003, p. 921. Bagenstos argues in this article that the courts have not failed the disability community in applying the ADA; rather, the original conception of the ADA was limited and lacked the mechanisms to move beyond mere protections.

————. "The Future of Disability Law." *Yale Law Journal*, vol. 114, no. 1, October 2004, p. 1. Bagenstos contends that the ADA has not been successful in ensuring employment for people with disabilities because it merely relies on passively mandating antidiscrimination. Accordingly, he argues that if the ADA is to have teeth, it must promote government intervention that addresses social welfare as well as discrimination.

Mezey, Susan Gluck. "The Federal Courts and Disability Rights: Judicial Interpretation of Title III of the Americans with Disabilities Act." *Journal of Disability Policy Studies*, vol. 15, no. 3, Winter 2004, p. 147. After examining all the federal cases filed under Title III of the ADA (concerning public accommodation), the author concludes that the court system has limited the power of the ADA. She contends, however, that part of the problem is Congress's original wording of the ADA to restrict plaintiffs to seeking only injunctive relief.

Myers, Randy. "Lack of Jobs, Accessible Homes Another Disability to Overcome: Advocates Continue Push for Equal Opportunities." *Contra Costa Times* (Walnut Creek, Calif.), February 18, 2007, p. 8. According to this article, more than a decade after the passage of the ADA, people with disabilities are still underemployed, cannot find affordable housing, and face transportation issues.

"New Ruling in ADA's Favor Has Limits: Impact on Mental Health Cases Unclear." *Mental Health Law Report*, vol. 22, no. 6, June 2004, p. 51. The

182

U.S. Supreme Court ruling in *Tennessee v. Lane* states that individuals can sue states for monetary damages under Title II of the ADA. This article assesses that the decision, however, is largely limited to the right of individuals with disabilities to access courtrooms and court buildings, making it inapplicable to those who have mental disabilities and are seeking damages in court.

Sidime, Aissatou. "Disabilities Act Marks 15 Years of Successes." *Houston Chronicle*, August 15, 2005, p. 5. In this article, several people with disabilities testify that the ADA has given them a taste of freedom and opportunity, but the law has much yet to accomplish.

ASSISTED SUICIDE AND HEALTH CARE

PERIODICALS

"California Assisted Suicide Bill Temporarily Defeated." *National Right to Life News*, vol. 32, no. 8, August 2005, p. 8. This article announces that a proposition in California to allow assisted suicide is squashed by right-to-life advocates and disabilities organizations.

Easton, Nina J. "Rights Groups for Disabled Join in Fight." *Boston Globe*, March 23, 2005, p. 3. Easton reports that disability rights groups and conservative Christians have made an uneasy alliance in advocating saving the life of Terry Schiavo, a Florida woman in a vegetative state who at that time was soon to be the victim of passive euthanasia.

Hentoff, Nat. "Devaluing Lives: The Culture of Death Imperils the Disabled." *Washington Times*, May 2, 2005, p. A19. Hentoff contends that the death of Terry Schiavo by passive euthanasia reveals that the more serious a person's disability is, the less protection he or she is granted. He further argues that those who cannot assert their right to live are the most vulnerable to passive euthanasia.

———. "The Legacy of Terri Schiavo: The Disabled Sound the Alarm for the Nonreligious." *Free Inquiry*, vol. 25, no. 5, August–September 2005, p. 33. Hentoff presents the disability community's argument that the fight to remove the feeding tubes from the vegetative body of Terry Schiavo had little to do with the supposed right-to-die and everything to do with a disregard for disability rights.

Higgins, Michael. "Shock Therapy Called Cruel: Kin Disagree." *Chicago Tribune*, March 8, 2007, p. 1. Higgins reports on a family that persuaded a judge to allow shock treatments for a relative because of his allergic reaction to psychiatric drugs.

Hunt, Paul, and Judith Mesquita. "Mental Disabilities and the Human Right to the Highest Attainable Standard of Health." *Human Rights Quarterly*, vol. 28, no. 2, May 2006, p. 332. The authors of this article propose a standard for health care for the mentally disabled based on human rights conventions and case law.

Johnson, Mary. "Terri Schiavo: A Disability Rights Case." *Death Studies*, vol. 30, no. 2, March 2006, p. 163. In this article, Johnson argues that the removal of feeding tubes from comatose and brain-damaged patient Terry Schiavo in 2005 was an act of discrimination against the disabled.

"Kansas Legislature Moves to End Guardians' Total Control over Life." *Report on Disability Law*, vol. 28, no. 4, April 2005, p. 32. This article reports that in light of the Terry Schiavo assisted suicide case, Kansas lawmakers are considering legislation to end legal guardians' control over the end of life wishes of severely disabled people who do not have a living will.

Leo, John. "An Autopsy Won't End It." *U.S. News & World Report*, vol. 138, no. 24, June 27, 2005, p. 60. Leo reviews an article by Joan Didion that discusses the death of Terry Schiavo and criticizes the government for getting involved in personal civil rights issues. Leo argues that Didion's argument—and others like it—miss the point that the morality of the nation still favors a disabled person's right to live.

Longmore, Paul K. "Assisted Suicide and Disability." *Chronicle of Higher Education*, vol. 52, no. 25, February 24, 2006, p. B13. Longmore contends that disability scholars do not reject legalized assisted suicide merely because of a right-to-life agenda; rather, opposition stems from concern that assisted suicide is becoming an industry and the medical profession is not conversely guaranteeing a right to health care.

Luna, Claire. "If Only We'd Known, Parents Say." *Los Angeles Times*, September 9, 2004, p. B1. In this article, Luna reports on parents that are suing obstetricians for failing to inform them about screening tests that might have detected specific birth defects. The parents claim that they would have chosen abortion rather than give birth to a disabled child.

"N.Y. Advocates Upset over Governor's Veto of Mental Health Bills: Advocates Hoping Lawmakers Will Override Veto." *Mental Health Weekly*, vol. 16, no. 34, August 28, 2006, p. 1. This article reports that state advocates decry Governor George Pataki's veto of bills that would potentially have increased housing and improved health services for people with mental disabilities and removed inmates with psychiatric disorders from solitary confinement.

Pelka, Fred. "Running the Transplant Gauntlet: Discrimination against People with Disabilities When They Seek an Organ Transplant." *Exceptional Parent*, vol. 34, no. 12, December 2004, p. 30. Organ transplants are difficult to come by, but people with disabilities seem to have more trouble receiving donated organs. Pelka posits that this is perhaps due to entrenched notions that people with disabilities are already considered unfixable and therefore are poor candidates for new organs.

Werth, James L. Jr. "Concerns about Decisions Related to Withholding/Withdrawing Life-Sustaining Treatment and Futility for Persons with Disabilities." *Journal of Disability Policy Studies*, vol. 16, no. 1, summer 2005, p. 31. The author argues that the decision to withhold treatment or life-sustaining care from patients with disabilities should not be made on an individual basis in which family or physician prejudice can interfere. Instead, a general withholding/withdrawing policy should be made applicable to all patients and should be drafted with the input of the disabled community.

INTERNET DOCUMENTS

Carter-Long, Lawrence. "Suicide beyond the Question of Choice." Ragged Edge Online. Available online. URL: http://www.raggededgemagazine.com/departments/mediacircusblog/000754.html. Posted January 19, 2006. Although assisted suicide may be a matter of choice to some, the media emphasis on the debate dangerously shifts the focus away from how people can learn to live with disability, according to this article.

Golden, Marilyn. "Why Assisted Suicide Must Not Be Legalized." Disability Rights Education & Defense Fund web site. Available online. URL: http://dredf.org/assisted_suicide/assistedsuicide.html. Downloaded March 25, 2007. Golden argues that legalizing assisted suicide would discriminate against low-income people with disabilities who might be perceived as a burden upon the health care system.

New York State Office of the Attorney General. "Hidden Cameras Reveal Neglect at Nursing Homes." New York State Office of the Attorney General web site. Available online. URL: http://www.oag.state.ny.us/press/2006/jan/jan05a_06.html. Posted January 5, 2006. This article reports that two New York nursing homes were cited for neglect of elderly patients in their care, and 19 employees were arrested for neglect and abuse.

Reynolds, Dave. "Advocates Angered as Supreme Court Upholds Oregon's Assisted-Suicide Law." *Inclusion Daily Express*. Available online. URL: http://www.inclusiondaily.com/archives/06/01/17/011706orsuicide.htm. Posted January 17, 2006. Reynolds reports that the U.S. Supreme Court has ruled that the federal government cannot interfere with Oregon doctors' prescription of drugs intended for assisted suicide because the state has legalized the practice.

Smith, Phil. "'There Is No Treatment Here': Disability and Health Needs in a State Prison System." *Disability Studies Quarterly*, vol. 25, no. 3. Available online. URL: http://www.dsq-sds.org/_articles_html/2005/fall/fleischer_zames.asp. Posted summer 2005. Smith presents the results of a survey of Vermont prison inmates revealing that most prisoners report having some disability and that the correctional services are inattentive to accommodating disability.

U.S. Department of Justice. "Justice Department and Commonwealth of Kentucky Reach Settlement Regarding Conditions at Developmental Center." *Disability Rights Online News*. Available online. URL: http://www.ada.gov/newsltr1006.htm. Posted October 2006. This article reports that the Department of Justice has reached an agreement with the Commonwealth of Kentucky to redress violations at the Communities at Oakwood, a center for people with developmental disabilities. The violations included numerous citations for issues involving preventable deaths, sexual abuse, and failure to provide services for residents' maladaptive behaviors.

"Why Disability Rights Activists Oppose Physician Assisted Suicide." Ragged Edge Online. Available online. URL: http://www.ragged edgemagazine.com/departments/closerlook/000749.html. Posted January 18, 2006. This article elaborates on the reasons why disability rights activists believe that assisted suicide is discriminatory toward the old and ill. According to this publication, if the government wants to legislate assisted suicide, then it must make it available to all people who want it, not just the disabled, infirm, or the terminally ill. Regardless, according to these activists, the message of assisted suicide is that an ill or disabled life is not valuable.

OTHER MEDIA

Conquest, Wendy, Bob Drake, and Deni Elliott. *The Burden of Knowledge: Moral Dilemmas in Prenatal Testing* (1994). Fanlight Productions, VHS, 1994. Interviews with seven couples reveal social attitudes toward prenatal testing and the ethics of detecting birth defects before birth.

BARRIERS TO SOCIAL INCLUSION

BOOKS

Barnes, Colin, Geof Mercer, and Tom Shakespeare. *Exploring Disability: A Sociological Introduction*. Malden, Mass.: Blackwell, 1999. This is an introductory primer on the sociological aspects of disability, including its manifestations in the political, social, medical, and cultural arenas. The authors note how disability is transforming from a medical problem to a social issue, but they chart how the medical model of disability still informs much of the debate on disability policy. The volume is an excellent starting point for those researching the evolution of social issues relating to disability.

Annotated Bibliography

Barton, Len, ed. *Disability, Politics and the Struggle for Change*. London: David Fulton, 2001. This collection of views concerns the struggle of the disabilities community to advance the notion of inclusion. The authors examine the persistence and power of the medical model of disability in hopes of overturning it to make disability a social issue that can be overcome through participation and unity. The cross-cultural aspect of the various essays adds a welcome dimension to the volume.

Bowe, Frank. *Handicapping America: Barriers to Disabled People*. New York: Harper & Row, 1978. A primary text to come out of the burgeoning disability rights movement in the 1970s, Bowe discusses how society chooses to discriminate against people with disabilities by allowing physical, architectural, and transportation barriers to exist. To make the world barrier-free, he contends, would require a complete change in social mindset.

———. *Rehabilitating America: Toward Independence for Disabled and Elderly People*. New York: Harper & Row, 1980. In this follow-up to *Handicapping America*, Bowe argues that America's unwillingness to invest in people with disabilities and the elderly has exacerbated the national problems of poverty, inflation, and bloated government. He proposes a plan to overcome these problems by changing America's perception of disability and by empowering the disabled to end troublesome dependency.

Bryan, Willie V. *In Search of Freedom: How Persons with Disabilities Have Been Disenfranchised from the Mainstream of American Society*. 2nd ed. Springfield, Ill.: Charles C. Thomas, 2006. Bryan examines issues that have kept people with disabilities from participating equally in mainstream society. In part, he blames society for not evolving its notions of disability from primitive views of "otherness" to one of inclusion. He asserts that exclusionary policies have traditionally separated the disabled in their own communities, where notions of difference (even helplessness) are perpetuated for lack of contact and involvement.

Charlton, James I. *Nothing about Us without Us: Disability Oppression and Empowerment*. Berkeley: University of California Press, 1998. Executive vice president of Access Living in Chicago, Charlton looks at the oppression of the disabled worldwide. Using interviews with disability activists in several countries, he examines how disability is often equated with powerlessness and how this has been reinforced through philosophy, politics, and cultural mores.

Covey, Herbert C. *Social Perceptions of People with Disabilities in History*. Springfield, Ill.: Charles C. Thomas, 1998. Dr. Covey writes of the social images of people with disabilities throughout history. He refers to literature, art, and historical record to display how disability has been presented, codified, and transferred through the ages. Given the limits of the historical record, however, Covey is often unable to show more than examples of social constructions without actually defining how these perceptions were generated or what impact they had on their societies.

Eisenberg, Myron, Cynthia Griggins, and Richard Duval, eds. *Disabled People as Second-Class Citizens*. New York: Springer, 1982. This anthology contends with obstacles that exist to people with disabilities. The authors discuss such topics as transportation, architectural access, employment, health care, and public attitudes. They also present the successes and failures of advocacy movements aimed at removing the barriers.

Gartner, Alan, and Tom Joe, eds. *Images of the Disabled, Disabling Images*. New York: Praeger, 1987. This collection of essays focuses on the way disability has been portrayed in society and literature. The authors primarily contend that stereotyped imagery of weakness, inability, and otherness have reinforced negative public attitudes toward the disabled. However, many assert that the able-bodied world and its created environments are what deprive people with disabilities from utilizing their capabilities, therefore never allowing people with disabilities to become anything other than less than human.

Ingstad, Benedicte, and Susan Reynolds Whyte, eds. *Disability and Culture*. Berkeley: University of California Press, 1995. The authors represented in this anthology discuss cultural assumptions about disability in various societies primarily in Africa but also in Europe, Asia, and America. The multicultural format, along with the focus on disability as a social construction in diverse social settings, makes this book a worthwhile, if dated, read.

Jaeger, Paul T., and Cynthia Ann Bowman. *Understanding Disability: Inclusion, Access, Diversity, and Civil Rights*. Westport, Conn.: Praeger, 2005. The authors of this volume argue that disability is too often relegated to medical science or abstract theory. They propose to show its connectedness to social concerns such as accessibility, education, media, and the law. Additionally, they attempt to examine the "otherness" of disability, question how people with disabilities have been marginalized, and determine what social barriers are keeping them isolated from the mainstream.

Johnson, Mary. *Make Them Go Away: Clint Eastwood, Christopher Reeve & the Case against Disability Rights*. Louisville, Ky.: Advocado, 2003. Written by the founder of the *Disability Rag* (now *Ragged Edge*), this engaging examination of the backlash against disability rights argues that the ADA has been poorly enforced and limited by court decisions. Johnson explains that the media and certain high-profile critics have spent time undercutting the disability rights movement, turning a lot of public sympathy into bad feelings by asserting that the disabilities community wants too much accommodation. Johnson suggests that the remedy lies in pushing forward a new paradigm of disability, one that is socially constructed rather than medically defined.

Annotated Bibliography

Liachowitz, Claire H. *Disability as a Social Construct: Legislative Roots.* Philadephia: University of Pennsylvania Press, 1988. The author examines various ways in which disability has been addressed by governmental law. She begins by showing how disabled veterans were recompensed through vocational training and living assistance; she then discusses workers compensation, the rehabilitation movement, and education for children with disabilities. Liachowitz contends that each attempt to cater to the needs of the disabled (or ignore them completely) has perpetuated the misconception that people with disabilities are inferior citizens who may be dismissed with charity.

Linton, Simi. *Claiming Disability: Knowledge and Identity.* New York: New York University Press, 1998. Linton makes the case for the legitimacy of disabilities studies in academic curriculum. She uses the disability rights movement as a springboard to argue that disability goes beyond the medical field and has become a type of social discourse that has its own theories, literature, arts, and social significance.

Murphy, Robert Francis. *The Body Silent: The Different World of the Disabled.* New York: Norton, 2001. The author, a quadriplegic, uses his own personal experiences to examine the ways in which people with disabilities have been discriminated against and isolated from participation in society. Murphy suggests that much of the fearful reaction to the disabled is based on society's misunderstanding of the disability experience and the capabilities of people with disabilities.

Oliver, Michael. *Understanding Disability: From Theory to Practice.* New York: St. Martin's Press, 1996. Oliver, a sociologist, provides a series of essays on various disability subjects including social policy, citizenship, education, and divisions within the disability movement. Using personal anecdotes about his own disability, which resulted from a spinal injury, he defines his relationship to the subject matter, emphasizing that collective action begins with the individual and that social change affects the person as well as society.

Priestley, Mark. *Disability: A Life Course Approach.* Malden, Mass.: Blackwell, 2003. Priestley describes disability as it is conceived through the stages of an individual's life. He offers a global perspective, touching on various societies' birth and death rituals, coming of age rites, marriage rites, and other aspects of moving from childhood to adulthood to old age. Priestley connects these personal maturation processes to various nations' views on disability, citizenship, and human rights.

Riley, Charles A. III. *Disability and the Media: Prescriptions for Change.* Lebanon, N.H.: University Press of New England, 2005. Riley maintains that images of disability in the media range from negative stereotypes to unrealistic and equally damaging portrayals of the supercrip. The latter is pervasive in current society, Riley contends, stimulating a focus on medical miracles (people who overcome the obvious limitations of their conditions) and ignoring the civil rights struggles that more accurately define the lives of people with disabilities.

Russell, Marta. *Beyond Ramps: Disability at the End of the Social Contract.* Monroe, Me.: Common Courage, 1998. Russell argues that America's social, political, and business worlds are geared to benefit the corporations that drive capitalism. She further contends that this emphasis has damaged social welfare programs and engendered a pervasive conformity in which the public is pigeonholed into specific types of consumers whose wants can be met by the corporate system. The book ties this criticism to the disabilities community by positing that such a system devalues difference and has no room for people with disabilities because they do not fit the mold of average, normal workers and consumers. She concludes the argument stating that in an era of corporate downsizing and runaway government spending, social services and entitlements for the disabled are jeopardized by this paradigm.

Shakespeare, Tom, ed. *The Disability Reader: Social Science Perspectives.* London: Cassell, 1998. This collection of essays presents changing views on disability in the sociologic and political realm. It offers insight into the process of inclusion, gender discrimination, the problematic implementation of the social model, and other topics relevant to the social sciences. Various authors discuss how disability is framed in current society, how inferiority and weakness are built into the social conception of disability, and how human-made environments are constructed to exclude or impede people with disabilities.

PERIODICALS

Drinan, Robert F. "World Law Aims to Protect Persons with Disabilities." *National Catholic Reporter*, vol. 43, no. 3, November 3, 2006, p. 18. Drinan's article details the United Nations's proposal for its own covenant on disability rights, one that spells out the rights of children, men, and women who face discrimination and poor treatment because of their disabilities. Questions about enforceability of this agreement are also presented.

Gostin, Lawrence O. "International Human Rights Law and Mental Disability." *Hastings Center Report*, vol. 34, no. 2, March–April 2004, p. 11. Gostin contends that disability rights are failing to bring equality to the mentally disabled. He suggests that the problem might be corrected if disability rights were equated with human rights instead of being framed as a social prerogative.

Haller, Beth, Bruce Dorries, and Jessica Rahn. "Media Labeling versus the U.S. Disability Community Identity: A Study of Shifting Cultural Language." *Disability & Society*, vol. 21, no. 1, January 2006, p. 61. A review of newspaper reporting reveals, according to the authors, that the media is still using outdated and damaging terminology when referring to people with disabilities. Haller, Dorries, and Rahn report that the disabilities community has had some influence on changing that vocabulary, but some stereotypical language remains.

Hays, Alicia. "People Power: International Exchange Finds that Individuals Are Catalysts in Helping Shape Disability Rights." *Paraplegia News*, vol. 58, no. 5, May 2004, p. 12. A visit to Japan helps the author see how the lack of a rights-based approach to disability is keeping the disabled from true participation in society. She does report, however, that some advocacy on the part of Japan's disabled community is bringing change.

Hernandez, Brigida, Christopher B. Keys, and Fabricio E. Balcazar. "Disability Rights: Attitudes of Private and Public Sector Representatives." *Journal of Rehabilitation*, vol. 70, no. 1, January–March 2004, p. 28. This article presents an ethnographic survey that reveals how a sample of ethnically diverse civic representatives and business people feel about disability rights. One conclusion drawn from the survey was that the more the respondents knew about the ADA, the more positive they felt about disability rights.

Johnson, Mary. "Scope of 'Disability Rights' Must Be Expanded." *Cincinnati Post*, August 1, 2005, p. A13. According to Johnson, disability rights is not about providing special treatment for a complaining special interest group; it is about making places and opportunities in America accessible to everyone.

Kaufman-Scarborough, Carol, and Stacey Menzel Baker. "Do People with Disabilities Believe the ADA Has Served Their Consumer Interests?" *Journal of Consumer Affairs*, vol. 39, no. 1, summer 2005, p. 1. Statistically, one in five consumers has some form of disability, and the ADA mandates that retail outlets and online merchandisers accommodate these disabled shoppers. The study presented by these authors concludes that few people with disabilities knew the law mandated accessibility of retail markets and that barriers still exist in the marketplace that keep people with disabilities from participating.

Koppelman, Susan. "Thinking about Disability." *Off Our Backs*, vol. 32, Issue 11/12, November/December 2002, p. 16. Koppelman discusses the distinctions between disability and chronic illness and why the separation exists even within the disabilities movement.

Lerner, Wayne, and Henry Betts. "Striving for Equity; Americans with Disabilities Act Still Not Fulfilling Promises to the Disabled." *Modern Healthcare*, vol. 35, no. 36, September 2005, p. 20. The ADA has made great strides in improving government-enforced accessibility for the disabled, but the law has not lived up to its promises in the business and health care arenas, according to the article.

"'Nothing about Us without Us': Recognizing the Rights of People with Disabilities." *UN Chronicle*, vol. 41, no. 4, December 2004, p. 10. According to this article, the United Nations recognizes the unique plight of the world's disabled, but the organization has yet to pass any specific agreements to spell out the rights of people with disabilities. The assembly is now considering such a convention; details are included in the article.

Pineda, Victor. "'A World Enabled': Fighting for the Human Rights of Persons with Disabilities." *UN Chronicle*, vol. 41, no. 4, December 2004, p. 12. The United Nations is considering a convention to recognize and protect the rights of people with disabilities worldwide. The article contends that this convention, however, would only be as strong as the governments that choose to enforce it.

Putnam, Michelle. "Developing a Framework for Political Disability Identity." *Journal of Disability Policy Studies*, vol. 16, no. 3, winter 2005, p. 188. The disability rights movement has long been a champion of disability identity politics, but there has been no theoretical approach to outline what such a construct would be. The author proposes some guidelines for building a framework that includes notions of pride, self-worth, and the experience of discrimination.

Wolbring, Gregor. "A Disability Rights Approach towards Sex Selection." *Development*, vol. 48, no. 4, December 2005, p. 106. Wolbring argues that the field of bioethics does not employ disability rights as a framework to shape its philosophies. The author further contends that such considerations should be included because of the potential for science to categorize disability as an abnormal, unwanted state.

INTERNET DOCUMENTS

Bowe, Frank. "Disability Meets the Boom." Ragged Edge Online. Available online. URL: http://www.raggededgemagazine.com/departments/closer look/000106.html. Posted September 27, 2005. According to the article, the baby boom generation will soon face disability due to aging. The author predicts that 76 million "boomers" will be a strong contingent that likely will make disability issues part of the national agenda.

Fleischer, Doris Zames. "Disability Rights: The Overlooked Civil Rights Issue." *Disability Studies Quarterly*, vol. 25, no. 4. Available online. URL: http://www.dsq-sds.org/_articles_html/2005/fall/fleischer_zames.asp. Posted fall 2005. Fleischer asks why disability rights are often overlooked in America and then tries to answer the question by examining the fight for disability rights and the public attitudes the fight has engendered.

Johnson, Mary. "'Disablism': A Closer Look." Ragged Edge Online. Available online. URL: http://www.raggededgemagazine.com/departments/closerlook/000947.html. Posted May 1, 2006. According to Johnson, disablism, the ingrained, socially structured discrimination against people with disabilities, is a controversial term and theory. Some deny that policies inherently promote disablism, but the backlash against the term itself has caused many to overlook the discrimination that exists, according to the author.

U.S. Department of Justice. "United Nations Adopts Disability Rights Treaty." Disability Rights Online News. Available online. URL: http://www.ada.gov/newsltr0107.htm. Posted February 2007. Details of the December 2006 United Nations adoption of the Convention on the Rights of Persons with Disabilities are given in this article. The treaty will give citizens the right to petition an international Committee on Rights of Persons with Disabilities once they have exhausted all avenues for relief within their own country.

DEAF CULTURE

BOOKS

Barnartt, Sharon N., and John B. Christiansen. *Deaf President Now! The 1988 Revolution at Gallaudet University*. Washington, D.C.: Gallaudet University Press, 2003. The authors describe the faculty commitment and student support for the insurrection on Gallaudet campus that compelled the university trustees to elect a deaf president. Barnartt and Christiansen also show connections to other student protest movements and disability rights demonstrations and explore the lasting impact of this successful, peaceful revolution.

Branson, Jan, and Don Miller. *Damned for Their Difference: The Social Construction of Deaf People as Disabled*. Washington, D.C.: Gallaudet University Press, 2002. Criticizing the label of "disabled" as it is applied to the hearing impaired, Branson and Miller explain why the Deaf do not perceive themselves as disabled and why they choose to shun a label that excludes people from society. They also question the hegemony of hearing/speaking traditions in Western society.

Lane, Harlan L. *The Mask of Benevolence: Disabling the Deaf Community*. San Diego: DawnSign, 1999. In this interesting history of the hearing world's subordination of the Deaf community, Lane passionately describes the hearing world's discrimination against the Deaf as a form of colonization. He advocates the recognition of the Deaf as a linguistic minority that have the right to administer to their own interests as a community.

Padden, Carol A., and Tom L. Humphries. *Deaf in America: Voices from a Culture*. Cambridge, Mass.: Harvard University Press, 1990. Written by two Deaf advocates, this book looks at the Deaf community and its values. It contains various first-person accounts of discrimination and the continual conflict between the expectations of the hearing world and the cultural defiance of the Deaf. The stories also attest to the celebratory aspects of Deaf arts, literature, and unity.

Van Cleve, John Vickrey, and Barry A. Crouch. *A Place of Their Own: Creating the Deaf Community in America*. Washington, D.C.: Gallaudet University Press, 1989. This concise history covers the experience of deaf individuals from ancient times to the modern age. The authors examine the changing views of deafness, the rise of American Sign Language, and the eventual recognition of Deaf culture.

Wilcox, Sherman, ed. *American Deaf Culture: An Anthology*. Burtonsville, Md: Linstok, 1989. The essays in this anthology detail Deaf culture in America, describing the language, social issues, and values of the Deaf community. Much of the focus is on the distinctness of Deaf culture and how its principles and projects are often misinterpreted by the hearing world. Some of the essays are personal accounts; others are scholarly papers.

PERIODICALS

Chayes, Matthew. "Gallaudet President Causes Stir: Foes—School's New Leader Unqualified." *Chicago Tribune*, May 10, 2006, p. 3. The new president of the deaf university has the power to speak, which according to the article, has touched off a debate among students concerning whether she is a deaf enough candidate to represent the school.

EDUCATION

BOOKS

Winzer, Margaret. *The History of Special Education: From Isolation to Integration*. Washington, D.C.: Gallaudet University Press, 1993. This work is a comprehensive examination of the education of the mentally retarded and other people with disabilities in North America. Winzer begins her narrative in the 18th century and moves through the eugenics movement and finally to the modern theories and practices of special education professionals. Although she reveals the social misconceptions that have led to the relative poor quality of education for the disabled, she also is not hesitant to point out how special education teachers have underestimated the capabilities of their students and therefore added to the restrictive nature of this field of instruction.

Annotated Bibliography

PERIODICALS

Boswell, Susan. "Speaking out on IDEA Regulations: Members Submit More than 1,600 Letters to U.S. Department of Education." *ASHA Leader*, vol. 10, no. 5, April 12, 2005, p. 1. Boswell reports on various members of the American Speech-Language-Hearing Association (ASHA) speaking out at meetings concerning the formalization of regulations for the Individuals with Disabilities Education Improvement Act of 2004 (IDEA). Most suggest the IDEA's attempts to mainstream children with disabilities may deprive them of the best education possible.

Cohen, Jodi S. "Colleges Feel Heat to Help Disabled: U. of C. Deal is Part of Crackdown by U.S." *Chicago Tribune*, August 31, 2006, p. 1. Cohen reports that universities are facing government pressure to make campuses accessible, including the employment of trained counselors, the clear marking of disabled services, and the creation of dorms for severely disabled students.

Cook, Glenn. "The Supreme Court Hands Schools a Special Education Win." *American School Board Journal*, vol. 193, no. 1, January 2006, p. 2. Cook reports on the U.S. Supreme Court ruling in *Schaffer v. Weast*, which finds that parents have the legal burden of proving that a school district's special education plan does not provide an appropriate education for their child.

Hetzner, Amy. "Suit to Stop New School for the Disabled Is Dismissed." *Milwaukee Journal Sentinel*, March 16, 2007, p. 14. The defeat of a disability rights group in its legal battle to stop the construction of a school for disabled students is the topic of this report. The group brought suit, questioning whether a separate school violated the rights of students to be educated in the most integrated setting possible.

Palley, Elizabeth. "Implementing the Least Restrictive Environment Mandate." *Journal of Disability Policy Studies*, vol. 16, no. 4, spring 2006, p. 229. The Individuals with Disabilities Education Act (IDEA) mandates that disabled children are to be educated in the least restrictive environment. Palley argues that in order to accomplish this, educational policies must look beyond individual cases and address stigmas that adhere to the treatment of all disabled students in academia.

Rubin, Bonnie Miller, and Grace Aduroja. "Educational Opportunities Grow for Disabled." *Los Angeles Times*, December 18, 2005, p. A22. According to this article, various schools and universities are expanding curricula for mentally and physically disabled students. As a result, more disabled students are graduating and moving into the professional workforce.

Weaver, Reg. "The Promise of a Fresh Start: A New Opportunity to Make ESEA/NCLB Work for All Students." *NEA Today*, vol. 25, no. 5, February 2007, p. 7. According to Weaver, the No Child Left Behind Act of

2001 has not lived up to its goals. He argues that congressional reauthorization of the act will allow advocates to get involved in shaping new legislation that can improve the educational outcome of children covered by the act.

INTERNET DOCUMENTS

Beratan, Gregg D. "Institutionalizing Inequity: Ableism, Racism and IDEA 2004." *Disability Studies Quarterly*, vol. 26, no. 2. Available online. URL: http://www.dsq-sds.org/_articles_html/2006/spring/beratan.asp. Posted spring 2006. The author argues that discriminatory views embedded within the language and ideas expressed in the Individuals with Disabilities Education Act (IDEA) keep the act from fulfilling its promise.

Reynolds, Dave. "School Can Ban Boy from Playground, Judge Says." *Inclusion Daily Express*. Available online. URL: http://www.inclusiondaily. com/archives/04/09/01/090104meplayground.htm. Posted September 1, 2004. Reynolds reports that a judge in Maine has ruled that a boy with Asperger's syndrome can be legally banned from the public school playground because of his disruptive behavior.

U.S. Department of Education. "Raising the Achievement of Students with Disabilities: New Ideas for IDEA." U.S. Department of Education web site. Available online. URL: http://www.ed.gov/admins/lead/speced/idea factsheet.html. Posted August 2006. After receiving input from lawmakers and educators, the Department of Education released newly revised guidelines for the Individuals with Disabilities Education Act, according to this article.

OTHER MEDIA

Kaplan, Marianne. *The Boy Inside* (2006). Fanlight Productions, VHS/DVD, 2006. A mother tells the story of her son who has Asperger's syndrome and his difficulties interacting with his peers at school.

HISTORIES OF THE DISABILITY RIGHTS MOVEMENT

BOOKS

Campbell, Jane, and Michael Oliver. *Disability Politics: Understanding Our Past, Changing Our Future*. New York: Routledge, 2006. In this engaging account of political action in the disabilities community, authors Campbell and Oliver combine their own and others' first hand accounts with

astute political and historical analysis to recount the way disability policies were shaped in the 1980s. First published in 1996, the new edition
brings the legacy of the struggle through the 21st century, highlighting
how the movement has slowed but not dissipated in the wake of backlash
against the ADA.

Fleischer, Doris Zames, and Frieda Zames. *The Disability Rights Movement:
From Charity to Confrontation.* Philadelphia: Temple University Press,
2001. Perhaps the best overview of the various interests that have been
lumped together as the disability rights movement, this book divides the
sociopolitical causes into topics of concern such as transportation, employment, veterans, services, and independent living, and provides excellent analysis of the accomplishments and setbacks experienced in each.
The volume ends with a discussion of disability as a cultural issue, which
is the one tie that binds all the various groups and activists discussed in
the previous chapters into a movement.

Jones, Ruth J. E. *Their Rightful Place: Society and Disability.* Toronto: Canadian Academy of the Arts, 1994. This book provides a brief overview of
the treatment of people with disabilities in history, with emphasis on the
19th and 20th centuries. Jones examines institutionalization policies,
changing employment opportunities, and medical treatment of the disabled. She also offers some predictions about how society and disability
policy will continue to shape each other in the future.

Longmore, Paul K., and Lauri Umanski, eds. *The New Disability History:
American Perspectives.* New York: New York University Press, 2001. The
authors in this anthology examine historical examples of the treatment of
people with disabilities in specific times and places. Whether contending
with hospitals at the end of the 19th century or the Blind Veterans Association at the end of World War II, these essays not only enlighten
historical moments, they also show a connection to the policies that continue to define disability in modern times.

Noll, Steven, and James W. Trent, Jr., eds. *Mental Retardation in America: A
Historical Reader.* New York: New York University Press, 2004. This anthology offers various essays on how mental retardation has been defined
and dealt with in America. The essays explore the institutionalization and
sterilization movements, as well as the general inclination to negatively
stereotype mental disability as idiocy. The authors also show positive
trends in the evolution of the treatment of the mentally retarded and attempts to make workplaces, living environments, and society as a whole
more inclusive.

Pelka, Fred. *The ABC-CLIO Companion to the Disability Rights Movement.*
Santa Barbara, Calif.: ABC-CLIO, 1997. This encyclopedia of people,
places, events, and terminology related to disability rights is a helpful

starting point for research. Though now somewhat out-of-date, the work covers the most active years of disability rights activism and is useful in quickly accessing information on a topic referenced but not fully explained in other disabilities studies.

Scotch, Richard K. *From Good Will to Civil Rights: Transforming Federal Disability Policy*. 2nd ed. Philadelphia: Temple University Press, 2001. A history of the treatment of people with disabilities in America, this book charts the transformation of public policy from institutionalization through the advent of the Rehabilitation Act of 1973. Scotch explains how grassroots advocacy brought attention to the plight of the disabled and how Section 504 of the Rehabilitation Act opened the door to expanded freedoms. The new second edition of this work (the first edition was published in 1984) adds an epilogue that examines the transformation of Section 504 policy brought on by the advent of the ADA.

Shapiro, Joseph P. *No Pity: People with Disabilities Forging a New Civil Rights Movement*. New York: Times Books, 1993. Considered a foundational text of disability history, the strength of Shapiro's work is his weaving of personal histories through the progress of the movement. This tactic reveals how the disability rights movement was fomented through individual will as well as collective action. The work is an excellent starting point for disability rights researchers.

Stiker, Henri-Jacques. *A History of Disability*. Translated by William Sayers. Ann Arbor: University of Michigan Press, 2002. Published in France in 1997, this volume traces disability and the treatment of the disabled from ancient history to modern times. Stiker maintains that Western societies have always prized conformity, and therefore people with disabilities have always been treated as exceptions that were either marginalized, made into grotesque entertainments, or eliminated. The author, however, offers his own countervailing theory that difference should be prized in society, for it not only reinforces individualism but also promises change.

Switzer, Jacqueline Vaughn. *Disabled Rights: American Disability Policy and the Fight for Equality*. Washington, D.C.: Georgetown University Press, 2003. Switzer, a political science professor, charts the history of the treatment of people with disabilities in the United States. She examines laws and public policies and their impact, while revealing the growth of the disabilities rights movement and its push for social change.

Treanor, Richard Bryant. *We Overcame: The Story of Civil Rights for Disabled People*. Falls Church, Va.: Regal Direct, 1993. An activist and author, Treanor has written a fairly thorough history of the disability rights movement focusing on the fight for key legislation and the debate surrounding prominent issues. Some of the writing is a bit unpolished, but the emphasis on details and the work of specific reformers makes up for any shortcomings.

Trent, James W., Jr. *Inventing the Feeble Mind: A History of Mental Retardation in the United States.* Berkeley: University of California Press, 1995. This is an academic history of the notion of feeblemindedness and the treatment of the mentally retarded in America. Trent provides graphic accounts of institutionalization, forced sterilization, and general neglect of a significant portion of the population. He also suggests that changing public policies and the advent of disability laws have not yet freed the mentally disabled from persecution and exclusion.

PERIODICALS

McCarthy, Henry. "The Disability Rights Movement: Experiences and Perspectives of Selected Leaders in the Disability Community." *Rehabilitation Counseling Bulletin*, vol. 46, no. 4, summer 2003, p. 209. Interviews with key members of the disability rights movement reveal the struggle of disability rights in America and the challenges that lay ahead.

INTERNET DOCUMENTS

Bowe, Frank. "The Time to Rise Will Come Again." Ragged Edge Online. Available online. URL: http://www.raggededgemagazine.com/departments/closerlook/000631.html. Posted November 21, 2005. Bowe, a lawyer and an old guard activist, responds to queries about why the disability protest movement of the 1970s and 1980s has lost momentum. Bowe contends that America has changed, other events have occupied public attention, and the climate for political action in Washington, D.C., has stagnated.

O'Toole, Corbett Joan. "Early Days in Berkeley, and Where We Are Now." Ragged Edge Online. Available online. URL: http://www.raggededgemagazine.com/departments/reflections/000499.html. Posted October 19, 2005. O'Toole, a member of the 1970s disability rights protest movement, traces the vitality of that movement to the shared sense that people mattered and a collective vision of needed change.

OTHER MEDIA

Ward, Irene M., and Associates. *A Little History Worth Knowing* (1998). Program Development Associates, VHS/DVD, 1998. A 22-minute history of the treatment of disabled people through history, this documentary focuses on the growth of the disability movement and its fight against discrimination and stereotyping.

PERSONAL NARRATIVES

BOOKS

Fries, Kenny, ed. *Staring Back: The Disability Experience from the Inside Out.* New York: Plume, 1997. This collection of essays, fiction, and poetry examines discrimination and otherness faced by people with disabilities. Some of the authors tackle society's misperceptions while others face their own misgivings about living with a disability.

Roth, William. *The Handicapped Speak.* Jefferson, N.C.: McFarland, 1981. Roth interviews several people with disabilities to understand their situations and the trials they've experienced living in an able-bodied world. Most of the stories presented push for social change and policy development, and Roth contends that only by listening to people with disabilities can society truly change to address their rights and needs.

Shaw, Barrett, ed. *The Ragged Edge: The Disability Experience from the Pages of the First Fifteen Years of the Disability Rag.* Louisville, Ky.: Advocado Press, 1994. This is an excellent collection of essays, fiction, and poetry from the *Disability Rag*, an influential disability periodical. While the authors focus on lively personal anecdotes (that range from the irate to the humorous), the issues are meaningful and complex. It is most interesting to see how these topics were explored and debated before serious interest in disability writing became codified in disabilities studies.

Zola, Irving Kenneth. *Missing Pieces: A Chronicle of Living with a Disability.* Philadelphia: Temple University Press, 1983. An often-cited work, Zola's autobiographical account of being confined to a wheelchair due to disability reveals many common experiences of the disabled living in a world not made for them. Zola, however, tries to rectify his situation by moving to a community in The Netherlands that is built entirely to accommodate the needs of people with disabilities. While living there, he discusses how the environment seems too good to be true and how the diversity of people is stimulating. But he remains aware that the community is an exception, a Utopian vision not shared by the majority of communities in the world.

PERIODICALS

Dinerstein, Robert D. "'Every Picture Tells a Story, Don't It?' The Complex Role of Narratives in Disability Cases." *Narrative*, vol. 15, no. 1, January 2007, p. 40. Dinerstein writes in this article about how personal narratives in legal cases involving disability have always been circumspect and have not always served people with disabilities well. The author contends that part of the problem exists in the way lawyers and the courts treat disabled litigants, an issue that has much to do with the negative stereotypes society has of disabled people.

O'Day, Bonnie, and Marcie Goldstein. "Advocacy Issues and Strategies for the 21st Century: Key Informant Interviews." *Journal of Disability Policy Studies*, vol. 15, no. 4, spring 2005, p. 240. Interviews with 16 disability activists reveal what they believe the focus of disability advocacy will be in the early 21st century. Health care ranked as the highest concern. Others included employment and accessible technology.

OTHER MEDIA

Brodie, James. *As I Am* (1990). Fanlight Productions, VHS, 1990. This 20-minute documentary records the thoughts of three young people with developmental disabilities as they deal with daily occurrences, challenges, and accomplishments.

Gould, Ron. *One of Us* (1992). Fanlight Productions, VHS, 1992. This public television documentary traces the lives of four people with disabilities who have benefited from communities that support integration into the school system, churches, housing, and other parts of the social network.

Greytak, Sharon. *Weirded Out and Blown Away* (1986). Cinema Guild, VHS, 1986. Interviews with five people with disabilities reveal the misconceptions the nondisabled community has about disability. The interviewees talk about job discrimination, identity, sexuality, and other aspects of their daily lives.

Mierendorf, Michael. *Without Pity: A Film about Abilities* (1996). Films Media Group, VHS/DVD, 1996. This HBO documentary narrated by Christopher Reeve tells of the accomplishments of several people with disabilities. Those depicted are successful parents, teachers, and business people who have overcome difficulties to take an active part in their communities.

Yu, Jessica. *Breathing Lessons* (1996). Fanlight Productions, VHS/DVD, 1996. This Academy Award-winning documentary focuses on the life and struggles of Mark O'Brien, a journalist and contributor to National Public Radio who has polio and spent much of his life in an iron lung.

PUBLIC POLICY

BOOKS

Berkowitz, Edward D. *Disabled Policy: America's Programs for the Handicapped*. New York: Cambridge University Press, 2003. Filled with anecdotes and details, Berkowitz's treatise makes public policy a readable subject. He traces the evolution of current income maintenance policy issues through decades of past laws, rulings, and public opinion. He notes that the maze of successive policies at both the federal and state levels have made it more difficult to apply consistent standards to disability security policy, but he is hopeful that the morass can be eliminated in the future by forcing governments to recognize that disability need not equal dependency.

Percy, Stephen. *Disability, Civil Rights, and Public Policy.* Tuscaloosa: University of Alabama Press, 1989. Written before the passage of the ADA, Percy's work could be seen as a foreshadowing of coming legislation. Percy discusses public policy and its implementation, focusing on how policy has been shaped, tempered, and finally put into practice, and what effect the policy has had. Especially notable is his discussion of Section 504 of the Rehabilitation Act, which includes a fine discussion of how disability has come to be defined.

PERIODICALS

"$1? $20? Only USA Makes Bills Hard for Blind to Use." *USA Today,* December 14, 2006, p. 17A. According to the article, blind people cannot differentiate U.S. paper currency denominations. It follows in reporting that the United States is one of the few countries in the world that does not use different sizes of engraving paper to distinguish paper currency denominations.

Fears, Darryl. "U.S. Sued over Dropping of Benefits for Disabled: Class-Action Case Filed on Behalf of Physically Handicapped People Granted Asylum and Awaiting U.S. Citizenship." *Washington Post,* December 21, 2006, p. A3. The author reports that disabled immigrants are losing aid benefits because they have missed the deadline to become U.S. citizens. The immigrants claim they cannot become citizens until the government clears them of lengthy background checks.

Jongbloed, Lyn. "Disability Policy in Canada: An Overview." *Journal of Disability Policy Studies,* vol. 13, no. 4, spring 2003, p. 203. Several models for conceptualizing disability have informed Canadian policy over the decades, but the lack of connection between these models has made the policies difficult to harmonize according to this article. Jongbloed argues that a new, uniform framework is needed.

Kantrowitz, Barbara, and Julie Scelfo. "What Happens When They Grow Up: Teenagers and Young Adults Are the Emerging Face of Autism as the Disorder Continues to Challenge Science and Unite Determined Families." *Newsweek,* November 27, 2006, p. 46. Kantrowitz and Scelfo report on a bill to fund autism research that sits in Congress, but maintain that legislation and therapies will likely not help those who face this disorder. Still, family members, who usually must provide all the care for autistic adults, are thankful for any help they can get, according to this article.

Richey, Warren. "In Next Round, Will Disability Rights be Broadened Further?" *Christian Science Monitor*, vol. 96, no. 129, May 28, 2004, p. 2. After the U.S. Supreme Court's ruling in *Tennessee v. Lane* that people with disabilities could collect damages from states, the author sees the potential for disability rights to be expanded as more power is given to those who press such suits.

INTERNET DOCUMENTS

Disability Rights Education & Defense Fund. "A Comparison of ADA, IDEA, and Section 504." Disability Rights Education & Defense Fund web site. Available online. URL: http://www.dredf.org/advocacy/comparison.html. Downloaded March 25, 2007. This table compares information regarding the ADA, the Individuals with Disabilities Education Act (IDEA), and Section 504 of the Rehabilitation Act, revealing who is protected under each law, what safeguards are in place, and what evaluating procedures exist.

Myers, Edward L. III. "Accessible Information Technology: An Overview of the Current State of Federal and State Laws and Policies." Rehabilitation Engineering and Assistive Technology Society of North America Technical Assistance Project. Available online. URL: http://www.resna.org/taproject/library/AccessibleIT.rtf. Posted February 2004. This document explains federal and state policy regarding accessible information technology through 2004. It includes discussions of closed captioning, hearing aids, voting technology, court cases regarding electronic and information technologies, and other topics.

National Council on Disability. "The Current State of Transportation for People with Disabilities in the United States." National Council on Disability web site. Available online. URL: http://www.ncd.gov/newsroom/publications/2005/pdf/current_state.pdf. Posted June 13, 2005. According to this document, millions of people with disabilities still report problems with accessible public transportation. This review of best practices and achievable goals is meant to advise the federal government on implementing new policies to correct the problems.

———. "National Disability Policy: A Progress Report." National Council on Disability web site. Available online. URL: http://www.ncd.gov/newsroom/publications/2006/progress_report.htm. Posted November 9, 2006. Examining the period between December 2004 and December 2005, the National Council on Disability concludes that government progress is slow in creating opportunities for people with disabilities and promoting a sense of social inclusion. The council offers suggestions on how to improve the federal disability agenda.

Reynolds, Dave. "Capra Craig Found Not Responsible for Daughter's Murder." *Inclusion Daily Express*. Available online. URL: http://www.inclusion daily.com/news/crime/capracraig.htm#022002. Posted February 20, 2002. This article presents the ruling of judge in Canada who found a mother not guilty of killing her daughter due to mental illness even though the woman admitted to poisoning the child, who had Rett syndrome, and herself.

———. "Executions of Convicts with Mental Retardation Are 'Cruel and Unusual' Punishment, High Court Rules." *Inclusion Daily Express*. Available online. URL: http://www.inclusiondaily.com/news/laws/deathpenalty. htm#062102ruling. Posted June 21, 2002. In *Atkins v. Virginia*, the U.S. Supreme Court ruled that the execution deaths of mentally retarded inmates constitutes cruel and unusual punishment and therefore violates the Eighth Amendment.

WOMEN AND OTHER MARGINALIZED DISABLED COMMUNITIES

BOOKS

Browne, Susan E., Debra Connors, and Nanci Stern, eds. *With the Power of Each Breath: A Disabled Women's Anthology*. Pittsburgh, Pa.: Cleis Press, 1990. This collection of essays, personal narratives, and poetry describes the lives of women with disabilities. The accounts are sometimes harrowing, sometimes humorous, but all stress not only the challenges of living with a disability but the added handicap of being a woman in a society that discriminates against both.

Deegan, Mary Jo, and Nancy A. Brooks, eds. *Women and Disability: The Double Handicap*. New Brunswick, N.J.: Transaction, 1985. Examining the status of women with various disabilities, the essays in this volume address how disabled women are a minority within a minority. The authors contend that women do not receive a fair share of disability benefits, how they suffer neglect more often than their male counterparts, and how their roles as actual and potential mothers is unjustly questioned by a society that views them as sick and limited in their ability to be caregivers.

Guter, Bob, and John R. Killacky, eds. *Queer Crips: Disabled Gay Men and their Stories*. Binghamton, N.Y.: Harrington Park Press, 2003. This volume presents many personal accounts from gay men who live with a variety of disabilities—from paraplegia to blindness. The stories are interesting for their forthright descriptions of problems encountered while dating, having sex, and building relationships with partners. Some authors also delve into the trials of having a disability in a society that privileges beauty and health.

Rousso, Harilyn, and Michael L. Wehmeyer, eds. *Double Jeopardy: Addressing Gender Equity in Special Education*. Albany: SUNY Press, 2001. This collection of essays discusses gender disparities in all curricula before focusing on special education. The various authors examine gender equity in special education and vocational training, noting that young women in these classes often lack role models, have fewer expectations placed on them to succeed, and are provided with fewer extracurricular activities.

Smith, Bonnie G., and Beth Hutchison, eds. *Gendering Disability*. New Brunswick, N.J.: Rutgers University Press, 2004. Providing a series of articles that address politics, arts, identity, and work, this volume examines the intersection of gender studies and disability studies. Both fields face the socially imposed models of weakness that have come to define the place of women and the disabled in society, yet the authors in this anthology look for ways to reshape academic curricula, government legislation, and public attitudes to counter these models. They also question their own identities within a culture that treats them as second-class participants.

PERIODICALS

Delson, Jennifer. "When the Safety Net Unravels." *Los Angeles Times*, November 1, 2006, p. B4. Delson reports on the story of a homeless woman in a wheelchair who finds that charities are having a difficult time finding housing for the disabled in California.

OTHER MEDIA

Harrison, Julie, and Harilyn Rousso. *Positive Images: Portraits of Women with Disabilities* (1989). Women Make Movies, VHS, 1989. This documentary portrays the unique problems faced by women with disabilities. The interviewees discuss education, employment, and motherhood, and tell how each is impacted by the intersection of gender, race, and disability.

WORKING WITH THE DISABLED

BOOKS

Batshaw, Mark L., Louis Pellegrino, and Nancy J. Roizen, eds. *Children with Disabilities*. 6th ed. Baltimore: Brookes Publishing Company, 2007. A compendium to aid those working with children who have disabilities, this exhaustive volume covers treatment, education, and family issues.

PERIODICALS

Gross, Jane. "Learning to Savor a Full Life, Love Life Included." *New York Times*, April 20, 2006, p. A1. The author reports on a social service agency that coaches people with mental disabilities in physical intimacy, an often overlooked but important aspect of personal development among the disabled.

WORKPLACE ISSUES

BOOKS

O'Brien, Ruth. *Crippled Justice: The History of Modern Disability Policy in the Workplace*. Chicago: University of Chicago Press, 2001. O'Brien examines disability policies in the workplace from the end of World War II to the beginning of the 21st century. In her assessment, the medical views that held sway in the 1940s—chiefly that disability was a personal matter requiring some government assistance but no accommodation—have remained intact even after the passage of such landmark legislation as the ADA. She believes that the failure of the ADA, the numerous setbacks experienced in the court system, and the backlash in the business world can be traced to these entrenched opinions.

Roulstone, Alan. *Enabling Technology: Disabled People, Work and New Technology*. Philadelphia, Pa.: Open University Press, 1998. This work argues that workplace policies have traditionally been shaped by attitudes that consider accommodation a form of welfare in which businesses make allowances for disabled workers. The author suggests, however, that new technologies can help reverse this way of thinking. If people with disabilities are involved in the creation and implementation of technological aids in the workplace, accommodation will be less of an issue and technology will become a form of social empowerment that eliminates differences between disabled and non-disabled employees.

PERIODICALS

Andrews, Linda Wasmer. "Hiring People with Intellectual Disabilities: Employers Are Discovering that with a Little Help, Workers with Such Disabilities Can Take on a Wide Array of Jobs." *HRMagazine*, vol. 50, no. 7, July 2005, p. 72. According to this article, people with intellectual disabilities are finally entering the workforce in record numbers. It concludes that employers, once fearful that such workers would not meet expectations, are now realizing the financial rewards of hiring the mentally disabled.

Appleby, Julie. "Wal-Mart Memo Sparks Criticism." *USA Today*, October 27, 2005, p. 3B. Appleby reports on a memo passed through management of the retailer outlets that implies that stores should dissuade unhealthy applicants from applying for jobs. The author states that the disabilities community is shocked by the implications of not hiring people based on level of fitness.

Berkman, Eric T. "1st U.S. Circuit Court of Appeals Rules Company Not Required to Allow Employee to Work Remotely." *Rhode Island Lawyers Weekly*, September 4, 2006, p. 6. This article reports on a circuit court's decision to hold that a manufacturing company is not required to permit an employee with asthma to work at home because of his claimed allergic reaction to plant chemicals.

Ceniceros, Roberto. "Court Puts Brakes on UPS Ban: Safety Plans that Bar Deaf Drivers Violate Bias Law, Ruling Says." *Business Insurance*, vol. 40, no. 42, October 16, 2006, p. 1. A circuit court of appeals found that United Postal Service violated the ADA by barring hearing impaired employees from driving delivery vans. Ceniceros reports that the ruling may have implications for other businesses with potentially discriminatory policies.

Danaher, Maria Greco. "Employer Must Accommodate Employee Perceived as Disabled." *HRMagazine*, vol. 50, no. 9, September 2005, p. 144. A U.S. circuit court case maintains that employees who are merely perceived as having a disability are protected by the ADA. Danaher reports that other rulings on similar cases, however, have not reached the same conclusion, proving that perceived disability is a debated concept.

Duman, Jill. "Bill to Limit Suits under ADA Fails." *Recorder*, May 4, 2005, p. 1. State senator Charles Poochigian's bill to allow California businesses a grace period to comply with infractions of the ADA was the subject of committee wrangling, according to this article.

Greenwald, Judy. "FedEx Disability Bias Case Dismissed; Injured Worker Insufficiently Impaired to Claim ADA Protection." *Business Insurance*, vol. 39, no. 48, November 28, 2005, p. 4. Greenwald reports on a former employee of FedEx who lost a lawsuit in which he claimed his on-the-job injuries proved reason for dismissal. According to this article, he intends to take the case before the U.S. Supreme Court in order to have some guidelines established that make clear how much burden of proof is necessary to claim protection under the ADA.

Kennedy, R. Bryan, and Nicole K. Harris. "Employing Persons with Severe Disabilities: Much Work Remains to Be Done." *Journal of Employment Counseling*, vol. 42, no. 3, September 2005, p. 133. A statistical evaluation by the authors shows the promise of a federal program that seeks to hire people with disabilities to work a Department of Defense installation.

Kleinfield, N. R. "Diabetics in the Workplace Confront a Tangle of Laws." *New York Times*, December 26, 2006, p. A1. Kleinfield reports that diabetics are facing job loss due to their condition. According to this article, the courts and businesses are struggling to decide if diabetes is a legitimate disability protected by law.

O'Brien, Ruth. "Other Voices at the Workplace: Gender, Disability, and an Alternative Ethic of Care." *Signs*, vol. 30, no. 2, winter 2005, p. 1529. The ADA was devised by Congress to enact sweeping change in employment policies regarding people with disabilities. O'Brien contends that the courts, however, have limited the power of the ADA, altering its intent to such a degree that it supports businesses in excluding people with disabilities from finding and holding jobs. Only a reworking by Congress can restore the ADA's original intent, according to this article.

Patel, Julie. "Veterans Health System Terminates Social Worker with Cerebral Palsy." *San Jose Mercury News*, August 1, 2006, p. 4. This article reports that a social worker with cerebral palsy was dismissed from her hospital position after breaking patient confidentiality. The social worker claims the hospital did not provide her with assistive devices that would have kept her from making the breach.

Scheck, Justin. "Mind Share: Once a Rarity, Mental Disability Claims Have Moved into the Mainstream." *Recorder*, March 17, 2005, p. 1. Mental disabilities now qualify as legitimate disorders protected by the ADA, according to this article. Scheck details case law that is mounting and proving the success of claims against employers who are unwilling to accommodate the needs of people with mental disabilities.

Zelek, Mark, and Anne Marie Estevez. "New ADA Guidelines Will Affect Many Employers." *Miami Daily Business Review*, September 28, 2004, p. 12. Changes to the accessibility guidelines of the ADA will likely cause headaches for employers who already struggle to keep up with all ADA codes, according to the article.

INTERNET DOCUMENTS

Foley, Nancy. "The Stigma of Not Working." Ragged Edge Online. Available online. URL: http://www.raggededgemagazine.com/departments/closerlook/001095.html. Posted May 24, 2006. A woman who suffers from chronic pain argues that many people have legitimate disabilities that keep them from working no matter how hard they try. The stigma of not being able to contribute to society through work, she asserts, is difficult to bear.

Reynolds, Dave. "Federal Programs Help Executives, Fail Workers with Disabilities." Ragged Edge Online. Available online. URL: http://www.raggededgemagazine.com/departments/closerlook/000567.html. Posted October 26, 2005. This article provides information concerning a federal program to provide jobs to people with disabilities which has disbursed funds of over $2 billion. Discrepancies between the amount of money allotted and the actual money distributed to the workers are also detailed. The 45,000 workers who were to benefit received wages of between $5 and $9, while the salaries of the executives of many of the nonprofit agencies involved were increased by nearly a third over three years.

Roberts, Gary. "My Unaccommodated Career." Ragged Edge Online. Available online. URL: http://www.raggededgemagazine.com/0500/b0500ft2.htm. Posted May/June 2000. A deaf social service worker employed by rehabilitative services finds that the agency is as discriminatory and unaccommodating toward people with disabilities as the general business world.

CHAPTER 8

ORGANIZATIONS AND AGENCIES

This chapter provides a list of advocacy organizations, government agencies, and other collectives that are connected to disability rights' issues. Government organizations have been given the task of monitoring the application of federal laws such as the Americans with Disabilities Act (ADA) and of disbursing federal aid to people with disabilities. Non-governmental organizations have had a much more pivotal role in expressing the need for federal protections. From the beginning of the disability rights movement, grassroots organizations fought for the passage of state and federal legislation that recognized the rights of the disabled. These organizations gave a face to the movement, and, with the members' tireless actions, gave the loose collective the momentum to effect change. Today, many of these organizations remain at the forefront of the struggle for education, employment, and health care, and of the fight against legalized assisted suicide.

Each listing in the following chapter provides (if available) the organization's web site (URL) and e-mail address, phone, TTY (or voice V/TTY), fax numbers, and postal address. Following the contact information is a brief description of the organization's mission or purpose. Researchers should be aware that contact information for an organization might change over time as the group relocates its headquarters or changes its Internet address. Occasionally, an organization may disband entirely or become dormant for a time. The best method of keeping up with such changes is to try and locate the desired organization through an Internet search engine and check the most recent posting of its contact information.

NATIONAL AND INTERNATIONAL ORGANIZATIONS

Adaptive Environments
URL: http://www.adaptenv.org

E-mail: info@
AdaptiveEnvironments.org

Phone: (617) 695-1225 (V/TTY)
Fax: (617) 482-8099
180-200 Portland Street
Suite 1
Boston, MA 02114
Since its founding in 1978, Adaptive Environments has worked to increase opportunities for individuals with disabilities through accessible design. While compliance with legal codes is one concern, the organization also promotes universal, or human-centered, design to make buildings and objects accessible to any individual, regardless of age or ability. In order to ensure the advance of accessible design, Adaptive Environments assists public and private entities in the design process, works closely with individuals with disabilities and the elderly in creating new designs, and provides educational materials and programs outlining the theories and practices of human-centered design. The organization's web site offers books for sale, links to project web sites, and other resources concerning accessible design.

Alexander Graham Bell
  Association for the Deaf and
  Hard of Hearing (AG Bell)
URL: http://www.agbell.org
E-mail: info@agbell.org
Phone: (202) 337-5220
TTY: (202) 337-5221
Fax: (202) 337-8314
3417 Volta Place, NW
Washington, DC 20007
AG Bell advocates for the independent living of individuals who are deaf or hard of hearing. The organization provides educational publications, scholarship and financial aid, and a network of support for individuals who are hearing impaired and their families. Their web site contains fact sheets on topics relating to hearing loss and impairment, as well as information on how to order the organization's books and periodicals, *The Volta Voice* and *The Volta Review.*

Alliance for Technology Access
  (ATA)
URL: http://www.ataccess.org
E-mail: ATAinfor@ATAccess.org
Phone: (707) 778-3011
TTY: (707) 778-3015
Fax: (707) 765-2080
1304 Southpoint Boulevard
Suite 240
Petaluma, CA 94954
ATA is a network promoting communication and cooperation between assistive technology resource centers, technology vendors and developers, and associate organizations and individuals. This interaction promotes the timely development of new and improved assistive technologies and ensures that these technologies are readily available to those who are in need. ATA resources for individuals, families, educators, and communities are available on the organization's web site, which provides information detailing the types of and ways in which accessible technologies can enhance lives.

American Association of the Deaf-Blind (AADB)
URL: http://www.aadb.org
E-mail: AADB-info@aadb.org
Phone: (301) 495-4403
TTY: (301) 495-4402
Fax: (301) 495-4404
8630 Fenton Street
Suite 121
Silver Spring, MD 20910
AADB is a nonprofit, consumer organization that works to promote independent living in an integrated community setting for individuals who have some combination of visual and hearing impairment. Through a mix of educational materials, outreach conferences, and advocacy projects, AADB works to ensure that opportunities for individuals who are deaf-blind are continued or increased. Fact sheets and archives of the organization's monthly newsletter can be found on the AADB web site.

American Association of People with Disabilities (AAPD)
URL: http://www.aapd-dc.org
E-mail: aapd@aol.com
Phone: (202) 457-0046 (V/TTY)
   (800) 840-8844 (V/TTY)
Fax: (202) 457-0473
1629 K Street, NW
Suite 503
Washington, DC 20006
Founded in 1995, five years after the passage of the ADA, AAPD advocates for the full societal integration of individuals with any type of disability. The organization provides an opportunity for individuals with disabilities to unite and exercise leadership to ensure that their voices and concerns are heard and taken seriously. Through advocacy efforts, the Justice for All e-mail network, and policy reports and activities, AAPD works to achieve nationwide compliance with legislation prohibiting discrimination based on disability. Fact sheets, toolkits providing suggestions on organizational involvement, and general resources are all available on the AAPD web site.

American Association on Intellectual and Developmental Disabilities (AAIDD)
URL: http://www.aaidd.org
Phone: (800) 424-3688
   (202) 387-1968
Fax: (202) 387-2193
444 North Capitol Street, NW
Suite 846
Washington, DC 20001
Formerly the American Association on Mental Retardation, AAIDD is dedicated to increasing and enhancing the opportunities available to individuals with intellectual and developmental disabilities. By advocating for improved health, education, and vocational services, the organization also works to ensure that the basic human rights of the developmentally disabled are not violated. AAIDD online bookstore offers publications on developmental disabilities and related topics for sale, and the AAIDD's web site provides resources such as fact sheets

and general information on topics such as the federal funding and government programs relating to issues concerning developmental disabilities.

American Bar Association Commission on Mental and Physical Disability Law
URL: http://www.abanet.org/ disability
E-mail: cmpdl@abanet.org
Phone: (202) 662-1570
Fax: (202) 662-1032
740 15th Street, NW
9th Floor
Washington, DC 20005
This commission within the American Bar Association (ABA) works not only to guarantee that the ABA is working to uphold and pursue the legal rights of individuals with disabilities, it also promotes full participation and nondiscrimination of lawyers with disabilities within the legal field. The commission offers the Comprehensive Disability Law Service (CDLS), a subscription-based service that offers a combination of periodicals and searchable online databases on pertinent legal events relating to disability law. The CDLS catalog includes the *Mental and Physical Disability Law Reporter,* the *Mental and Physical Disability Law Digest*, the *Monograph on State Disability Discrimination Laws*, and access to the *Online Reporter Research Database* and the *Online Digest*. The commission's web site also maintains a directory of disability lawyers.

American Council of the Blind (ACB)
URL: http://www.acb.org
E-mail: info@acb.org
Phone: (202) 467-5081
　(800) 424-8666
Fax: (202) 467-5085
1155 15th Street, NW
Suite 1004
Washington, DC 20005
Through its numerous and varied programs, ACB works to provide ever-increasing and improving opportunities for individuals who are blind or visually impaired. All positions on the ACB Board of Directors, except that of secretary and treasurer, are required to be filled by individuals who are legally blind. To advance its cause, the organization uses educational materials and services, government advocacy, and training seminars on issues relating to visual impairment. ACB publishes the monthly magazine *The Braille Forum* and produces *ACB Reports*, a monthly, 30-minute informational radio program, in addition to other radio and television public service announcements. Back issues of the magazine, ACB radio, and numerous fact sheets and general information resources are available on the ACB web site.

American Deafness and Rehabilitation Association (ADARA)
URL: http://www.adara.org
E-mail: ADARAorgn@aol.com
P.O. Box 480
Myersville, MD 21773

ADARA is an organization dedicated to enhancing the lives of individuals who are deaf or hard of hearing through the expansion of professional opportunities for these individuals. A biennial conference and publications such as *JADARA: The Journal for Professionals Networking for Excellence in Service Delivery with Individuals who are Deaf and Hard of Hearing*, and *ADARA Update* are utilized by the organization to promote expanded opportunities and outreach.

American Disabled for Attendant Programs Today (ADAPT)
URL: http://www.adapt.org
E-mail: adapt@adapt.org
Phone: (303) 733-9324
201 South Cherokee
Denver, CO 80223
Founded in 1983 to fight for accessible public transportation in Denver, Colorado, the acronym ADAPT first stood for American Disabled for Accessible Public Transit. Following the passage of the ADA in 1990, the organization redefined its goals and renamed itself. Encouraging deinstitutionalization and the promotion of community-based attendant service programs form the core of ADAPT's new mission. Information on organized events and training sessions as well as brochures on ADAPT and the *ADAPT Action Report* are all available on the group's web site.

American Foundation for the Blind (AFB)
URL: http://www.afb.org
E-mail: afbinfo@afb.net
Phone: (212) 502-7600
Fax: (212) 502-7777
11 Penn Plaza
Suite 300
New York, NY 10001
The nonprofit organization AFB provides national public policy advocacy, enhanced access to assistive technologies, and other services to enhance the lives of individuals with vision loss. Helen Keller was closely associated with AFB during her life, and a collection of her works and belongings are retained by the organization to honor her commitment to the blind community. Additionally, AFB's web site provides articles and fact sheets on topics such as education, employment, and living with vision loss.

American Society for Deaf Children (ASDC)
URL: http://www.deafchildren.org
E-mail: asdc@deafchildren.org
Phone: (717) 703-0073
(866) 895-4206
Fax: (717) 909-5599
3820 Hartzdale Drive
Camp Hill, PA 17011
Founded in 1967 as a parent support group, the primary goals of ASDC continue to focus on providing families of deaf children with a community of understanding and encouragement. The organization's web site provides online links to articles pertaining to raising deaf children, as well as numerous resources providing general information on

issues relating to education and assistive technology. ASDC advocacy efforts are also detailed on the web site.

The Arc
URL: http://www.thearc.org
E-mail: info@thearc.org
Phone: (301) 565-3842
   (800) 433-5255
Fax: (301) 565-3843
1010 Wayne Avenue
Suite 650
Silver Spring, MD 20910
Founded in 1950, making it the oldest advocacy organization of its kind, The Arc was originally formed by parents of children with developmental disabilities. It was originally known as the National Association for Retarded Children (NARC) but was often abbreviated as the ARC. It again changed its name in 1991 to The Arc because members wished to avoid the stigmatizing term "retarded." The Arc works to ensure that individuals with intellectual and developmental disabilities are granted the same rights and opportunities in society as all other people. The organization provides a community of support for individuals, parents, and families and encourages participation in activities that create positive changes in governmental policies impacting these individuals. Fact sheets and family guides are available on The Arc's web site.

Association of Programs for Rural
   Independent Living (APRIL)
URL: http://www.april-rural.org

E-mail: april-elissa@neo.rr.com
Phone: (330) 678-7648
Fax: (330) 678-7658
5903 Powdermill Road
Kent, OH 44240
APRIL is a grassroots coalition of organizations and individuals nationwide, all with the shared goal of promoting and aiding independent living for individuals with disabilities in rural areas. The organization's national advocacy efforts are aimed at improving the independent living options of these individuals. Some cornerstone issues include accessible transportation and increasing access to assistive technology. APRIL's yearly newsletter and reports can be found on the group's web site, along with links to web sites on transit accessibility.

Association of University
   Centers on Disabilities
   (AUCD)
URL: http://www.aucd.org
E-mail: aucdinfo@aucd.org
Phone: (301) 588-8252
Fax: (301) 588-2842
1010 Wayne Avenue
Suite 920
Silver Spring, MD 20910
AUCD is a coalition of university-based programs addressing issues related to developmental and other forms of disabilities. This organization fosters the cooperation of the university centers with their surrounding communities, encouraging strategies of advocacy, networking, and leadership to address the needs and problems faced by

the disability community. Publications, newsletters, and brochures can be accessed on the AUCD web site.

Association on Higher Education and Disability (AHEAD)
URL: http://www.ahead.org
E-mail: ahead@ahead.org
Phone: (704) 947-7779
Fax: (704) 948-7779
107 Commerce Center Drive
Suite 204
Huntersville, NC 28078
AHEAD, an organization of education professionals, works to ensure that individuals with disabilities are afforded equal opportunities in postsecondary education. *The Journal of Postsecondary Education and Disability* in combination with an e-mail newsletter, brochures, and multimedia productions keep educators abreast of new developments in the field. Conferences and training seminars provide individuals the opportunity to discuss, learn, and promote the opportunities available for individuals with disabilities in a collegiate setting.

Autism Society of American (ASA)
URL: http://www.autism-society.org
Phone: (301) 657-0881
(800) 328-8476
7910 Woodmont Avenue
Suite 300
Bethesda, MD 20814

Founded in 1965 following the publication of *Infantile Autism: The Syndrome and Its Implications for a Neural Theory of Behavior*, by Bernard Rimland, ASA continues to serve as a support and resource center for individuals with autism, their families, and professionals who work with autistic individuals. Through the dissemination of educational materials, promotion of research, and advocacy efforts, ASA strives to inform the public and society at large about autism and related issues. Fact sheets and current events about autism are provided on the ASA web site, and members can access *Autism Advocate* magazine.

Center for Accessible Technology (CforAT)
URL: http://www.cforat.org
E-mail: info1@cforat.org
Phone: (510) 841-3224
TTY: (510) 841-5621
Fax: (510) 841-7956
CforAT Computer Lab
2525 8th Street
Suite 12-A
Berkeley, CA 94710
The CforAT, formerly known as the Disabled Children's Computer Group, works to ensure that individuals with disabilities have access to computers. Through its web site consultation and testing services, this organization is dedicated to increasing the availability of accessible computer technology for individuals with disabilities. Details about CforAT's programs are available on the organization's web site.

Center for Universal Design (CUD)
URL: http://www.design.ncsu.
edu/cud
Phone: (919) 515-3082
(800) 647-6777
Fax: (919) 515-8951
College of Design
North Carolina State University
Campus Box 8613
Raleigh, NC 27695

The Center for Universal Design, part of the College of Design at North Carolina State University, was founded to advance the principles of universal design, pioneered by Ronald Mace. The center promotes design that is accessible to all individuals, regardless or age or ability. To achieve this end, consultation with builders and manufacturers as well as extensive research (including publication of informational and educational materials) serves as the basis for much of the center's work. Many of these publications and materials are available on the center's web site.

Consortium for Citizens with Disabilities (CCD)
URL: http://www.c-c-d.org
E-mail: info@c-c-d.org
Phone: (202) 783-2229
Fax: (202) 783-8250
1660 L Street, NW
Suite 700
Washington, DC 20036

CCD is an advocacy organization comprised of member organizations, all with the shared goal of increasing federal legislation that protects and increases the rights and independence of individuals with disabilities in American society. To achieve this goal, the coalition works directly with members of Congress to increase government awareness of disability rights issues. Additionally, CCD helps individuals become involved on a grassroots level and have their voices heard in the legislative process. CCD provides numerous fact sheets, articles, testimony, and press releases on its web site.

Council for Disability Rights (CDR)
URL: http://www.
disabilityrights.org
Phone: (312) 444-9484
TTY: (312) 444-1967
Fax: (312) 444-1977
30 East Adams
Suite 1130
Chicago, IL 60603

CDR works to promote integrated, independent living for individuals with disabilities. It believes participation by these individuals and their families is essential to forward the independent living movement. The council takes stands on pertinent issues within the disability rights community such as assisted suicide, attendant care, and employment. CDR's web site provides links to reading lists, current events articles, and other organization and informational web sites.

Council for Exceptional Children (CEC)
URL: http://www.cec.sped.org
Phone: (888) 232-7733
TTY: (866) 915-5000
Fax: (703) 264-9494
1110 North Glebe Road
Suite 300
Arlington, VA 22201
An international organization of education professionals, CEC provides guidelines and standards to ensure the best educational opportunities for students with disabilities or who are gifted. Advocacy efforts focus on creating or amending government policies so that these parameters will be enforced on a national level. Many resources and articles relating to current projects are available on the CEC web site, and additional publications can be purchased from the organization's online bookstore.

DisabilityInfo.gov
URL: http://www.disabilityinfo. gov
E-mail: disabilityinfo@dol.gov
Phone: (800) 333-4636 (V/TTY)
This online resource for disability-related government information was formed in 2002 with President George W. Bush's New Freedom Initiative. Visitors to the web site can search for government policy relating to programs for individuals with disabilities in the fields of education, employment, housing, and transportation, among others.

Disability Resources, Inc.
URL: http://www. disabilityresources.org
E-mail: info@disabilityresources. org
Disability Resources, Inc., is an online database of information sources related to disability rights, compiled to raise awareness of disability issues. Topics are arranged alphabetically, and can be searched by state, disability, or organization. The monthly newsletter, *Disability Resources Monthly*, offers reviews of informative independent living publications and guides.

Disability Rights Advocates (DRA)
URL: http://www.dralegal.org
E-mail: general@dralegal.org
Phone: (510) 665-8644
TTY: (510) 665-8716
Fax: (510) 665-8511
2001 Center Street
Third Floor
Berkeley, CA 94704
DRA provides legal aid and general advocacy for individuals with disabilities nationwide through class action lawsuits as well as research and education efforts. Many of the projects taken on by the organization provide increased opportunities in all areas of life including education, employment, transportation, and health care. In order to ensure that individuals with disabilities are aware of their rights, DRA publishes "Know Your Rights" handbooks, and these are available through its web site. Information

on current DRA projects and links to additional resources can also be found on the web site.

Disability Rights Education and Defense Fund (DREDF)
URL: http://www.dredf.org
E-mail: info@dredf.org
Phone: (800) 348-4232 (V/TTY)
(510) 644-2555 (V/TTY)
Fax: (510) 841-8645
2212 Sixth Street
Berkeley, CA 94710
DREDF works to ensure that the civil and human rights of individuals with disabilities are observed and upheld in all aspects of life. Through activities such as national advocacy, awareness raising, and support of new legislation, the organization provides a voice for individuals with disabilities and their families. DREDF is dedicated to redefining social conceptions of disability to create a society in which complete integration and inclusion are possible. Press releases and publications on related activities are available on the DREDF web site.

Disabled Peoples' International (DPI)
URL: http://www.dpi.org
E-mail: info@dpi.org
Phone: (204) 287-8010
Fax: (204) 783-6270
902-388 Portage Avenue
Winnipeg, Manitoba
Canada R3C 0C8
DPI is a global coalition of organizations working together to ad-vance the rights of individuals with disabilities, establish full inclusion in society, and create new organizations to forward these goals. Articles, position papers, and information on topics such as education, bioethics, and rehabilitation can be found on the DPI web site.

Hearing Loss Association of America
URL: http://www.shhh.org
Phone: (301) 657-2248 (V/TTY)
Fax: (301) 913-9413
7910 Woodmont Avenue
Suite 1200
Bethesda, MD 20814
Formerly Self Help for Hard of Hearing People, Inc., the Hearing Loss Association of America seeks increased communication outlets for individuals with hearing impairments. Utilizing a network of state chapters, the organization disseminates information in an attempt to raise awareness about hearing loss and the need for assistive technology. Numerous resources on topics such as accessibility and education, as well as position papers, are available on the group's web site.

Job Accommodation Network (JAN)
URL: http://www.jan.wvu.edu
Phone: (304) 293-7186
(800) 526-7234
TTY: (877) 781-9403
Fax: (304) 293-5407
PO Box 6080
Morgantown, WV 26506

JAN, a project of the Office of Disability Employment Policy, provides aid to both individuals with disabilities and their employers to ensure equal opportunity and compliance with antidiscrimination laws. Individuals can call JAN and receive knowledgeable answers to questions related to workplace accommodations required by law, options to address accommodation shortcomings, and opportunities for self-employment. The JAN web site offers comprehensive information on the ADA, as well as specific information pertaining to employability of individuals with disabilities.

**Judge David L. Bazelon Center
  for Mental Health Law**
URL: http://www.bazelon.org
E-mail: info@bazelon.org
Phone: (202) 467-5730
TTY: (202) 467-4232
Fax: (202) 223-0409
1101 15th Street, NW
Suite 1212
Washington, DC 20005
The Bazelon Center for Mental Health Law serves as a legal advocacy organization for individuals with mental disabilities. The center provides litigation services in cases concerning the rights of individuals with disabilities. Additionally, the center's lobbying efforts have increased education, employment, and housing opportunities, enabling individuals with mental disabilities to live more integrated and independent lives. Some reports and

publications are available online, while others can be ordered from the center's bookstore. Current events articles regarding disability law are also available on the center's web site.

League for the Hard of Hearing
URL: http://www.lhh.org
E-mail: info@lhh.org
Phone: (917) 305-7700
TTY: (917) 305-7999
Fax: (917) 305-7888
50 Broadway
6th Floor
New York, NY 10004
The League for the Hard of Hearing is an advocacy organization dedicated to advancing and promoting hearing rehabilitation for all individuals with any form of hearing impairment, visual impairment, or combination of the two. Professionals at the league aid individuals in enhancing their ability to communicate. The league's web site provides fact sheets on hearing loss, assistive hearing devices, and other related topics.

**Learning Disabilities
  Association of America (LDA)**
URL: http://www.ldanatl.org
Phone: (412) 341-1515
Fax: (412) 344-0224
4156 Library Road
Pittsburgh, PA 15234
LDA advocates on behalf of individuals with learning disabilities and their families to promote societal equality. Additionally, the organization seeks a more complete under-

standing of learning disabilities in order to reduce their occurrence and to offer more appropriate methods of aiding individuals who have them. LDA offers a variety of services to aid individuals with learning disabilities and their families, and publishes many of their position papers and educational resources on the organization's web site.

**Mental Disability Rights
   International (MDRI)**
URL: http://www.mdri.org
E-mail: mdri@mdri.org
Phone: (202) 296-0800
Fax: (202) 728-3053
1156 15th Street, NW
Suite 1001
Washington, DC 20005
MDRI works to ensure that the rights of individuals with mental disabilities worldwide are protected and observed. By working closely with individuals with mental disabilities and their families, mental health care providers, legal experts, and human rights advocates, MDRI promotes appropriate legal reform. Exposé-style reports detailing human rights abuses of individuals with mental disability in various countries are available on the MDRI web site, as are reports detailing the projects aimed at correcting these problems.

Mental Health America
URL: http://www.
   mentalhealthamerica.net
Phone: (800) 969-6642
TTY: (800) 433-5959
Fax: (703) 684-5968

2000 North Beauregard Street
6th Floor
Alexandria, VA 22311
Formerly the National Mental Health Association, Mental Health America was renamed to convey the necessity of mental well-being for improved health and happiness for all Americans. The organization works to provide education on the importance of good mental health, increase access to appropriate care and treatment, reduce and end the stigma associated with mental illness and addiction, and encourage innovative research in mental health fields. Many fact sheets, organized by category, can be browsed on the organization's web site.

**Mobility International USA
   (MIUSA)**
URL: http://www.miusa.org
Phone: (541) 343-1284 (V/TTY)
Fax: (541) 343-6812
132 East Broadway
Suite 343
Eugene, OR 97401
Mobility International USA encourages individuals with disabilities and their supporters worldwide to take control of their lives and demand equal human rights. The organization fosters international conversation through educational exchange programs, offering individuals with disabilities the opportunity to learn and live in a culture outside of their own. Reports and articles detailing the benefits of these exchange programs are available in the National Clearinghouse

on Disability and Exchange, an information dissemination project sponsored by the U.S. Bureau of Educational and Cultural Affairs and run by MIUSA.

National Alliance on Mental Illness (NAMI)
URL: http://www.nami.org
Phone: (703) 524-7600
TTY: (703) 516-7227
Fax: (703) 524-9094
2107 Wilson Boulevard
Suite 300
Arlington, VA 22201
NAMI works to improve the lives of individuals with mental illness through a coalition of grassroots chapters, with the ultimate goal of eliminating mental illness entirely. These organizations cooperate to provide advocacy and support at the national, state, and local levels to advance the rights of individuals with mental illnesses and reduce the stigma attached to these conditions. Fact sheets are available on the NAMI web site, and members can access publications such as *Advocate* magazine online.

National Association for Visually Handicapped (NAVH)
URL: http://www.navh.org
E-mail: navh@navh.org
Phone: (212) 255-2804
Fax: (212) 727-2931
22 West 21st Street
6th Floor
New York, NY 10010
NAVH seeks to provide services for individuals who have lost only part of their sight, a subpopulation that the organization believes is neglected by many other groups dedicated to aiding individuals who are blind. NAVH encourages and aids individuals in using what sight ability they retain in order to continue living independently. The organization also promotes the use of low vision aids and large print publications to assist in the transition from full sighted to limited sighted life. Additionally, the organization offers a large print loan library.

National Association of the Deaf (NAD)
URL: http://www.nad.org
Phone: (301) 587-1788
TTY: (301) 587-1789
Fax: (301) 587-1791
8630 Fenton Street
Suite 820
Silver Spring, MD 20910
NAD works to ensure that individuals who are deaf enjoy the same rights and opportunities as individuals who have the ability to hear. The organization's web site provides information on numerous issues, such as housing, education, and employment, and encourages individuals to become self advocates, using this information to further their own rights and goals. Subscriptions to online newsletters are available for free on the NAD web site.

National Center for Dissemination of Disability Research (NCDDR)
URL: http://www.ncddr.org

Phone: (512) 476-6861 (V/TTY)
(800) 266-1832 (V/TTY)
Fax: (512) 476-2286
Southwest Educational
Development Laboratory
211 East 7th Street
Suite 448
Austin, TX 78701
NCDDR is a project of the Southwest Educational Development Laboratory (SEDL) that seeks to provide cutting edge disability research to organizations that receive grants from the National Institute on Disability and Rehabilitation Research to make improved products for individuals with disabilities. NCDDR also works to ensure that the research adheres to uniform test standards (and review processes) and is widely available to consumers. Guidelines outlining the standards that define quality research can be found on the NCDDR web site.

National Council on Disability
(NCD)
URL: http://www.ncd.gov
E-mail: ncd@ncd.gov
Phone: (202) 272-2004
TTY: (202) 272-2074
Fax: (202) 272-2022
1331 F Street, NW
Suite 850
Washington, DC 20004
Through their reports to the U.S. government, this independent government agency works to ensure that all Americans are afforded equal opportunity to pursue an independent and integrated life within U.S. society. One such report, *Towards Independence*, proposed in 1986 the implementation of national legislation to protect the civil rights of citizens with disabilities; this led to the passage of the ADA. At present, NCD is working on the project *Investing in Independence* in correlation with President George W. Bush's New Freedom Initiative, details of which can be found on the NCD web site.

National Council on
Independent Living (NCIL)
URL: http://www.ncil.org
E-mail: ncil@ncil.org
Phone: (202) 207-0334
TTY: (202) 207-0340
Fax: (202) 207-0341
1710 Rhode Island Avenue, NW
5th Floor
Washington, DC 20036
NCIL is the grassroots, umbrella organization for more than 700 Centers for Independent Living (CILs), Statewide Independent Living Councils (SILCs), individuals with disabilities, and various other organizations nationwide that advocate on their behalf. NCIL was formed following the passage of the 1978 amendments to the Rehabilitation Act in order to ensure that the funding allocated for independent living centers was used properly and that the building of CILs continued. NCIL continues to advocate for improved disability rights legislation, much of which is outlined on the organization's web site.

National Disability Rights Network (NDRN)
URL: http://www.ndrn.org
E-mail: info@ndrn.org
Phone: (202) 408-9514
TTY: (202) 408-9521
Fax: (202) 408-9520
900 Second Street, NE
Suite 211
Washington, DC 20002
NDRN provides legal advocacy for individuals with disabilities and attempts to increase the opportunities for individuals with disabilities to live fully participatory lives in American society with all the rights and protections afforded to all citizens. The membership consists of organizations created under the federal Protection and Advocacy (P&A) Systems and Client Assistance Programs (CAP). The parent organization offers training seminars for P&A and CAP professionals to ensure that advocacy efforts on behalf of individuals with disabilities nationwide are addressing issues of the disability community appropriately.

National Down Syndrome Society (NDSS)
URL: http://www.ndss.org
E-mail: info@ndss.org
Phone: (800) 221-4602
Fax: (212) 979-2873
666 Broadway
New York, NY 10012
NDSS is a national organization dedicated to engaging in programs and policies that provide enhanced opportunities for individuals with Down syndrome and their families to live inclusive, integrated lives. In order to improve the quality of life of these individuals, NDSS promotes national advocacy, research, and education. The NDSS web site serves as a starting point for those interested in learning about Down syndrome; numerous articles containing general information about the condition are located there.

National Easter Seals Society
URL: http://www.easterseals.com
Phone: (312) 726-6200
   (800) 221-6827
TTY: (312) 726-4258
Fax: (312) 726-1494
230 West Monroe Street
Suite 1800
Chicago, IL 60606
Founded in 1907, Easter Seals has provided aid to individuals with disabilities and their families for nearly a century. At Easter Seals chapters nationwide, individuals can receive anything from medical rehabilitation to job training to child care to adult day services. The legislative advocacy center of the organization works to promote the passage of various federal bills and programs to ensure the continued enhancement of quality of life for individuals with disabilities and their families. Information on specific, current Easter Seals projects can be found on the organization's web site, along with general facts and information on disability.

National Federation of the Blind (NFB)
URL: http://www.nfb.org
Phone: (410) 659-9314
Fax: (410) 685-5653
1800 Johnson Street
Baltimore, MD 21230
The programs and advocacy of NFB are intended to promote and secure increased opportunities for individuals who are blind. Independence is an important aspect of NFB's platforms, and the organization works hard to encourage and support individuals who seek independent living. Access to the publications *Braille Monitor*, *Future Reflections*, and other general information resources about vision loss, related technology, and reports are available on the NFB web site.

National Organization on Disability (NOD)
URL: http://www.nod.org
E-mail: ability@nod.org
Phone: (202) 293-5960
TTY: (202) 293-5968
Fax: (202) 293-7999
910 16th Street, NW
Suite 600
Washington, DC 20006
NOD works through its grassroots outreach programs to help individuals with disabilities achieve more complete integration and inclusion in their communities and society. These outreach programs—the Community Partnership Program and the National Partnership Program—are only two of the many specialized programs sponsored by NOD to raise awareness about disability rights. Other programs include the Religion and Disability Program, the World Committee on Disability, and the Start on Success Student Internship Program. The NOD web site provides comprehensive information on these programs and others.

National Spinal Cord Injury Association (NSCIA)
URL: http://www.spinalcord.org
E-mail: info@spinalcord.org
Phone: (301) 214-4006
(800) 962-9629
Fax: (301) 990-0445
6701 Democracy Boulevard
Suite 300-9
Bethesda, MD 20817
Formed in 1948, NSCIA utilizes education and support to promote independent living for individuals who have received severe spinal cord injuries. The association works to raise awareness nationwide with regard to the ongoing research developments, public policies, and education relating to spinal cord injury. The publication of the organization, *SCI Life*, is available online with free membership registration.

National Theater for the Deaf (NTD)
URL: http://www.ntd.org
E-mail: ntd-info@ntd.org
Phone: (860) 236-4193 (V/TTY)
Fax: (860) 236-4163
139 North Main Street
West Hartford, CT 06107

Using American Sign Language in its productions, NTD has been presenting theater performances internationally for nearly 40 years. The organization runs the NTD Professional Theater School to train deaf individuals in performance arts, and it sponsors a similar program for deaf actors in junior high and high school. Details about current projects and performances can be found on the NTD web site.

National Wheelchair Basketball Association (NWBA)
URL: http://www.nwba.org
Phone: (719) 266-4082
Fax: (719) 266-4876
6165 Lehman Drive
Suite 101
Colorado Springs, CO 80918
NWBA is the governing organization that directs 181 teams and 22 conferences of wheelchair basketball players in the United States. There are teams for men and women, and they compete on the intercollegiate as well as youth levels. As the oldest disability sports organization, NWBA has worked since its founding in 1948 to increase the opportunity for individuals with disabilities to participate in competitive sports. Team lists and the organization's history can be found on the NWBA web site.

Not Dead Yet (NDY)
URL: http://www.notdeadyet.
org
Phone: (708) 209-1500
TTY: (708) 209-1826

Fax: (708) 209-1735
7521 Madison Street
Forest Park, IL 60130
Formed in 1996 following the acquittal of Jack Kevorkian on charges of assisted suicide, NDY is the premier organization leading the disability rights community's opposition to assisted suicide. NDY has led many demonstrations protesting "Right to Die" court cases and the portrayal of assisted suicide in films such as *Million Dollar Baby*. Articles on assisted suicide issues can be found on the NDY web site.

Office of Disability Employment Policy (ODEP)
URL: http://www.dol.gov/odep
Phone: (866) 633-7365
TTY: (877) 889-5627
200 Constitution Avenue, NW
Washington, DC 20210
ODEP is an agency within the U.S. Department of Labor charged with creating, evaluating, and suggesting reform for federal policies regarding the employment of individuals with disabilities. Information about these policies can be found on the ODEP web site.

Paralyzed Veterans of American (PVA)
URL: http://www.pva.org
E-mail: info@pva.org
Phone: (800) 424-8200
TTY: (800) 795-4327
801 18th Street, NW
Washington, DC 20006
PVA advocates for increased and improved health care options, re-

search, civil rights, and services for veterans of the U.S. armed forces who are paralyzed as a result of spinal cord injury or dysfunction. Information regarding specific areas of interest including architectural barriers, sports and recreation, and veterans benefits can be found on the PVA web site.

Rehabilitation International (RI)
URL: http://www.
   rehab-international.org
E-mail: ri@riglobal.org
Phone: (212) 420-1500
Fax: (212) 505-0871
25 East 21st Street
4th Floor
New York, NY 10010
RI is an organization fostering the cooperation and partnership of disability organizations worldwide in order to more completely address the needs of individuals with disabilities and their families. The promotion of global disability rights leads RI to work closely with the United Nations (UN), and the organization encourages UN member states to adhere to guidelines set forth by UN committees on disability. Additionally, educational, research, and training programs worldwide form an important part of RI's international outreach. RI publications and information detailing the organization's projects can be found on the official web site.

Society for Disability Studies
   (SDS)
URL: http://www.uic.edu/orgs/sds

Phone: (312) 996-4664
Fax: (312) 996-7743
Department of Disability and
   Human Development
University of Illinois at Chicago
   (MC 626)
1640 W. Roosevelt Road, #236
Chicago, IL 60608
SDS is an academic organization dedicated to advancing scholarship in the field of disability studies. The official publication of the organization, *Disability Studies Quarterly*, provides articles from scholars' perspectives on disability related issues, as well as articles from the perspectives of individuals directly involved in the disability rights movement. Cross disciplinary study forms the basis for this field, and submissions from a diverse, international community are encouraged. The SDS web site provides information on the society and its ongoing activities.

TASH
URL: http://www.tash.org
Phone: (202) 263-5600
Fax: (202) 637-0138
1025 Vermont Avenue
Floor 7
Washington, DC 20005
TASH, a worldwide civil rights organization working on behalf of individuals with any type of disability, is dedicated to achieving full societal integration and participation for individuals with disabilities. Formerly known as The Association for Persons with Severe Handicaps, the organization dropped its full name in 1995 but kept its well-known

acronym. Through advocacy efforts, educational outreach, and government policy development, TASH has been successful in shaping the world into one that is more accepting and accommodating to individuals with disabilities. TASH has been at the forefront in the fight to eliminate barriers to people with disabilities, and it continues to work to ensure that the civil and human rights of individuals with disabilities are observed. Articles on specific advocacy projects and positions of the organization can be found on its web site.

United Cerebral Palsy (UCP)
URL: http://www.ucp.org
E-mail: info@ucp.org
Phone: (202) 776-0406
(800) 872-5827
Fax: (202) 776-0414
1660 L Street, NW
Suite 700
Washington, DC 20036
Since its founding in 1949, UCP has worked to ensure a high quality of life for individuals with cerebral palsy, focusing on issues such as access to gainful employment and education. As a charity, the organization utilizes the funds it receives to promote the independence and integration of individuals with disabilities. Access to public policy reports, press releases, and UCP newsletters is available for free on the organization's web site.

United Spinal Association
URL: http://www.unitedspinal.org
E-mail: info@unitedspinal.org

Phone: (718) 803-3782
Fax: (718) 803-0414
75-20 Astoria Boulevard
Jackson Heights, NY 11370
United Spinal Association encourages individuals with spinal injury or disease to actively pursue their goals and participate fully in their communities. Through research, education, advocacy, and support the association provides opportunities for members to integrate into society. Articles from the online magazine *Action* can be accessed through the United Spinal Association's web site, which also archives fact sheets and informative resources on spinal injury and advocacy projects.

United States Access Board
URL: http://www.access-board.
gov
E-mail: info@access-board.gov
Phone: (202) 272-0080
(800) 872-2253
TTY: (202) 272-0082
(800) 993-2822
Fax: (202) 272-0081
1331 F Street, NW
Suite 1000
Washington, DC 20004
An independent federal agency created in 1973, the U.S. Access Board determines the accessibility guidelines for all buildings, vehicles, and technology in the United States. The board, which consists of both government and public members, enforces these standards and provides training and consultation to aid entities in achieving

accessible design standards. Documents defining these guidelines are available on the Access Board's web site.

**United States Equal
  Employment Opportunity
  Commission (EEOC)**
URL: http://www.eeoc.gov
E-mail: info@ask.eeoc.gov
Phone: (800) 669-4000
TTY: (800) 669-6820
1801 L Street, NW
Washington, DC 20507
The EEOC is charged with creating policy ensuring equal employment opportunities for all Americans. Additionally the commission, comprised of five members (who must first be appointed by the president and then approved by the Senate), approves litigation relating to employment discrimination claims based on national legislation such as the ADA. The EEOC web site provides facts about discrimination and links to the texts of germane laws.

Very Special Arts (VSA)
URL: http://www.vsarts.org
E-mail: info@vsarts.org
Phone: (202) 628-2800
    (800) 933-8721
TTY: (202) 737-0645
Fax: (202) 429-0868
818 Connecticut Avenue, NW
Suite 600
Washington, DC 20006
VSA provides arts education and performance opportunities for individuals with disabilities. VSA awards scholarships and grants every year, recognizing the abilities of artists with disabilities and encouraging them to pursue artistic careers. Details on different programs and awards are available on the VSA web site.

Wheelchair Sports, USA
URL: http://www.wsusa.org
E-mail: wsusa@aol.com
Phone/Fax: (732) 422-4546
P.O. Box 5266
Kendall Park, NJ 08824
Wheelchair Sports, USA strives to make a variety of competitive sports opportunities available to athletes in wheelchairs. Run by and for wheelchair athletes and their supporters and fans, this organization seeks to provide competitions for individuals competing at all levels from novice to professional. The Wheelchair Sports, USA web site provides comprehensive information concerning the programs available.

**World Institute on Disability
  (WID)**
URL: http://www.wid.org
E-mail: wid@wid.org
Phone: (510) 763-4100
TTY: (510) 208-9496
Fax: (510) 763-4109
510 16th Street
Suite 100
Oakland, CA 94612
WID is a civil rights organization for individuals with disabilities. Many of their projects have the stated goal of promoting integration into society through economic

independence, appropriate health care services, assistive technology, and the addressing of disability rights issues on a global scale. WID works to advance its goals through the dissemination of research and education that encourages society as a whole to embrace disability rights issues. Publications are available for order online.

PART III

APPENDICES

APPENDIX A

THE REHABILITATION ACT OF 1973 (29 U.S.C. § 701 ET SEQ.): SECTION 504

Section 504 of the Rehabilitation Act of 1973 is the foundation of civil rights law for people with disabilities. The brief section was originally a sentence in the Rehabilitation Act, but the concise phrasing seemed to provide unlimited opportunity for disabled individuals to participate in any program or service receiving federal funds. Most significantly, schools and public transportation (that operated on federal funds) would have to expand their services so that people with disabilities could access them. In addition, the law required courts, hopsitals, museums, airports, and other federally funded institutions to become accessible. Section 504 did have its shortcomings, however. Its wording did not specify any enforcement procedures or institute compliance deadlines. The law also did not apply to any services or institutions not receiving federal aid. The text of Section 504 has been amended over time and appears in its current form below.

(a) Promulgation of rules and regulations

No otherwise qualified individual with a disability in the United States, as defined in section 705 (20) of this title [Title 29], shall, solely by reason of her or his disability, be excluded from the participation in, be denied the benefits of, or be subjected to discrimination under any program or activity receiving Federal financial assistance or under any program or activity conducted by any Executive agency or by the United States Postal Service. The head of each such agency shall promulgate such regulations as may be necessary to carry out the amendments to this section made by the Rehabilitation, Comprehensive Services, and Developmental Disabilities Act of 1978. Copies of any proposed regulation shall be submitted to appropriate authorizing committees of the Congress, and such regulation may take effect no earlier than the thirtieth day after the date on which such regulation is so submitted to such committees.

(b) "Program or activity" defined

For the purposes of this section, the term "program or activity" means all of the operations of—

(1)

(A) a department, agency, special purpose district, or other instrumentality of a State or of a local government; or

(B) the entity of such State or local government that distributes such assistance and each such department or agency (and each other State or local government entity) to which the assistance is extended, in the case of assistance to a State or local government;

(2)

(A) a college, university, or other postsecondary institution, or a public system of higher education; or

(B) a local educational agency (as defined in section 7801 of title 20), system of vocational education, or other school system;

(3)

(A) an entire corporation, partnership, or other private organization, or an entire sole proprietorship—

(i) if assistance is extended to such corporation, partnership, private organization, or sole proprietorship as a whole; or

(ii) which is principally engaged in the business of providing education, health care, housing, social services, or parks and recreation; or

(B) the entire plant or other comparable, geographically separate facility to which Federal financial assistance is extended, in the case of any other corporation, partnership, private organization, or sole proprietorship; or

(4) any other entity which is established by two or more of the entities described in paragraph (1), (2), or (3); any part of which is extended Federal financial assistance.

(c) Significant structural alterations by small providers

Small providers are not required by subsection (a) of this section to make significant structural alterations to their existing facilities for the purpose of assuring program accessibility, if alternative means of providing the services are available. The terms used in this subsection shall be construed with reference to the regulations existing on March 22, 1988.

(d) Standards used in determining violation of section

The standards used to determine whether this section has been violated in a complaint alleging employment discrimination under this section shall be the standards applied under title I of the Americans with Disabilities Act of 1990 (42 U.S.C. 12111 et seq.) and the provisions of sections 501 through 504, and 510, of the Americans with Disabilities Act of 1990 (42 U.S.C. 12201–12204 and 12210), as such sections relate to employment.

Source: U.S. House of Representatives, Office of the Law Revision Counsel. http://uscode.house.gov.

APPENDIX B

THE AMERICANS WITH DISABILITIES ACT OF 1990 (42 U.S.C. § 12101 ET SEQ.): TITLE I EXCERPTS PROHIBITING DISCRIMINATION IN EMPLOYMENT

The Americans with Disabilities Act of 1990 (Public Law 101-336) is the cornerstone of disability rights. The act is divided into five titles, of which Title I prohibits discrimination against people with disabilities in the workplace. This title specifically protects against discrimination in job application procedures, hiring or discharge, compensation, advancement, training, and other privileges of employment. These protections are afforded to qualified disabled individuals as defined by the title. The wording of the title also introduced the concepts of "undue hardship" and "reasonable accommodation," which have proved controversial in applying the law.

SEC. 101. DEFINITIONS.

As used in this title:

(1) COMMISSION- The term 'Commission' means the Equal Employment Opportunity Commission established by section 705 of the Civil Rights Act of 1964 (42 U.S.C. 2000e-4).

(2) COVERED ENTITY- The term 'covered entity' means an employer, employment agency, labor organization, or joint labor-management committee.

(3) EMPLOYEE- The term 'employee' means an individual employed by an employer.

Appendix B

(4) EMPLOYER-

(A) The term 'employer' means a person engaged in an industry affecting commerce who has 15 or more employees for each working day in each of 20 or more calendar weeks in the current or preceding calendar year, and any agent of such person, except that, for two years following the effective date of this title, an employer means a person engaged in an industry affecting commerce who has 25 or more employees for each working day in each of 20 or more calendar weeks in the current or preceding year, and any agent of such person.

(B) EXCEPTIONS- The term 'employer' does not include--

(i) the United States, a corporation wholly owned by the government of the United States, or an Indian tribe; or

(ii) a bona fide private membership club (other than a labor organization) that is exempt from taxation under section 501(c) of the Internal Revenue Code of 1986. . . .

(6) PERSON, ETC- The terms 'person', 'labor organization', 'employment agency', 'commerce', and 'industry affecting commerce', shall have the same meaning given such terms in section 701 of the Civil Rights Act of 1964 (42 U.S.C. 2000e).

(7) QUALIFIED INDIVIDUAL WITH A DISABILITY- The term 'qualified individual with a disability' means an individual with a disability who, with or without reasonable accommodation, can perform the essential functions of the employment position that such individual holds or desires.

(8) REASONABLE ACCOMMODATION- The term 'reasonable accommodation' may include—

(A) making existing facilities used by employees readily accessible to and usable by individuals with disabilities; and

(B) job restructuring, part-time or modified work schedules, reassignment to a vacant position, acquisition or modification of equipment or devices, appropriate adjustment or modifications of examinations, training materials or policies, the provision of qualified readers or interpreters, and other similar accommodations for individuals with disabilities.

(9) UNDUE HARDSHIP-

(A) IN GENERAL- The term 'undue hardship' means an action requiring significant difficulty or expense.

(B) DETERMINATION- In determining whether an accommodation would impose an undue hardship on a covered entity, factors to be considered include—

(i) the overall size of the business of a covered entity with respect to the number of employees, number and type of facilities, and the size of the budget;

(ii) the type of operation maintained by the covered entity, including the composition and structure of the workforce of such entity; and

(iii) the nature and cost of the accommodation needed under this Act.

SEC. 102. DISCRIMINATION.

(a) GENERAL RULE- No covered entity shall discriminate against a qualified individual with a disability because of the disability of such individual in regard to job application procedures, the hiring or discharge of employees, employee compensation, advancement, job training, and other terms, conditions, and privileges of employment.

(b) CONSTRUCTION- As used in subsection (a), the term 'discrimination' includes—

(1) limiting, segregating, or classifying a job applicant or employee in a way that adversely affects the opportunities or status of such applicant or employee because of the disability of such applicant or employee;

(2) participating in a contractual or other arrangement or relationship that has the effect of subjecting a qualified applicant or employee with a disability to the discrimination prohibited by this title (such relationship includes a relationship with an employment or referral agency, labor union, an organization providing fringe benefits to an employee of the covered entity, or an organization providing training and apprenticeship programs);

(3) utilizing standards, criteria, or methods of administration—

(A) that have the effect of discrimination on the basis of disability; or

(B) that perpetuate the discrimination of others who are subject to common administrative control;

(4) excluding or otherwise denying equal jobs or benefits to a qualified individual because of the known disability of an individual with whom the qualified individual is known to have a relationship or association;

(5) not making reasonable accommodations to the known physical or mental limitations of a qualified individual who is an applicant or employee, unless such covered entity can demonstrate that the accommodation would impose an undue hardship on the operation of the business of such covered entity;

(6) denying employment opportunities to a job applicant or employee who is a qualified individual with a disability, if such denial is based on the need of such covered entity to make reasonable accommodation to the physical or mental impairments of the employee or applicant;

(7) using employment tests or other selection criteria that screen out or tend to screen out an individual with a disability or a class of individuals with disabilities unless the test or other selection criteria, as used by the covered entity, is shown to be job-related for the position in question and is consistent with business necessity; and

(8) failing to select and administer tests concerning employment in the most effective manner to ensure that, when such test is administered to a job applicant or employee who has a disability that impairs sensory, manual, or speaking skills, such test results accurately reflect the skills, aptitude, or whatever other factor of such applicant or employee that such test purports to measure, rather than reflecting the impaired sensory, manual, or speaking skills of such employee or applicant (except where such skills are the factors that the test purports to measure).

(c) MEDICAL EXAMINATIONS AND INQUIRIES-

(1) IN GENERAL- The prohibition against discrimination as referred to in subsection (a) shall include medical examinations and inquiries.

(2) PREEMPLOYMENT-

(A) PROHIBITED EXAMINATION OR INQUIRY- Except as provided in paragraph (3), a covered entity shall not conduct a medical examination or make inquiries of a job applicant or employee as to whether such applicant or employee is an individual with a disability or as to the nature or severity of such disability.

(B) ACCEPTABLE INQUIRY- A covered entity may make pre-employment inquiries into the ability of an applicant to perform job-related functions.

(3) EMPLOYMENT ENTRANCE EXAMINATION- A covered entity may require a medical examination after an offer of employment has been made to a job applicant and prior to the commencement of the employment duties of such applicant, and may condition an offer of employment on the results of such examination, if—

(A) all entering employees are subjected to such an examination regardless of disability;

(B) information obtained regarding the medical condition or history of the applicant is collected and maintained on separate forms and in separate medical files and is treated as a confidential medical record, except that—

(i) supervisors and managers may be informed regarding necessary restrictions on the work or duties of the employee and necessary accommodations;

(ii) first aid and safety personnel may be informed, when appropriate, if the disability might require emergency treatment; and

(iii) government officials investigating compliance with this Act shall be provided relevant information on request; and

(C) the results of such physical examination are used only in accordance with this title.

(4) EXAMINATION AND INQUIRY-

(A) PROHIBITED EXAMINATIONS AND INQUIRIES- A covered entity shall not conduct or require a medical examination and shall not make inquiries of an employee as to whether such employee is an individual with a disability or as to the nature or severity of the disability, unless such examination or inquiry is shown to be job-related and consistent with business necessity.

(B) ACCEPTABLE INQUIRIES- A covered entity may make inquiries into the ability of an employee to perform job-related functions.

SEC. 103. DEFENSES.

(a) IN GENERAL- It may be a defense to a charge of discrimination under this Act that an alleged application of qualification standards, tests, or selection criteria that screen out or tend to screen out or otherwise deny a job or benefit to an individual with a disability has been shown to be job-related and consistent with business necessity, and such performance cannot be accomplished by reasonable accommodation.

(b) QUALIFICATION STANDARDS- The term 'qualification standards' may include a requirement that an individual with a currently contagious disease or infection shall not pose a direct threat to the health or safety of other individuals in the workplace.

(c) RELIGIOUS ENTITIES-

(1) IN GENERAL- This title shall not prohibit a religious corporation, association, educational institution, or society from giving preference in employment to individuals of a particular religion to perform work connected with the carrying on by such corporation, association, educational institution, or society of its activities.

(2) QUALIFICATION STANDARD- Under this title, a religious organization may require, as a qualification standard to employment, that all applicants and employees conform to the religious tenets of such organization.

(d) LIST OF INFECTIOUS AND COMMUNICABLE DISEASES-

(1) IN GENERAL- The Secretary of Health and Human Services, not later than 6 months after July 26, 1990, shall

(A) review all infectious and communicable diseases which may be transmitted through handling the food supply;

(B) publish a list of infectious and communicable diseases which are transmitted through handling the food supply;

(C) publish the methods by which such diseases are transmitted; and

(D) widely disseminate such information regarding the list of diseases and their modes of transmissibility to the general public.
Such list shall be updated annually.

(2) APPLICATIONS- In any case in which an individual has an infectious or communicable disease that is transmitted to others through the handling of food, that is included on the list developed by the Secretary of Health and Human Services under paragraph (1), and which cannot be eliminated by reasonable accommodation, a covered entity may refuse to assign or continue to assign such individual to a job involving food handling.

(3) CONSTRUCTION- Nothing in this title shall be construed to preempt, modify, or amend any State, county, or local law, ordinance, or regulation applicable to food handling which is designed to protect the public health from individuals who pose a significant risk to the health or safety of others, which cannot be eliminated by reasonable accommodation, pursuant to the list of infectious or communicable diseases and the modes of transmissibility published by the Secretary of Health and Human Services.

SEC. 104. ILLEGAL USE OF DRUGS AND ALCOHOL.

(a) QUALIFIED INDIVIDUAL WITH A DISABILITY- For purposes of this title, the term "qualified individual with a disability" shall not include any employee or applicant who is currently engaging in the illegal use of drugs, when the covered entity acts on the basis of such use.

(b) RULES OF CONSTRUCTION- Nothing in subsection (a) of this section shall be construed to exclude as a qualified individual with a disability an individual who

(1) has successfully completed a supervised drug rehabilitation program and is no longer engaging in the illegal use of drugs, or has otherwise been rehabilitated successfully and is no longer engaging in such use;

(2) is participating in a supervised rehabilitation program and is no longer engaging in such use; or

(3) is erroneously regarded as engaging in such use, but is not engaging in such use; except that it shall not be a violation of this title for a covered entity to adopt or administer reasonable policies or procedures, including but not limited to drug testing, designed to ensure that an individual described in paragraph (1) or (2) is no longer engaging in the illegal use of drugs.

(c) AUTHORITY OF COVERED ENTITY- A covered entity

(1) may prohibit the illegal use of drugs and the use of alcohol at the workplace by all employees;

(2) may require that employees shall not be under the influence of alcohol or be engaging in the illegal use of drugs at the workplace;

(3) may require that employees behave in conformance with the requirements established under the Drug-Free Workplace Act of 1988 (41 U.S.C. 701 et seq.);

(4) may hold an employee who engages in the illegal use of drugs or who is an alcoholic to the same qualification standards for employment or job performance and behavior that such entity holds other employees, even if any unsatisfactory performance or behavior is related to the drug use or alcoholism of such employee; and

(5) may, with respect to Federal regulations regarding alcohol and the illegal use of drugs, require that

(A) employees comply with the standards established in such regulations of the Department of Defense, if the employees of the covered entity are employed in an industry subject to such regulations, including complying with regulations (if any) that apply to employment in sensitive positions in such an industry, in the case of employees of the covered entity who are employed in such positions (as defined in the regulations of the Department of Defense);

(B) employees comply with the standards established in such regulations of the Nuclear Regulatory Commission, if the employees of the covered entity are employed in an industry subject to such regulations, including complying with regulations (if any) that apply to employment in sensitive positions in such an industry, in the case of employees of the covered entity who are employed in such positions (as defined in the regulations of the Nuclear Regulatory Commission); and

(C) employees comply with the standards established in such regulations of the Department of Transportation, if the employees of the covered entity are employed in a transportation industry subject to such regulations, including complying with such regulations (if any) that apply to employment in sensitive positions in such an industry, in the case of employees of the covered entity who are employed in such positions (as defined in the regulations of the Department of Transportation).

(d) DRUG TESTING-

(1) IN GENERAL- For purposes of this title, a test to determine the illegal use of drugs shall not be considered a medical examination.

(2) CONSTRUCTION- Nothing in this title shall be construed to encourage, prohibit, or authorize the conducting of drug testing for

the illegal use of drugs by job applicants or employees or making employment decisions based on such test results.

(e) TRANSPORTATION EMPLOYEES- Nothing in this title shall be construed to encourage, prohibit, restrict, or authorize the otherwise lawful exercise by entities subject to the jurisdiction of the Department of Transportation of authority to

(1) test employees of such entities in, and applicants for, positions involving safety-sensitive duties for the illegal use of drugs and for on-duty impairment by alcohol; and

(2) remove such persons who test positive for illegal use of drugs and on-duty impairment by alcohol pursuant to paragraph (1) from safety-sensitive duties in implementing subsection (c) of this section. . . .

Source: U.S. House of Representatives, Office of the Law Revision Counsel. http://uscode.house.gov.

APPENDIX C

THE AMERICANS WITH DISABILITIES ACT OF 1990 (42 U.S.C. § 12101 ET SEQ.): TITLE II EXCERPTS PROHIBITING DISCRIMINATION IN PUBLIC SERVICES

Title II of the Americans with Disabilities Act of 1990 (Public Law 101-336) prohibits discrimination against people with disabilities in public services funded or operated by the federal government as well as state and local governments. This title maintains that no qualified individual with a disability can be denied access to public transportation vehicles and stations or government-operated communications services. The title specifically states that transportation entities must conform to accessibility requirements by providing paratransit options where normal routes do not extend unless such changes would cause "undue financial burden" to the service provider.

SEC. 201. DEFINITION.

As used in this title, the term 'qualified individual with a disability' means an individual with a disability who, with or without reasonable modifications to rules, policies, and practices, the removal of architectural, communication, and transportation barriers, or the provision of auxiliary aids and services, meets the essential eligibility requirements for the receipt of services or the participation in programs or activities provided by a department, agency, special purpose district, or other instrumentality of a State or a local government.

Appendix C

SEC. 202. DISCRIMINATION.

No qualified individual with a disability shall, by reason of such disability, be excluded from the participation in, be denied the benefits of, or be subjected to discrimination by a department, agency, special purpose district, or other instrumentality of a State or a local government.

SEC. 203. ACTIONS APPLICABLE TO PUBLIC TRANSPORTATION PROVIDED BY PUBLIC ENTITIES CONSIDERED DISCRIMINATORY.

(a) DEFINITION- As used in this title, the term 'public transportation' means transportation by bus or rail, or by any other conveyance (other than air travel) that provides the general public with general or special service (including charter service) on a regular and continuing basis.

(b) VEHICLES-

(1) NEW BUSES, RAIL VEHICLES, AND OTHER FIXED ROUTE VEHICLES- It shall be considered discrimination for purposes of this Act and section 504 of the Rehabilitation Act of 1973 (29 U.S.C. 794) for a public entity to purchase or lease a new fixed route bus of any size, a new intercity rail vehicle, a new commuter rail vehicle, a new rapid rail vehicle, a new light rail vehicle to be used for public transportation, or any other new fixed route vehicle to be used for public transportation and for which a solicitation is made later than 30 days after the date of enactment of this Act, if such bus, rail, or other vehicle is not readily accessible to and usable by individuals with disabilities, including individuals who use wheelchairs.

(2) USED VEHICLES- If a public entity purchases or leases a used vehicle to be used for public transportation after the date of enactment of this Act, such individual or entity shall make demonstrated good faith efforts to purchase or lease such a used vehicle that is readily accessible to and usable by individuals with disabilities, including individuals who use wheelchairs.

(3) REMANUFACTURED VEHICLES- If a public entity remanufactures a vehicle, or purchases or leases a remanufactured vehicle to be used for public transportation, so as to extend its usable life for 5 years or more, the vehicle shall, to the maximum extent feasible, be readily accessible to and usable by individuals with disabilities, including individuals who use wheelchairs.

(c) PARATRANSIT AS A SUPPLEMENT TO FIXED ROUTE PUBLIC TRANSPORTATION SYSTEM-

(1) IN GENERAL- If a public entity operates a fixed route public transportation system to provide public transportation, it shall be considered discrimination, for purposes of this Act and section 504

of the Rehabilitation Act of 1973 (29 U.S.C. 794), for a public transit entity that is responsible for providing public transportation to fail to provide paratransit or other special transportation services sufficient to provide a comparable level of services as is provided to individuals using fixed route public transportation to individuals with disabilities, including individuals who use wheelchairs, who cannot otherwise use fixed route public transportation and to other individuals associated with such individuals with disabilities in accordance with service criteria established under regulations promulgated by the Secretary of Transportation unless the public transit entity can demonstrate that the provision of paratransit or other special transportation services would impose an undue financial burden on the public transit entity.

(2) UNDUE FINANCIAL BURDEN- If the provision of comparable paratransit or other special transportation services would impose an undue financial burden on the public transit entity, such entity must provide paratransit and other special transportation services to the extent that providing such services would not impose an undue financial burden on such entity.

(3) REGULATIONS-

(A) FORMULA- Regulations promulgated by the Secretary of Transportation to determine what constitutes an undue financial burden, for purposes of this subsection, may include a flexible numerical formula that incorporates appropriate local characteristics such as population.

(B) ADDITIONAL PARATRANSIT SERVICES- Notwithstanding paragraphs (1) and (2), the Secretary may require, at the discretion of the Secretary, a public transit authority to provide paratransit services beyond the amount determined by such formula. . . .

(g) NEW FACILITIES- For purposes of this Act and section 504 of the Rehabilitation Act of 1973 (29 U.S.C. 794), it shall be considered discrimination for a public entity to build a new facility that will be used to provide public transportation services, including bus service, intercity rail service, rapid rail service, commuter rail service, light rail service, and other service used for public transportation that is not readily accessible to and usable by individuals with disabilities, including individuals who use wheelchairs.

(h) ALTERATIONS OF EXISTING FACILITIES- With respect to a facility or any part thereof that is used for public transportation and that is altered by, on behalf of, or for the use of a public entity in a manner that affects or could affect the usability of the facility or part thereof, it shall be considered discrimination, for purposes of this title and section

Appendix C

504 of the Rehabilitation Act of 1973 (29 U.S.C. 794), for such individual or entity to fail to make the alterations in such a manner that, to the maximum extent feasible, the altered portions of the facility are readily accessible to and usable by individuals with disabilities, including individuals who use wheelchairs. If such public entity is undertaking major structural alterations that affect or could affect the usability of the facility (as defined under criteria established by the Secretary of Transportation), such public entity shall also make the alterations in such a manner that, to the maximum extent feasible, the path of travel to the altered area, and the bathrooms, telephones, and drinking fountains serving such area, are readily accessible to and usable by individuals with disabilities, including individuals who use wheelchairs. . . .

SEC. 204. REGULATIONS.
(a) ATTORNEY GENERAL- Not later than 1 year after the date of enactment of this Act, the Attorney General shall promulgate regulations in an accessible format that implement this title (other than section 203), and such regulations shall be consistent with this title and with the coordination regulations under part 41 of title 28, Code of Federal Regulations (as promulgated by the Department of Health, Education, and Welfare on January 13, 1978), applicable to recipients of Federal financial assistance under section 504 of the Rehabilitation Act of 1973 (29 U.S.C. 794) except, with respect to 'program accessibility, existing facilities', and 'communications', such regulations shall be consistent with regulations and analysis as in part 39 of title 28 of the Code of Federal Regulations, applicable to federally conducted activities under section 504 of the Rehabilitation Act of 1973 (29 U.S.C. 794).
(b) SECRETARY OF TRANSPORTATION-
(1) IN GENERAL- Not later than 1 year after the date of enactment of this Act, the Secretary of Transportation shall promulgate regulations in an accessible format that include standards applicable to facilities and vehicles covered under section 203 of this title.
(2) CONFORMANCE OF STANDARDS- Such standards shall be consistent with the minimum guidelines and requirements issued by the Architectural and Transportation Barriers Compliance Board in accordance with section 504.

SEC. 205. ENFORCEMENT.
The remedies, procedures, and rights set forth in section 505 of the Rehabilitation Act of 1973 (29 U.S.C. 794a) shall be available with respect to any individual who believes that he or she is being subjected to discrimination on the basis of disability in violation of this Act, or regulations promulgated under section 204, concerning public services.

247

SEC. 206. EFFECTIVE DATE.

(a) IN GENERAL- Except as provided in subsection (b), this title shall become effective 18 months after the date of enactment of this Act.

(b) FIXED ROUTE VEHICLES- Section 203(b)(1), as regarding new fixed route vehicles, shall become effective on the date of enactment of this Act.

Source: U.S. House of Representatives, Office of the Law Revision Counsel. http://uscode.house.gov.

APPENDIX D

THE AMERICANS WITH DISABILITIES ACT OF 1990 (42 U.S.C. § 12101 ET SEQ.): TITLE III EXCERPTS PROHIBITING DISCRIMINATION IN PUBLIC ACCOMMODATIONS AND SERVICES OPERATED BY PRIVATE ENTITIES

Title III of the Americans with Disabilities Act of 1990 (Public Law 101-336) prohibits discrimination against people with disabilities in places of public accommodation or in places that provide services to the public. In general, the title protects the right of people with disabilities to have access to hotels, restaurants, bars, theaters, stores, schools, museums, and any other venue open to the public. These entities are required to make "reasonable modifications" to avoid discrimination against people with disabilities and to remove barriers to access (including architectural barriers) when "readily achievable."

SEC. 301. DEFINITIONS.
As used in this title:

(1) COMMERCE- The term 'commerce' means travel, trade, traffic, commerce, transportation, or communication—

(A) among the several States;

(B) between any foreign country or any territory or possession and any State; or

(C) between points in the same State but through another State or foreign country.

(2) POTENTIAL PLACES OF EMPLOYMENT- The term 'potential places of employment' means facilities—

(A) that are intended for nonresidential use; and

(B) whose operations will affect commerce.

Such term shall not include facilities that are covered or expressly exempted from coverage under the Fair Housing Act of 1968 (42 U.S.C. 3601 et seq.).

(3) PUBLIC ACCOMMODATION- The following privately operated entities are considered public accommodations for purposes of this title, if the operations of such entities affect commerce—

(A) an inn, hotel, motel, or other similar place of lodging, except for an establishment located within a building that contains not more than five rooms for rent or hire and that is actually occupied by the proprietor of such establishment as the residence of such proprietor;

(B) a restaurant, bar, or other establishment serving food or drink;

(C) a motion picture house, theater, concert hall, stadium, or other place of exhibition or entertainment;

(D) an auditorium, convention center, or lecture hall;

(E) a bakery, grocery store, clothing store, hardware store, shopping center, or other similar retail sales establishment;

(F) a laundromat, dry-cleaners, bank, barber shop, beauty shop, travel service, shoe repair service, funeral parlor, gas station, office of an accountant or lawyer, pharmacy, insurance office, professional office of a health care provider, hospital, or other similar service establishment;

(G) a terminal used for public transportation;

(H) a museum, library, gallery, and other similar place of public display or collection;

(I) a park or zoo;

(J) a nursery, elementary, secondary, undergraduate, or postgraduate private school;

(K) a day care center, senior citizen center, homeless shelter, food bank, adoption program, or other similar social service center; and

(L) a gymnasium, health spa, bowling alley, golf course, or other similar place of exercise or recreation.

(4) PUBLIC TRANSPORTATION- The term 'public transportation' means transportation by bus or rail, or by any other conveyance (other than by air travel) that provides the general public with general or special service (including charter service) on a regular and continuing basis.

(5) READILY ACHIEVABLE-
(A) IN GENERAL- The term 'readily achievable' means easily accomplishable and able to be carried out without much difficulty or expense.
(B) DETERMINATION- In determining whether an action is readily achievable, factors to be considered include—
(i) the overall size of the covered entity with respect to number of employees, number and type of facilities, and the size of budget;
(ii) the type of operation of the covered entity, including the composition and structure of the entity; and
(iii) the nature and cost of the action needed.

SEC. 302. PROHIBITION OF DISCRIMINATION BY PUBLIC ACCOMMODATIONS.

(a) GENERAL RULE- No individual shall be discriminated against on the basis of disability in the full and equal enjoyment of the goods, services, facilities, privileges, advantages, and accommodations of any place of public accommodation.
(b) CONSTRUCTION-
(1) GENERAL PROHIBITION-
(A) ACTIVITIES-
(i) DENIAL OF PARTICIPATION- It shall be discriminatory to subject an individual or class of individuals on the basis of a disability or disabilities of such individual or class, directly, or through contractual, licensing, or other arrangements, to a denial of the opportunity of the individual or class to participate in or benefit from the goods, services, facilities, privileges, advantages, and accommodations of an entity.
(ii) PARTICIPATION IN UNEQUAL BENEFIT- It shall be discriminatory to afford an individual or class of individuals, on the basis of a disability or disabilities of such individual or class, directly, or through contractual, licensing, or other arrangements with the opportunity to participate in or benefit from a good, service, facility, privilege, advantage, and accommodation that is not equal to that afforded to other individuals.
(iii) SEPARATE BENEFIT- It shall be discriminatory to provide an individual or class of individuals, on the basis of a disability or disabilities of such individual or class, directly, or through contractual, licensing, or other arrangements with a good, service, facility, privilege, advantage, or accommodation that is different or separate from that provided to other individuals, unless such action is necessary to provide the individual or class of individuals with a good, service, facility, privilege,

advantage, or accommodation, or other opportunity that is as effective as that provided to others.

(B) INTEGRATED SETTINGS- Goods, facilities, privileges, advantages, accommodations, and services shall be afforded to an individual with a disability in the most integrated setting appropriate to the needs of the individual.

(C) OPPORTUNITY TO PARTICIPATE- Notwithstanding the existence of separate or different programs or activities provided in accordance with this section, an individual with a disability shall not be denied the opportunity to participate in such programs or activities that are not separate or different.

(D) ADMINISTRATIVE METHODS- An individual or entity shall not, directly or through contractual or other arrangements, utilize standards or criteria or methods of administration—

(i) that have the effect of discriminating on the basis of disability; or

(ii) that perpetuate the discrimination of others who are subject to common administrative control.

(E) ASSOCIATION- It shall be discriminatory to exclude or otherwise deny equal goods, services, facilities, privileges, advantages, and accommodations, or other opportunities to an individual or entity because of the known disability of an individual with whom the individual or entity is known to have a relationship or association.

(2) SPECIFIC PROHIBITIONS-

(A) DISCRIMINATION- As used in subsection (a), the term 'discrimination' shall include—

(i) the imposition or application of eligibility criteria that screen out or tend to screen out an individual with a disability or any class of individuals with disabilities from fully and equally enjoying any goods, services, facilities, privileges, advantages, and accommodations, unless such criteria can be shown to be necessary for the provision of the goods, services, facilities, privileges, advantages, or accommodations being offered;

(ii) a failure to make reasonable modifications in policies, practices, procedures, when such modifications are necessary to afford such goods, services, facilities, privileges, advantages, and accommodations to individuals with disabilities, unless the entity can demonstrate that making such modifications would fundamentally alter the nature of such goods, services, facilities, privileges, advantages, and accommodations;

(iii) a failure to take such steps as may be necessary to ensure that no individual with a disability is excluded, denied services, segregated or otherwise treated differently than other individuals because of the absence of auxiliary aids and services, unless the entity can demonstrate that taking such steps would fundamentally alter the nature of the good, service, facility, privilege, advantage, or accommodation being offered or would result in undue burden;

(iv) a failure to remove architectural barriers, and communication barriers that are structural in nature, in existing facilities, and transportation barriers in existing vehicles used by an establishment for transporting individuals (not including barriers that can only be removed through the retrofitting of vehicles by the installation of a hydraulic or other lift), where such removal is readily achievable;

(v) where an entity can demonstrate that the removal of a barrier under clause (iv) is not readily achievable, a failure to make such goods, services, facilities, privileges, advantages, and accommodations available through alternative methods if such methods are readily achievable;

(vi) with respect to a facility or part thereof that is altered by, on behalf of, or for the use of an establishment in a manner that affects or could affect the usability of the facility or part thereof, a failure to make alterations in such a manner that, to the maximum extent feasible, the altered portions of the facility are readily accessible to and usable by individuals with disabilities, including individuals who use wheelchairs, and where the entity is undertaking major structural alterations that affect or could affect the usability of the facility (as defined under criteria established by the Attorney General), the entity shall also make the alterations in such a manner that, to the maximum extent feasible, the path of travel to the altered area and the bathrooms, telephones, and drinking fountains serving the remodeled area, are readily accessible to and usable by individuals with disabilities, except that this paragraph shall not be construed to require the installation of an elevator for facilities that are less than three stories or that have less than 3,000 square feet per story unless the building is a shopping center, a shopping mall, or the professional office of a health care provider or unless the Attorney General determines that a particular category of such facilities requires the installation of elevators based on the usage of such facilities. . . .

Source: U.S. House of Representatives, Office of the Law Revision Counsel. http://uscode.house.gov.

APPENDIX E

EDUCATION OF INDIVIDUALS WITH DISABILITIES (20 U.S.C. § 1400): EXCERPTS FROM THE 1990 CONGRESSIONAL FINDINGS EXPLAINING THE NEED FOR LEGISLATION

The Education for All Handicapped Children Act (EAHCA) was signed into law in 1975 and went into effect in 1978. The act was designed to provide public education for all children with disabilities in integrated classroom settings. In 1990 the EAHCA was renamed the Individuals with Disabilities Education Act (IDEA) after having been amended. The IDEA has been numbered as part of the Education title (Chapter 33 of Title 20) of the U.S. Code and has been amended several times subsequently. In codifying the law, Congress documented its findings that explained the need for such legislation.

Congress finds the following:
(1) Disability is a natural part of the human experience and in no way diminishes the right of individuals to participate in or contribute to society. Improving educational results for children with disabilities is an essential element of our national policy of ensuring equality of opportunity, full participation, independent living, and economic self-sufficiency for individuals with disabilities.
(2) Before the date of enactment of the Education for All Handicapped Children Act of 1975 (Public Law 94-142), the educational needs of millions of children with disabilities were not being fully met because -

(A) the children did not receive appropriate educational services;

(B) the children were excluded entirely from the public school system and from being educated with their peers;

(C) undiagnosed disabilities prevented the children from having a successful educational experience; or

(D) a lack of adequate resources within the public school system forced families to find services outside the public school system.

(3) Since the enactment and implementation of the Education for All Handicapped Children Act of 1975, this chapter has been successful in ensuring children with disabilities and the families of such children access to a free appropriate public education and in improving educational results for children with disabilities.

(4) However, the implementation of this chapter has been impeded by low expectations, and an insufficient focus on applying replicable research on proven methods of teaching and learning for children with disabilities.

(5) Almost 30 years of research and experience has demonstrated that the education of children with disabilities can be made more effective by -

(A) having high expectations for such children and ensuring their access to the general education curriculum in the regular classroom, to the maximum extent possible, in order to -

(i) meet developmental goals and, to the maximum extent possible, the challenging expectations that have been established for all children; and

(ii) be prepared to lead productive and independent adult lives, to the maximum extent possible;

(B) strengthening the role and responsibility of parents and ensuring that families of such children have meaningful opportunities to participate in the education of their children at school and at home;

(C) coordinating this chapter with other local, educational service agency, State, and Federal school improvement efforts, including improvement efforts under the Elementary and Secondary Education Act of 1965 [20 U.S.C. 6301 et seq.], in order to ensure that such children benefit from such efforts and that special education can become a service for such children rather than a place where such children are sent;

(D) providing appropriate special education and related services, and aids and supports in the regular classroom, to such children, whenever appropriate;

(E) supporting high-quality, intensive preservice preparation and professional development for all personnel who work with children with disabilities in order to ensure that such personnel have the skills and knowledge necessary to improve the academic achievement and functional performance of children with disabilities, including the use of scientifically based instructional practices, to the maximum extent possible;

(F) providing incentives for whole-school approaches, scientifically based early reading programs, positive behavioral interventions and supports, and early intervening services to reduce the need to label children as disabled in order to address the learning and behavioral needs of such children;

(G) focusing resources on teaching and learning while reducing paperwork and requirements that do not assist in improving educational results; and

(H) supporting the development and use of technology, including assistive technology devices and assistive technology services, to maximize accessibility for children with disabilities.

(6) While States, local educational agencies, and educational service agencies are primarily responsible for providing an education for all children with disabilities, it is in the national interest that the Federal Government have a supporting role in assisting State and local efforts to educate children with disabilities in order to improve results for such children and to ensure equal protection of the law.

(7) A more equitable allocation of resources is essential for the Federal Government to meet its responsibility to provide an equal educational opportunity for all individuals.

(8) Parents and schools should be given expanded opportunities to resolve their disagreements in positive and constructive ways.

(9) Teachers, schools, local educational agencies, and States should be relieved of irrelevant and unnecessary paperwork burdens that do not lead to improved educational outcomes. . . .

Source: U.S. House of Representatives, Office of the Law Revision Counsel. http://uscode.house.gov.

APPENDIX F

REMARKS BY PRESIDENT GEORGE H. W. BUSH AT THE SIGNING OF THE AMERICANS WITH DISABILITIES ACT OF 1990

On July 26, President George H. W. Bush held a ceremony on the South Lawn of the White House to formalize the signing of the Americans with Disabilities Act (ADA). Before an audience of reporters, congressional leaders, administration officials, and more than 2,000 representatives from the disabilities community, he made the following speech prior to affixing his name to the historic legislation.

Evan, thank you so much. And welcome to every one of you, out there in this splendid scene of hope, spread across the South Lawn of the White House. I want to salute the Members of the United States Congress, the House and the Senate who are with us today—active participants in making this day come true. This is, indeed, an incredible day—especially for the thousands of people across the nation who have given so much of their time, their vision, and their courage to see this act become a reality.

You know, I started trying to put together a list of all the people who should be mentioned today. But when the list started looking a little longer than the Senate testimony for the bill, I decided I better give up, or that we'd never get out of here before sunset. So, even though so many deserve credit, I will single out but a tiny handful. And I take those who have guided me personally over the years: of course, my friends [presidential adviser] Evan Kemp and [chairperson of the President's Committee on Employment of People with Disabilities] Justin Dart, up here on the platform with me; and of course—I hope you'll forgive me for also saying a special word of thanks to two from the White House, but again, this is personal, so I don't want to offend those omitted—two from the White House, [legal counsel] Boyden Gray and [director of the Centers for Disease Control] Bill Roper, who labored long and hard. And I want to thank [chairperson of the National Council on the Handicapped] Sandy Parrino, of course, for her leadership. And I again—it is very risky with all these Members of Congress here who worked so hard, but I can say on a very personal basis, [senator from Kansas] Bob Dole has inspired me.

This is an immensely important day, a day that belongs to all of you. Everywhere I look, I see people who have dedicated themselves to making sure that this day would come to pass: my friends from Congress, as I say, who worked so diligently with the best interest of all at heart, Democrats and Republicans; members of this administration—and I'm pleased to see so many top officials and members of my Cabinet here today who brought their caring and expertise to this fight; and then, the organizations—so many dedicated organizations for people with disabilities, who gave their time and their strength; and perhaps most of all, everyone out there and others—across the breadth of this nation are 43 million Americans with disabilities. You have made this happen. All of you have made this happen. To all of you, I just want to say your triumph is that your bill will now be law, and that this day belongs to you. On behalf of our nation, thank you very, very much.

Three weeks ago we celebrated our nation's Independence Day. Today we're here to rejoice in and celebrate another "independence day," one that is long overdue. With today's signing of the landmark Americans for Disabilities Act, every man, woman, and child with a disability can now pass through once-closed doors into a bright new era of equality, independence, and freedom. As I look around at all these joyous faces, I remember clearly how many years of dedicated commitment have gone into making this historic new civil rights act a reality. It's been the work of a true coalition, a strong and inspiring coalition of people who have shared both a dream and a passionate determination to make that dream come true. It's been a coalition in the finest spirit—a joining of Democrats and Republicans, of the legislative and the executive branches, of Federal and State agencies, of public officials and private citizens, of people with disabilities and without.

This historic act is the world's first comprehensive declaration of equality for people with disabilities—the first. Its passage has made the United States the international leader on this human rights issue. Already, leaders of several other countries, including Sweden, Japan, the Soviet Union, and all 12 members of the EEC [European Economic Community], have announced that they hope to enact now similar legislation. Our success with this act proves that we are keeping faith with the spirit of our courageous forefathers who wrote in the Declaration of Independence: "We hold these truths to be self-evident, that all men are created equal, that they are endowed by their Creator with certain unalienable rights." These words have been our guide for more than two centuries as we've labored to form our more perfect union. But tragically, for too many Americans, the blessings of liberty have been limited or even denied. The Civil Rights Act of '64 took a bold step towards righting that wrong. But the stark fact remained that people with disabilities were still victims of segregation and discrimination, and this was intolerable. Today's legislation brings us closer to that day when no Americans will ever again be deprived of their basic guarantee of life, liberty, and the pursuit of happiness.

This act is powerful in its simplicity. It will ensure that people with disabilities are given the basic guarantees for which they have worked so long and so hard: independence, freedom of choice, control of their lives, the opportunity to blend fully and equally into the rich mosaic of the American mainstream. Legally, it will provide our disabled community with a powerful expansion of protections and then basic civil rights. It will guarantee fair and just access to the fruits of American life which we all must be able to enjoy. And then, specifically, first the ADA ensures that employers covered by the act cannot discriminate against qualified individuals with disabilities. Second, the ADA ensures access to public accommodations such as restaurants, hotels, shopping centers, and offices. And third, the ADA ensures expanded access to transportation services. And fourth, the ADA ensures equivalent telephone services for people with speech or hearing impediments.

These provisions mean so much to so many. To one brave girl in particular, they will mean the world. Lisa Carl, a young Washington State woman with cerebral palsy, who I'm told is with us today, now will always be admitted to her hometown theater. Lisa, you might not have been welcome at your theater, but I'll tell you—welcome to the White House. We're glad you're here. The ADA is a dramatic renewal not only for those with disabilities but for all of us, because along with the precious privilege of being an American comes a sacred duty to ensure that every other American's rights are also guaranteed.

Together, we must remove the physical barriers we have created and the social barriers that we have accepted. For ours will never be a truly prosperous nation until all within it prosper. For inspiration, we need look no further than our own neighbors. With us in that wonderful crowd out there are people representing 18 of the daily Points of Light [a community leadership organization] that I've named for their extraordinary involvement with the disabled community. We applaud you and your shining example. Thank you for your leadership for all that are here today.

Now, let me just tell you a wonderful story, a story about children already working in the spirit of the ADA—a story that really touched me. Across the nation, some 10,000 youngsters with disabilities are part of Little League's Challenger Division. Their teams play just like others, but—and this is the most remarkable part—as they play, at their sides are volunteer buddies from conventional Little League teams. All of these players work together. They team up to wheel around the bases and to field grounders together and, most of all, just to play and become friends. We must let these children be our guides and inspiration.

I also want to say a special word to our friends in the business community. You have in your hands the key to the success of this act, for you can unlock a splendid resource of untapped human potential that, when freed, will enrich us all. I know there have been concerns that the ADA may be vague or costly, or may lead endlessly to litigation. But I want to reassure you right now that my administration and the United States Congress have carefully crafted this Act. We've all been determined to ensure that it gives flexibility, particularly in terms of the timetable of implementation, and we've been committed to containing the costs that may be incurred.

This act does something important for American business, though—and remember this: You've called for new sources of workers. Well, many of our fellow citizens with disabilities are unemployed. They want to work, and they can work, and this is a tremendous pool of people. And remember, this is a tremendous pool of people who will bring to jobs diversity, loyalty, proven low turnover rate, and only one request: the chance to prove themselves. And when you add together Federal, State, local, and private funds, it costs almost $200 billion annually to support Americans with disabilities—in effect, to keep them dependent. Well, when given the opportunity to be independent, they will move proudly into the economic mainstream of American life, and that's what this legislation is all about.

Our problems are large, but our unified heart is larger. Our challenges are great, but our will is greater. And in our America, the most generous, optimistic nation on the face of the Earth, we must not and will not rest until every man and woman with a dream has the means to achieve it.

And today, America welcomes into the mainstream of life all of our fellow citizens with disabilities. We embrace you for your abilities and for your disabilities, for our similarities and indeed for our differences, for your past courage and your future dreams. Last year, we celebrated a victory of international freedom. Even the strongest person couldn't scale the Berlin Wall to gain the elusive promise of independence that lay just beyond. And so, together we rejoiced when that barrier fell.

And now I sign legislation which takes a sledgehammer to another wall, one which has for too many generations separated Americans with disabilities from the freedom they could glimpse, but not grasp. Once again, we rejoice as this barrier falls for claiming together we will not accept, we will not excuse, we will not tolerate discrimination in America. With, again, great thanks to the Members of the United States Senate, leaders of whom are here today, and those who worked so tirelessly for this legislation on both sides of the aisles. And to those Members of the House of Representatives with us here today, Democrats and Republicans as well, I salute you. And on your behalf, as well as the behalf of this entire country, I now lift my pen to sign this Americans with Disabilities Act and say: Let the shameful wall of exclusion finally come tumbling down. God bless you all.

Source: Remarks of President George Bush at the signing of the Americans with Disabilities Act, U.S. Equal Employment Opportunity Commission. http://www.eeoc.gov/ada/bushspeech.html.

APPENDIX G

PRESIDENT GEORGE W. BUSH ANNOUNCES THE NEW FREEDOM INITIATIVE OF 2001

In 2001, President George W. Bush launched a new federal plan to improve the quality of civic participation for Americans with disabilities. He called the plan the New Freedom Initiative because it promised to bring greater independence to the millions of people with disabilities. Specifically, the president wanted to correct the woeful unemployment levels of people with disabilities and to bring more disabled individuals out of institutions and group homes and into the nation's communities. He also asserted that the lack of educational opportunities was keeping many people with disabilities from utilizing their full capabilities, and he saw the proliferation of assistive technologies as a way to counter this trend. Since the launch of the president's plan, his administration has secured funds to help many people with disabilities acquire assistive technologies and technological aids to allow them to telework. The New Freedom Initiative has also attained funds to assist in finding community-based housing for people with disabilities and to aid in the removal of transportation barriers.

On February 1, 2001, President Bush made the following remarks in the East Room of the White House to inaugurate the New Freedom Initiative.

One of the things I enjoy most about my new job is the walk I get to take every single morning, up the colonnade from the residence to the Oval Office. I say "up," because the path rises just slightly. It's been that way since they took out the steps, so that Franklin Roosevelt could make it to his place of work.

This house is among the first places in America to accommodate people with disabilities. And we have come a long way since the days when only a President could hope for that consideration. We are more mindful now of the hardships that come with disability, more generous in responding to the needs of our citizens, more grateful for the contributions you make to our society.

262

Appendix G

Old misconceptions about physical and mental disability are being discredited. Old barriers are falling away. Our task is now clear: We must speed up the day when the last barrier has been removed to full and independent lives for every American with or without disability.

I am proud that the last great reform in this cause, the Americans With Disability Act, bears the signature of my dad [President George H. W. Bush, who signed the legislation in 1990]. I see many in this audience who helped him get this important legislation through Congress, and I want to thank you for coming. Because of that law, millions of Americans can now compete for jobs once denied them; enter buildings once closed to them; travel on buses and trains once unequipped for them.

For those who have hearing or visual impairments, for those who use walkers and wheelchairs or have mental retardation and mental illnesses, your own country now seems a more welcoming place as a result of that law. Eleven years after the ADA, we are a better country for it.

But there is more to do, and today I propose we move forward. This morning I sent to Congress a set of proposals called the New Freedom Initiative. It is an important step in ensuring that all Americans with disabilities, whether young or old, can participate more fully in the life of their communities and of our country.

Wherever a door is closed to anyone because of a disability, we must work to open it. Wherever any job or home, or means of transportation is unfairly denied because of a disability, we must work to change it. Wherever any barrier stands between you and the full rights and dignity of citizenship, we must work to remove it, in the name of simple decency and simple justice.

Often, as you know, such barriers are unintentional. One is the high cost of assistive technologies. For many people with disabilities, new technologies are helping to defeat dependence and frustration and isolation: Text telephones for those with hearing impairments. Computer monitors for those with visual impairments. Infrared pointers for people who cannot use their hands, allowing them to operate computers by pointing at functions on the monitor or the keyboard. Lighter wheelchairs. Lighter artificial limbs. These modern wonders make the world more accessible; yet, they are often inaccessible to people who need, but cannot afford them. These technologies were once beyond the dreams of Americans with disabilities. Today, they're only beyond their means; and we can help.

In our New Freedom Initiative, we're asking Congress to significantly increase federal funding for low-interest loans so that more Americans with disabilities can purchase assistive technology. And to ensure that even better technologies are available in the future, we're asking Congress to increase federal investment in assistive technology research and development.

My administration will also work with businesses to bring more assisting technologies to the marketplace. Once available, these technologies will allow Americans with disabilities to use more of their own gifts, make more of their own choices and lead lives of greater independence.

Many Americans with disabilities work, or would like to have more freedom to do so. And you know that the greatest challenges are often not in the job itself, but in the distance between your job and your home. For some people with disabilities, this challenge means no job at all; no opportunity to work and to contribute and to use their talents.

This is changing as more Americans work at home. Yet here, too, the cost of computers and telecommuting are sometimes beyond the means of those with disabilities. And we can help. In our New Freedom Initiative, we are asking Congress to create a fund to help people with disabilities to buy the equipment they need to telecommute. We will provide tax incentives to encourage employers to provide such equipment. And we will protect home offices from needless OSHA [Occupational Safety and Health Administration] regulations.

Some 40 million Americans today work out of their homes. For most, it is a convenience. For workers with disabilities, it is a revolution. And we want as many Americans as possible to share in this revolution of independence.

Our plans also include transportation solutions and we want as many Americans as possible to share in this revolution of independence. Our plans also include transportation solutions for people with disabilities. Specifically, we're asking Congress to fund pilot programs for innovative transportation plans that serve people with disabilities. And we'll provide federal matching grants to community groups to provide alternative methods of transportation.

There are several additional proposals in this package, but let me just mention one more. We will provide additional funding each year to help churches, synagogues, mosques and other civic groups become more fully accessible to all Americans. In many houses of worship and civic centers, intentions are good, but resources are scarce. We can help make these community places open to all.

I've often talked about the goal of a welcoming society, a nation where no one is dismissed or forgotten. Our progress toward that goal is really the great American story. It is a story of inclusion and protection extending across our history to more and more Americans.

And that story's not over. There is still work to do. We must all do our duty and play our part. And I hope today we have made a good beginning.

Source: Remarks by the President in Announcement of New Freedom Initiative, White House, February 1, 2001. http://www.whitehouse.gov/news/releases/20010201-3.html.

APPENDIX H

STATISTICS

Rights of the Disabled

In 2005, the U.S. Census Bureau conducted its annual American Community Survey to acquire data that helps communities and local government discern how they are changing demographically. Part of the survey reports the number of people within the population who are over five years old and who have one or more disabilities. That information is displayed in the following table.

ESTIMATED NUMBER OF AMERICANS WITH DISABILITIES

Population	United States	
	Estimate	Margin of Error
Total:	267,387,983	+/-18,647
Male:	130,301,787	+/-22,500
5 to 15 years:	22,810,520	+/-27,874
Without any disability	20,976,844	+/-34,779
With one type of disability	1,462,329	+/-19,965
With two or more types of disability	371,347	+/-11,764
16 to 64 years:	92,647,138	+/-30,554
Without any disability	81,516,786	+/-61,024
With one type of disability	4,977,289	+/-37,797
With two or more types of disability	6,153,063	+/-39,753
65 to 74 years:	8,400,634	+/-10,635
Without any disability	5,878,133	+/-19,991
With one type of disability	1,411,676	+/-15,434
With two or more types of disability	1,110,825	+/-14,009
75 years and over:	6,443,495	+/-8,196
Without any disability	3,288,169	+/-20,304
With one type of disability	1,344,408	+/-13,623
With two or more types of disability	1,810,918	+/-19,207
Female:	137,086,196	+/-20,361
5 to 15 years:	21,775,627	+/-23,066
Without any disability	20,722,769	+/-30,106
With one type of disability	812,247	+/-15,704
With two or more types of disability	240,611	+/-9,218
16 to 64 years:	95,394,171	+/-25,786
Without any disability	83,734,224	+/-62,626
With one type of disability	4,876,806	+/-37,541
With two or more types of disability	6,783,141	+/-44,946
65 to 74 years:	9,959,175	+/-10,585
Without any disability	6,925,352	+/-24,589
With one type of disability	1,586,324	+/-18,201
With two or more types of disability	1,447,499	+/-16,012
75 years and over:	9,957,223	+/-9,865
Without any disability	4,604,997	+/-25,826
With one type of disability	1,901,800	+/-18,595
With two or more types of disability	3,450,426	+/-22,404

Note: Data are limited to the household population and exclude the population living in institutions, college dormitories, and other group quarters.

Source: U.S. Census Bureau, 2005 American Community Survey

Appendix H

In 2005, the U.S. Census Bureau conducted its annual American Community Survey to acquire data that helps communities and local government discern how they are changing demographically. Part of the survey reports the level of academic learning achieved by people between the ages of 18 and 34 who report having a disability. That information is displayed in the following table.

ACADEMIC ACHIEVEMENT LEVEL OF AMERICANS WITH DISABILITIES

Population	United States	
	Estimate	Margin of Error
Total:	64,647,330	+/-32,573
With a disability:	4,505,696	+/-38,758
Enrolled in school:	943,341	+/-19,626
Below college	315,275	+/-10,078
College or graduate school	628,066	+/-15,344
Not enrolled in school:	3,562,355	+/-36,775
Less than high school graduate	1,028,260	+/-21,291
High school graduate (includes equivalency)	1,473,170	+/-23,598
Some college or associate's degree	797,800	+/-14,878
Bachelor's degree or higher	263,125	+/-8,635
No disability:	60,141,634	+/-48,867
Enrolled in school:	15,684,523	+/-63,864
Below college	2,593,345	+/-24,835
College or graduate school	13,091,178	+/-58,427
Not enrolled in school:	44,457,111	+/-83,496
Less than high school graduate	7,369,787	+/-70,712
High school graduate (includes equivalency)	14,704,903	+/-90,592
Some college or associate's degree	11,614,674	+/-59,313
Bachelor's degree or higher	10,767,747	+/-68,260

Note: Data are limited to the household population and exclude the population living in institutions, college dormitories, and other group quarters.

Source: U.S. Census Bureau, 2005 American Community Survey

Rights of the Disabled

In 2005, the U.S. Census Bureau conducted its annual American Community Survey to acquire data that helps communities and local government discern how they are changing demographically. Part of the survey reports the employment status of people between the ages of 16 and 64 who have an employment disability. That information is displayed in the following table.

EMPLOYMENT STATUS OF AMERICANS WITH DISABILITIES

Population	United States	
	Estimate	Margin of Error
Total:	188,041,309	+/-35,238
Male:	92,647,138	+/-30,554
16 to 20 years:	9,789,354	+/-38,514
With an employment disability:	260,993	+/-8,583
Employed	44,316	+/-3,429
Not employed	216,677	+/-8,284
No employment disability:	9,528,361	+/-38,991
Employed	4,016,022	+/-31,390
Not employed	5,512,339	+/-27,941
21 to 64 years:	82,857,784	+/-31,616
With an employment disability:	5,838,698	+/-41,258
Employed	1,130,907	+/-17,948
Not employed	4,707,791	+/-36,235
No employment disability:	77,019,086	+/-50,775
Employed	65,238,713	+/-75,218
Not employed	11,780,373	+/-65,600
Female:	95,394,171	+/-25,786
16 to 20 years:	9,249,304	+/-32,444
With an employment disability:	212,416	+/-7,876
Employed	39,031	+/-3,209
Not employed	173,385	+/-7,159
No employment disability:	9,036,888	+/-33,389
Employed	3,817,202	+/-25,479
Not employed	5,219,686	+/-28,971
21 to 64 years:	86,144,867	+/-31,307
With an employment disability:	6,524,724	+/-41,934
Employed	1,065,289	+/-16,298
Not employed	5,459,435	+/-40,797
No employment disability:	79,620,143	+/-49,559
Employed	56,203,367	+/-84,570
Not employed	23,416,776	+/-77,313

Note: Data are limited to the household population and exclude the population living in institutions, college dormitories, and other group quarters.

Source: U.S. Census Bureau, 2005 American Community Survey

Appendix H

In 2005, the U.S. Census Bureau conducted its annual American Community Survey to acquire data that helps communities and local government discern how they are changing demographically. Part of the survey reports the employment status of African Americans between the ages of 16 and 64 who have an employment disability. That information is displayed in the following table.

EMPLOYMENT STATUS OF AFRICAN-AMERICANS WITH DISABILITIES

African-American Population	United States	
	Estimate	Margin of Error
Total:	22,376,728	+/-27,914
With any disability:	3,554,531	+/-38,292
Male:	1,594,519	+/-22,525
16 to 34 years:	420,175	+/-13,632
Employed	121,802	+/-7,627
Not employed	298,373	+/-10,392
35 to 64 years:	1,174,344	+/-18,414
Employed	328,296	+/-9,260
Not employed	846,048	+/-16,679
Female:	1,960,012	+/-27,869
16 to 34 years:	401,938	+/-11,555
Employed	129,046	+/-6,430
Not employed	272,892	+/-9,716
35 to 64 years:	1,558,074	+/-23,339
Employed	449,155	+/-14,253
Not employed	1,108,919	+/-19,865
No disability:	18,822,197	+/-48,943
Male:	8,554,381	+/-29,331
16 to 34 years:	4,006,216	+/-21,861
Employed	2,404,114	+/-23,660
Not employed	1,602,102	+/-22,272
35 to 64 years:	4,548,165	+/-20,657
Employed	3,638,090	+/-22,636
Not employed	910,075	+/-15,546
Female:	10,267,816	+/-33,068
16 to 34 years:	4,732,527	+/-22,631
Employed	2,773,569	+/-27,651
Not employed	1,958,958	+/-22,842
35 to 64 years:	5,535,289	+/-26,044
Employed	4,155,273	+/-25,933
Not employed	1,380,016	+/-20,666

Note: Data are limited to the household population and exclude the population living in institutions, college dormitories, and other group quarters.

Source: U.S. Census Bureau, 2005 American Community Survey

Rights of the Disabled

In 2005, the U.S. Census Bureau conducted its annual American Community Survey to acquire data that helps communities and local government discern how they are changing demographically. Part of the survey reports the employment status of people between the ages of 16 and 64 who have a mental disability. That information is displayed in the following table.

EMPLOYMENT STATUS OF AMERICANS WITH MENTAL DISABILITIES

Population	United States	
	Estimate	Margin of Error
Total:	188,041,309	+/-35,238
With a mental disability:	8,398,104	+/-48,509
Male:	4,135,685	+/-30,429
16 to 34 years:	1,479,397	+/-22,002
Employed	560,392	+/-12,611
Not employed	919,005	+/-19,749
35 to 64 years:	2,656,288	+/-25,239
Employed	724,681	+/-12,749
Not employed	1,931,607	+/-22,867
Female:	4,262,419	+/-30,656
16 to 34 years:	1,166,612	+/-19,312
Employed	396,167	+/-9,508
Not employed	770,445	+/-14,905
35 to 64 years:	3,095,807	+/-29,195
Employed	726,920	+/-13,598
Not employed	2,368,887	+/-25,794
No mental disability:	179,643,205	+/-55,252
Male:	88,511,453	+/-43,565
16 to 34 years:	35,077,998	+/-38,691
Employed	25,387,394	+/-50,784
Not employed	9,690,604	+/-43,720
35 to 64 years:	53,433,455	+/-31,557
Employed	43,757,491	+/-59,071
Not employed	9,675,964	+/-48,699
Female:	91,131,752	+/-38,039
16 to 34 years:	35,200,715	+/-31,611
Employed	21,789,027	+/-48,084
Not employed	13,411,688	+/-46,495
35 to 64 years:	55,931,037	+/-38,224
Employed	38,212,775	+/-64,243
Not employed	17,718,262	+/-64,480

Note: Data are limited to the household population and exclude the population living in institutions, college dormitories, and other group quarters.

Source: U.S. Census Bureau, 2005 American Community Survey

Appendix H

The 2005 Disability Status Reports released by the Rehabilitation Research and Training Center on Disability Demographics and Statistics at Cornell University uses data from the U.S. Census Bureau to show trends in statistics regarding working-age people with disabilities in America. The following table shows the percentage of state populations comprised of working-age (ages 21–64) people with disabilities.

PERCENTAGE OF STATE POPULATIONS COMPRISED OF PEOPLE WITH DISABILITIES

Location 2005	Percentage of Working-Age People with Disabilities	Location 2005	Percentage of Working-Age People with Disabilities
United States	12.6	Missouri	15.3
Alabama	18.1	Montana	13.3
Alaska	14.9	Nebraska	11.4
Arizona	12.1	Nevada	9.9
Arkansas	19.1	New Hampshire	11.7
California	10.8	New Jersey	9.4
Colorado	10.1	New Mexico	15.1
Connecticut	10.0	New York	11.4
District of Columbia	10.9	North Carolina	14.5
Delaware	12.2	North Dakota	11.1
Florida	12.7	Ohio	13.8
Georgia	12.9	Oklahoma	17.3
Hawaii	9.7	Oregon	13.6
Idaho	14.1	Pennsylvania	12.9
Illinois	10.2	Rhode Island	12.6
Indiana	13.7	South Carolina	15.7
Iowa	11.5	South Dakota	11.9
Kansas	12.0	Tennessee	17.1
Kentucky	19.7	Texas	12.3
Louisiana	16.4	Utah	10.6
Maine	15.4	Vermont	13.1
Maryland	10.4	Virginia	11.3
Massachusetts	10.7	Washington	13.9
Michigan	13.3	West Virginia	21.7
Minnesota	9.8	Wisconsin	10.8
Mississippi	18.9	Wyoming	14.1

Note: Calculations by the Rehabilitation Research and Training Center on Disability Demographics and Statistics (StatsRRTC) using the 2005 American Community Survey Public Use Microdata Samples (PUMS).

Source: Houtenville, Andrew J. 2005. "Disability Statistics in the United States." Ithaca, NY: Cornell University Rehabilitation Research and Training Center on Disability Statistics and Demographics, http://www.disabilitystatistics.org. Posted May 15, 2003. Accessed March 28, 2005.

Rights of the Disabled

The 2005 Disability Status Reports released by the Rehabilitation Research and Training Center on Disability Demographics and Statistics at Cornell University uses data from the U.S. Census Bureau to show trends in statistics regarding working-age people with disabilities in America. The following graphs show comparisons between the employment, income, and poverty level of working-age (ages 21–64) people with disabilities and those without disabilities.

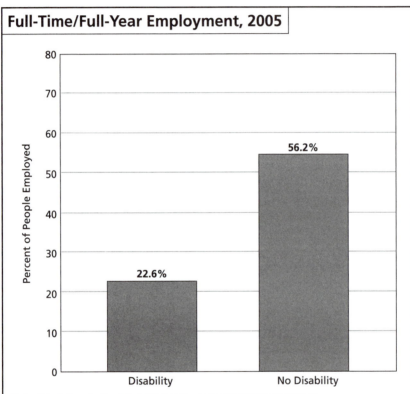

Full-Time/Full-Year Employment, 2005

Note: Calculations by the Rehabilitation Research and Training Center on Disability Demographics and Statistics (StatsRRTC) using the 2005 American Community Survey Public Use Microdata Samples (PUMS).

Source: Data from Houtenville, Andrew J. 2005. "Disability Statistics in the United States." Ithaca, N.Y.: Cornell University Rehabilitation Research and Training Center on Disability Statistics and Demographics. Available online. URL: http://www.disabilitystatistics.org. Accessed March 28, 2005.

© Infobase Publishing

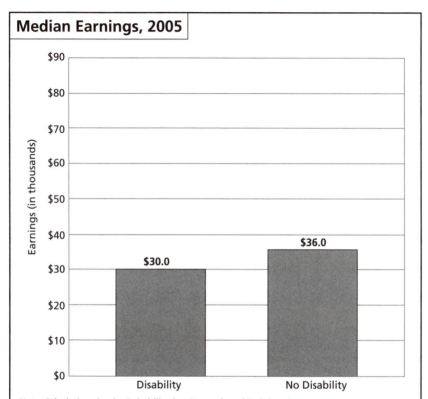

Median Earnings, 2005

Note: Calculations by the Rehabilitation Research and Training Center on Disability Demographics and Statistics (StatsRRTC) using the 2005 American Community Survey Public Use Microdata Samples (PUMS).

Source: Data from Houtenville, Andrew J. 2005. "Disability Statistics in the United States." Ithaca, N.Y.: Cornell University Rehabilitation Research and Training Center on Disability Statistics and Demographics. Available online.
URL: http://www.disabilitystatistics.org. Accessed March 28, 2005.

© Infobase Publishing

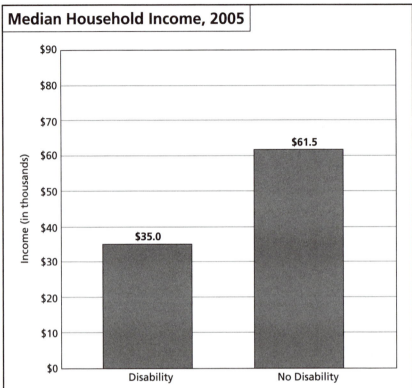

Median Household Income, 2005

Note: Calculations by the Rehabilitation Research and Training Center on Disability Demographics and Statistics (StatsRRTC) using the 2005 American Community Survey Public Use Microdata Samples (PUMS).

Source: Data from Houtenville, Andrew J. 2005. "Disability Statistics in the United States." Ithaca, N.Y.: Cornell University Rehabilitation Research and Training Center on Disability Statistics and Demographics. Available online. URL: http://www.disabilitystatistics.org. Accessed March 28, 2005.

© Infobase Publishing

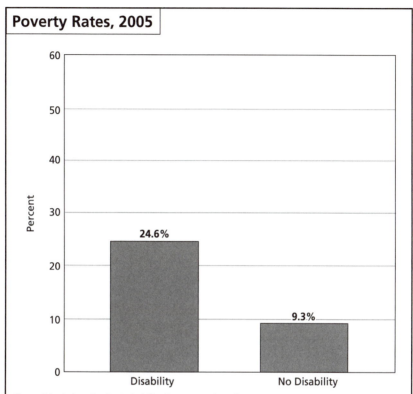

Poverty Rates, 2005

Note: Calculations by the Rehabilitation Research and Training Center on Disability Demographics and Statistics (StatsRRTC) using the 2005 American Community Survey Public Use Microdata Samples (PUMS).

Source: Data from Houtenville, Andrew J. 2005. "Disability Statistics in the United States." Ithaca, N.Y.: Cornell University Rehabilitation Research and Training Center on Disability Statistics and Demographics. Available online.URL: http://www.disabilitystatistics.org. Accessed March 28, 2005.

© Infobase Publishing

INDEX

Locators in **boldface** indicate main topics. Locators followed by *c* indicate chronology entries. Locators followed by *b* indicate biographical entries. Locators followed by *g* indicate glossary entries. Locators followed by *t* refer to tables.

Index

Index

Index

Index

Index

Index

Index

Index

Index

For Reference

Not to be taken from this room.